The Power Capabilities of Nation-States

International Conflict and War

Wayne H. Ferris
International Research Group, Ltd.

Lexington Books
D.C. Heath and Company
Lexington, Massachusetts
Toronto   London

Library of Congress Cataloging in Publication Data

Ferris, Wayne H.
  The power capabilities of nation states.

  (A Foreign Policy Research Institute book)
  Bibliography: p.
  1. International relations–Research. 2. War.
I. Title. II. Title: International conflict and war.
JX1291.F45   327'.11   73-1007
ISBN 0-669-86819-1

Published simultaneously in Canada.

Printed in the United States of America.

International Standard Book Number: 0-669-86819-1

Library of Congress Catalog Card Number: 73-1007

To My Parents

Contents

List of Tables

Foreword

Perhaps the most significant problem toward which students of international relations can direct their efforts is that of conflict among nations. This problem seems at the same time both simple to resolve and impossibly difficult. It is simple in the sense that nations can be admonished to behave pacifically toward each other, in which case peace will prevail when policy-makers heed these admonitions. Presumably, if all nations, as most claim, desire peace, then peace ought to be forthcoming. But while all nations may claim to seek peace, it is always a "peace under certain conditions," and these conditions seem rarely to exist in the world of nations to the satisfaction of everyone. Thus, hortatory efforts to bring about peace in the world have never succeeded in the past, and it is unlikely that they will succeed in the future. The problem of resolving conflict among nations is difficult in the sense that peace has never held sway in the world of nations for long.

Since peace itself seems too elusive and general a notion, scholars interested in attaining it have tried to focus attention on the more specific causes of conflict. This attempt to designate causes of conflict has enlisted the aid of many disciplines: anthropology, sociology, history, political science, and psychology. Many methodologies have been utilized in the effort at explanation, including case studies, historical description, systems analysis, content analysis, simulation, and mathematical techniques. The work has focused on many levels of analysis: on the nation, the group, and the individual. The present work focuses, for example, on nations, but it extends this focus somewhat by treating nations relative to other nations in terms of their power capabilities. It is likely that all academic disciplines and all of these methodologies are necessary in the ongoing effort to explain the causes of war, because whatever the propensities of the individual researcher, he is at least aware by now that monocausal explanations are unlikely to contain more than a germ of the truth.

Since the pioneering efforts of Lewis Fry Richardson, a number of scholars have continued to explore the avenues he opened through quantitative techniques. As with all other techniques, of course, quantification has shortcomings, some of which are discussed at length by Professor Ferris. At the same time, a number of advantages are offered by quantification and mathematization, and those who are willing to tackle the immense task of data collection may profit by these. Among the advantages is the intellectual effort that must be expended to define concepts in operational terms. Often this effort reveals that our concepts, which may have inspired heated "great debates" in the past, are too ill-defined to be meaningful. This initial task is a great aid to clarity. Most important in this book is the operationalization of the concept "power," which provides a power capabilities score for nations which marks their position relative to the other nations coexisting in the system. This data-generating work augments the increasing body of data available to other researchers, a cumulative enterprise that owes a debt to Richardson, of course, the Dimensionality of Nations Project, J. David Singer and Melvin Small, Arthur S. Banks and Robert B. Textor, the many contributors to the Yale data bank, and a host of others.

It is often remarked that the findings of quantitative efforts are trivial in the sense that we already knew the answers derived. But while such an hypothesis as "the side possessing the greater power capabilities . . . will almost always be victorious" may seem fairly obvious, the findings based on the historical experience marshaled in this book suggest a slighter relationship than we may have suspected. Some of the hypotheses discussed in the course of the book have to do with whether the relationships in power capabilities among nations have any effect in escalating conflict to the level of war. Other hypotheses add a dynamic aspect by positing that changes in these power capabilities may lead to war. All of these questions are important, and they have all furnished material for speculation in the past. Some relevant answers to these hypotheses are provided by Professor Ferris. These answers are not expected to terminate speculation, of course, but dissenters will find that the task of trying to disprove the results of this research has been greatly facilitated by the lucid operationalization of concepts and the utilization of a research technique that reveals rather than obfuscates its processes. Replication has been made less difficult. It is in this sense that the findings in this study may be regarded as cumulative, for they are derived through a method that may be duplicated; in short, they are fully open to refutation.

A remaining question is the extent to which the results in this study might relate to policy-making. In a general sense, it is valuable to know that "as power capabilities disparity increases . . . the prospects of violent international conflict rise." If he is aware of this, the policy-maker will avoid generalizing contradicting propositions that might hold in exceptional cases of conflict to the general population of international wars. But this implies that the policy-maker, as he deals with each unique case, is still thrown to some degree onto his own intellectual resources based on the single case at hand. Where hypotheses have been supported in this study, the variance in war events explained may be something like 10 to 20 percent, which leaves much to unexplained variance. Yet, the findings presented here are not simply "academic." They add to the growing fund of knowledge about conflict among nations, and it is to be hoped that they may be added to the growing arsenal of knowledge of those policy-makers that seek to understand and mitigate conflict among nations.

Willard D. Keim

Preface

Within the broad scope of recorded history, war has been the most deplorable pattern in the interactions of peoples. Some of the most heroic examples of human behavior have been associated with war, yet war certainly remains the most destructive kind of interaction that historians have found worth recording. There is scarcely a history book—outside the realm of biographical treatises—that does not give prominence to the occurrence of war. Alexander the Great, Peter the Great, Catherine the Great, Frederick the Great—none of these would have earned their places in history or been judged "great" had it not been for the violent conquests prompted by their decisions. Nor would Caesar, Napoleon, Bismarck, or so many others. One of the supreme ironies of history, insofar as it records the actions of mankind, is that many "household names" are those of generals who won and lost battles by plotting the destruction of men and women, including civilians. Lee, Grant, Pétain, Rommel, MacArthur, Eisenhower come most readily to mind. Some of them, and many others that could be mentioned, became statesmen on the merits of the reputations they gained in war.

This is not to say, of course, that war is invariably used for personal aggrandizement, or that some nations did not rise to greatness without making war on others. It is to say that *some* wars have been launched for personal or national aggrandizement.

Many potential wars have been avoided because the weaker nation recognized that its only choice was to compromise with, or yield to, the stronger one. In similar instances, on the other hand, war broke out between strong and weak states, because the weaker ones saw no way of preserving their national existence without defending themselves against the stronger ones by force of arms. This was the case, for instance, in the Russo-Finnish War of 1939 and the Italo-Ethiopian War of 1935, among others.

Wars have been started by weaker states against stronger coalitions, like that launched by Nazi Germany against what came to be the strongest allied war machine ever known, or by Israel against the Arab world, each for different reasons. If only by contrast, it might be noted that there have been weak and strong states coexisting with each other for more than a century, settling their disputes (and many there have been) by peaceful means.

To cap off this short exercise in illustrating dichotomies, at the time of this writing one of the world's smallest states, Iceland, has chosen to take its stand in conflict with one of the world's most powerful ones, nuclear-armed Great Britain, in what has come to be called the "Cod War." Every knowledgeable observer, including this writer, would be surprised if the "Cod War" were to escalate into armed conflict between the strong and the weak by the time this book goes to press, or any time thereafter. And yet too many wars may have been fought among nations in which the outcome was clearly predictable at the outset, yet for various reasons the leaders of the probable losing side deemed war nonetheless important to the national interest of their own state and to their own personal ambition.

The causes of war are so numerous that it is difficult to abstract and combine them into any general model or into a meaningful theory. Many studies of war have been published. Many thoughtful contributions to knowledge and understanding have been made. Yet a great deal of systematic research and analysis remains necessary for a comprehensive understanding of war. Among the contributions yet to be made are systematic analyses of a range of supporting factors, those factors that endow nations with the ability to pursue national interests or to settle international conflicts by resorting to war. High on the list of supporting factors is, of course, the power of nations relative to one another.

No concept has been more important to the study of international politics than that of "power," yet as the decade of the 1970s approached, the discipline still lacked an empirical interpretation of the concept of power in general and of the power capabilities of nation-states in particular. As a result, theory embodying power-related variables had yet to be subjected to systematic inquiry. It was in this context that I first decided in the summer of 1969 to operationalize the power capabilities of nation-states for a period of more than a century and relate the results to the involvement of states in international conflict and war.

The purpose of this book, then, is to present a systematic empirical analysis of how national power capabilities have been related to the involvement of nation-states in conflict and war during the 116-year period from 1850 to 1965. Considering the time span, the number of conflicts that have occurred, and the number of sovereign nations in the universe, it has been necessary to rely heavily on bases from previously published scholarly works. To this end, the works of Lewis Richardson, Quincy Wright, K.J. Holsti, Arthur S. Banks, J. David Singer, and Melvin Small have been especially valuable.

My own research focused on filling the gaps in the existing data that make up the power capabilities of all the world's nation-states that were sovereign and recognized members of the international community and combining them into a single index which could then be correlated with the occurrence of international conflict and war according to a comprehensive set of explicitly defined hypotheses. It is in this admittedly limited realm that this book seeks to make a contribution. This book presents the analytical results of the author's endeavor, including a review of previous theoretical notions and findings relevant to the subject, the hypotheses formulated for testing and the theoretical rationale upon which they rest, and the results of the empirical testing of the hypotheses. In a second volume, to be published in the near future,[a] are recorded the original

---

[a]Wayne H. Ferris, *Nation-State Power and Economic Variable Data* (Lexington, Mass.: D.C. Heath and Company, forthcoming).

data compiled for operationalizing the power capabilities of nation-states for the years 1850 to 1966 and the power capabilities variable data generated in the course of the analysis. This latter volume incorporates a report on the procedures and sources used in the collection of the data, and the methods developed and utilized for filling data gaps that remained after considerable expenditure of time and energy by the many individuals who assisted in the data gathering.

The substance of this study was submitted as a Ph.D. dissertation to, and accepted by, the Graduate Group in Political Science of the University of Pennsylvania in August 1972. Both that and the revised version for this publication owe their completion to the advice, assistance, and encouragement of many individuals and several institutions.

The National Science Foundation (Contract No. NSF-GS-3060) and the Rena and Angelius Anspach Institute for Diplomacy and Foreign Affairs provided research grants that made possible the collection of data for the index on the power capabilities of nation-states. The University of Pennsylvania supplied work-study students, and the Foreign Policy Research Institute supplied research funds and important fellowship support as well. Dr. William R. Kintner and Dr. Robert L. Pfaltzgraff, Director and Deputy Director respectively of the Institute, provided shop, materials, and sustenance for the enterprise. This study would not have reached its present stage were it not for their patient and generous support over the past several years.

More recently, International Research Group, Ltd., has provided the time and resources necessary to pull together many of the threads of the present endeavor and to reflect on their implications.

I want to express my appreciation to Dorothy Brady, Neal Cutler, Charles D. Elder, Jack M. Guttentag, Michael Haas, Kenneth Janda, Lawrence R. Klein, Irving B. Kravis, Frank Lee, Vincent E. McHale, Dennis H. Paranzino, and most importantly, Willard D. Keim for critical counsel in working through the problems of the research design.

For invaluable assistance in collecting and preparing the indicator-variable data on the power capabilities of states, a task that proved to be among the most difficult and frustrating aspects of the entire study, and in preparing the data for various stages in the analysis phase of the project, I am grateful to the following individuals: Martin Burke, Tea-Haw Chang, Robert Chirenko, Janet Czarnecki, Barbara Fair, Paul Fetterman, Gordon Fine, Sally Garris, Mary Gooderham, Stephanie Gooderham, Christine Hill, Robert Langenbrunner, Janice Orfe, Ruth Ann Price, Marlene Prost, Oswald Roach, Alana Stark, and Julia Steele. A great debt of gratitude is owed to Janice Orfe and Stephanie Gooderham. Their labor, diligence, and perserverance made this work possible.

I would like to acknowledge Mary Toelke, Marcia Dissinger, and Marie Burke for their skill and patience in typing various drafts of the manuscript.

Still others who were of valuable assistance at various stages of the study and provided general sympathetic advice and assistance include Anne Clancy, Bradford Greene, Della Grossman, Lawrence Jacksina, John Nagy, Richard Werbeck, and Gerald West.

Special mention is due Judithann Cole, who edited the manuscript in its entirety, and from whom I learned considerably in the process.

I have benefited richly from the criticisms and suggestions made of a previous draft of the manuscript by Michael Haas, Leo Hazlewood, Mark LeVine, Jack Nagel, and R.J. Rummel.

I wish especially to acknowledge my intellectual debt to Wolfgang Klaiber, friend and colleague, who has profoundly stimulated my thinking about problems of international politics over a period of many years and has provided invaluable assistance in carefully reviewing and critiquing the final manuscript. And, similarly and most importantly, my dissertation advisor and colleague, Willard Keim, whose support of the research idea from its inception proved to be of immeasurable material and ideational value. He commented in detail on successive drafts of the study, was always available to provide counsel when such was needed, and, more than anyone else, supplied insight into the difficult theoretical and methodological obstacles encountered along the way.

Needless to say, any shortcomings present in the study are my own responsibility.

Washington, D.C.   **Wayne H. Ferris**
June, 1973

The Power Capabilities of Nation-States

1

Power and the Power Capabilities of Nation States

Introduction

"Power" is a concept long used in the explanation of political science and international relations. In the view of some analysts it is power that distinguishes "politics" from other human activities. Harold Lasswell and Abraham Kaplan, for example, have defined the empirical discipline of political science as "the study of the shaping and sharing of power."[1]

In the study of international relations a "major school of thought has developed around the power concept . . . and it has been accepted for several decades by many scholars that power is the organizing idea for the whole discipline of political science."[2]

In recent years considerable progress has been made toward clarification of the concept of power. Highlights of this progress will be touched upon within this chapter. But it would be superfluous to trace its evolution in detail, since other theorists have already done so.[3]

Power as a concept has obstructed efforts aimed at explaining the subject matter of politics, and for at least two principal reasons. First, power is a complex variable that subsumes within its meaning diverse phenomena. A partial listing of these includes force, authority, influence, deterrence, persuasion, coercion, and compulsion. Robert Dahl has designated such concepts "power terms" and observed that the great variety and heterogeneity of the human relations which they comprise may "make it impossible—or at any rate not very fruitful—to develop general theories of power intended to cover them all."[4]

The problem stems not only from the fact that power has many faces but also from the relatively frequent failure of investigators to specify verbally which aspect or aspects they have in mind in the context of their discourse. A well-known case in point is the literature on the concept of "balance of power." Some of the many meanings that have been attached to this concept include: *distribution* of power in the international system, whether balanced or unbalanced; *equilibrium*, or a situation in which the power relationship between states or groups of states is one of more or less approximate equality; *disequilibrium*, or a favorable balance or superiority in power for one state or group of states in the international system; a *policy* pursued by states aimed at securing a position of either equality or superiority; a *system* of international politics; a *theoretical principle* acting as a guide to foreign policy-makers in any and all international situations so that the preponderance of any one state can be avoided; *power politics* generally; *stability and peace*; and *instability and war*.[5]

1

It cannot be denied that inquiry into a theoretical concept is necessarily hampered when multiple meanings are attached to the concept by different investigators and when even individual investigators use the term to designate different phenomena within the same study. For the purpose of clarity and cross-fertilization of thought among various users of the concept, it would be desirable if investigators agreed upon and employed a standard definition.

Although considerable effort has been addressed to clarification of the concept of power, much ambiguity continues to characterize its usage. Disagreement persists on how the general concept is to be defined, and there is a lack of standardized classification scheme and nomenclature.[6] Precise definitions used by theorists who have investigated the concept with rigor vary considerably.[7] For example, some theorists have argued that influence and power represent qualitatively different phenomena and should be differentiated accordingly.[8] Others continue to use the two more or less interchangeably.[9]

Although ambiguity continues to cloud the power concept, some underlying unity is inherent in various approaches to the analysis of power. Investigators have employed rather similar elements in describing and explaining patterns of power,[10] and although the precise definitions of power vary considerably, it has been suggested that

their common sophistication by now should include the tenets that power is a relation among people, not an attribute or possession of a person or group, and that an adequate description of a power situation at a specified time must refer to (a) the extension or domain of power of each actor (that is, the set of persons over whom he has power); (b) the range or scope of power (the responses of B which A can influence); (c) the bases of power, both in B's motives and in the behaviors and objects which A can supply to satisfy those motives; (d) the strength of power (can A affect B's value position greatly or only slightly?); (e) the amount and direction of power (to what extent measured in probability or frequency can A get B to change his response, and is the change in the intended direction?); (f) the means of power (how does A mediate between his power base and B's actions?); and (g) the costs to A of exercising power.[11]

Intimately associated with the verbal problem is an empirical one. Investigators have seldom operationalized power in meaningful terms. Because empirical references have infrequently been assigned to the concept, even simple hypotheses employing the variable have scarcely been tested systematically against the real world. The scant operational attention the concept has received to date is perhaps not surprising. The elements comprising power are so many, and so interrelated, that extraordinarily complex models are probably required to explain and verify adequately their interaction in the real world.[12] The problem is compounded by the difficulty of securing relevant observations on many of the aspects of power, a problem that arises in part from the sensitivity attached to power relationships by individuals in the actual world. Since power relationships account for who gets what, when, and how, individuals involved in the process of effecting power relationships frequently conceal their activities with a veil of secrecy.

Can the concept of power be operationalized meaningfully? Some observers have thought not.[13] Final judgment must be reserved until the systematic effort to do so has been fully explored.

Purpose and Scope of this Study

The purpose of this book is to contribute to a theoretical-empirical elucidation of the concept of power by: focusing on one aspect of the overall phenomenon of power, namely, the power capabilities of nation-states; devising an index for measuring the power capabilities of nation-states; setting forth a theory that relates the power capabilities of states to the occurrence of conflict, especially war, and to the outcome of the latter; and testing the theory systematically against evidence drawn from the real world. It should be noted that "theory" here refers to a series of interrelated propositions that seek to explain, in part, some phenomenon. It does not refer to propositions so interrelated that one or more deductions can automatically be made.

Conflict occurs when two or more entities "seek to possess the same object, occupy the same space or the same exclusive position, play incompatible roles, maintain incompatible goals, or undertake mutually incompatible means for achieving their purposes."[14] In international politics conflict arises when actors pursue a variety of objectives, some of which can be realized only at the expense of the interests and values of other parties. The actors are typically, but not always, governments of nation-states. Other actors are private citizens and interest groups within states, including rebellious movements, and, external to states, dependent political entities such as colonies and trusteeships, and independent actors such as multinational corporations and the United Nations.

In this book only those conflicts and wars in which at least one participant to each side of the conflict is both a sovereign state and a member of the international system will be examined. For those conflicts that do qualify, only those participants that are independent states and members of the international system are studied. Civil wars, revolutionary wars, and wars between sovereign and dependent states will be excluded.

The geographical area under review is the world of sovereign nation-states.[15] Chronologically the study covers the period from 1850 to 1965. There are several reasons for the choice of this time frame. First, war is a relatively infrequent event in the sum total of relations between nation-states. By selecting a 116-year period it was possible to secure a set of wars sufficiently large for statistically testing the validity of the hypotheses. Second, a universe of wars covering this time frame had already been defined in the works of Lewis Richardson, Quincy Wright, and J. David Singer and Melvin Small. Third, with these data already available, it was possible to launch the still remaining large-scale data-collecting effort necessary for operationalizing the concept of power capabilities for all nation-states between 1850 and 1966.

Power Defined

Conventional wisdom equates power with the ability to influence others. But some theorists long ago rejected this definition on the grounds that influence and power are qualitatively different in several key respects.[16] Two other concepts have frequently been used more or less interchangeably with that of power and are integral to the controversy over how best to define power. They are "force" and "authority." It is not necessary for the purpose of this study to reexamine in detail the arguments that have been advanced for how these four concepts can be best employed,[17] but a brief review in this chapter of some of the important distinctions that have been made is useful in providing an appreciation of the complexities and difficulties inherent in efforts to grasp theoretically what the essence of power is and to subject the concept to empirical analysis.

Perhaps the clearest explication of the differentiating aspects of power, influence, force, and authority is that outlined by Bachrach and Baratz, and consequently this short review will draw heavily upon their interpretation.[18] Power, as they define it, is relational and involves three characteristics.

1. There must be a conflict of interests or values between two or more persons or groups.

2. One group, A, must threaten sanctions to be applied to the second group, B, if B does not conform to A's wishes.

3. B must be aware of what is expected, must regard the threatened sanctions as a deprivation, and must accede to the wishes of A because greater value would be sacrificed should it disobey rather than comply. If B is aware and does regard the threatened sanctions as deprivation, but refuses to obey, then A's attempt to effect a power relationship collapses. It collapses because A fails to control B's behavior. "A" may accept the failure or can again seek to assert a power relationship by *using* force to make B comply.

Force is a second type of relationship. It involves the actual application of sanctions and results in an establishment of a power relationship if the party, B, to which the sanctions are applied, gives in to the objectives of the enforcer so as to end the deprivation. The power relationship is not established if the enforcer is unable to cause the target of its sanctions to submit to its will.[19]

Influence is different from power and force in that if A has influence over B, B's behavior conforms to A's wishes, but not as a response to deprivations threatened by A nor as a result of the application of force by A. B acts in accord with A's wishes because B finds A's objectives attractive in their own light or because A is able to proffer rewards that are valued highly enough by B to warrant compliance.[20]

Finally, in an authority relationship one party, A, has authority over another party, B, when the latter sees A's command as reasonable in terms of its overall value system. Expressed differently, in B's set of values A has "rightful" authority to command B to perform certain acts.[21] As an example, B, a citizen, regularly observes certain laws laid down by his community, A, not because of threatened deprivation (the laws are unenforceable or at any rate B knows he can violate them without being detected and caught, much less prosecuted and convicted), nor because of A's influence (B in fact thinks some of the laws are nonsensical), nor because of the exertion of force (B does not disobey, so A does not apply force), but because A's command is viewed as legitimate.

Some critics may object to the above conception of power on the basis of what is known as the rule of anticipated reaction. According to this rule, B *anticipates* that A will act in a specific way, i.e., apply sanctions if B does not perform a certain action, x. Without any communication between the two, B performs action x because it wants to avoid the expected deprivation. In this situation, according to these critics, A is said to have power over B, even though A may in fact not have planned to apply sanctions if B did not do x. Indeed, one can imagine an extreme case in which A is not even aware of B's existence.[22] It cannot be denied that in this illustration B's compliance arises from his estimation of A's behavior. On the other hand, B conceivably might react differently to a situation in which A threatens sanctions if compliance with a given set of actions is not forthcoming than in a situation where B thinks A will eventually demand compliance and impose sanctions if B does not comply. In the latter case B could decide to await A's demand, thinking that he perhaps could persuade A to modify its objectives. In the former case, B may be so enraged by A's threat as to refuse to obey. Hence, there appears to be good reason for distinguishing between the two types of situations.

Other critics may object to the above differentiation of power, force, influence, and authority on the grounds that two or more of the elements will be inherent in many relationships and, consequently, that it will be difficult to draw the line between them. This objection, while accurate, is perhaps not sufficient for overriding the distinctions. It is well accepted that human behavior springs from multiple motivations. What is important is that in some situations all four elements will be present, whereas in other cases various combinations of less than four will account for the behavior expressed. To explain behavior fully, one must know which elements co-occur and under what circumstances. On the other hand, one can only sympathize with the empirical analyst faced with the task of compiling valid observations of ongoing power, influence, authority, and force relationships, much less those that have existed in the past. Many of the relevant actors under purview may themselves equate two or more of the elements, and in any case not clearly differentiate among the four unless requested or required to do so. Moreover, behavioral responses to the different kinds of relationships will frequently be the same, so that, unless the exact sequence of events which preceded the behavior, including the perceptions and intimate thoughts of the actors, are known, one will be at a loss about how to categorize any given relationship, with the possible exception of the force relation. The latter involves an act of physical compulsion in the face of active resistance and thus typically results in readily observable manifestations.

Whether or not it is possible to distinguish meaningfully, empirically as well as theoretically, among power, influence, force, and authority is in the final sense an empirical question that can only be answered by the results of rigorous and concerted efforts to do so. For the purpose of this book the author's position regarding the definition of power is to adhere to the general interpretation provided above, while employing the caveat that this usage is essentially academic. As previously noted, the primary focus of this endeavor is the power capabilities of nation-states and, hence, the bases of power relevant to the effectation of power relationships among states.

What is important about this focus in terms of our discussion is that power capabilities are highly relevant to all four types of relationships. Power capabilities are required if force is to be exerted and if a threat to use force is to be made. The base for authority rests upon the notion of legitimacy and is manifest in the existence of particular value structures, but authority also typically depends on the ability to exact sanctions when its tenets are violated. (The difference between the sanctions of an authority relationship and those of a power relationship is that in the former the sanctions are perceived as legitimate by the community within which it is applied, if not always by the actual target of the sanctions, whereas in the latter the community within which or against which sanctions are applied denies rightfulness to the actions.) Finally, influence relationships arise at least partly out of the ability to tender rewards, and power capabilities can provide a base for the making of rewards. As an example, a state well endowed with power capabilities can afford to enter into alliances with other states in exchange for favors it desires.

Power Capabilities Defined

Adhering to the above interpretation of power, then, power capabilities can be defined as those factors that enable one entity to threaten sanctions vis-à-vis another. Power capabilities are a prerequisite for the assertion of a power relationship but are not synonymous with such a relationship. It is a truism that without the means for threatening deprivation upon another, a power relationship cannot be established. Yet to possess the means for enforcing deprivation upon another is not equivalent to a power relationship, since one must seek to effect a relationship and successfully secure it. As noted above, one party may enforce significant deprivation upon a second party yet fail to force the latter to accede to its demands.[23] Some existing evidence points to the importance of the mere possession of power capabilities. The simple existence of punitive options has been found to exacerbate conflict by arousing fear. If this holds across the board, it may be that over the short run, at least, power capabilities contribute more frequently to a breakdown of power relationships than an assertion of such a relationship.[24]

The factors that an individual or group can utilize in an effort to assert a power relationship depend upon those things highly valued by the threatened party and upon the former's ability to jeopardize the continued or future fulfillment of these values. Conceivably, anything that a given entity values is a potential object that another can threaten to deprive it of, provided that the former already possesses the valued object or will possess it in the future, and assuming no interference by an outside party. Robert Dahl has suggested that the offer of rewards by one party, A, to another party, B, in return for B's compliance with some act, desired by A, be considered a power relationship. If B is "offered a very large reward for compliance, *then once his expectations are adjusted to this large reward*, he suffers a prospective loss if he does not comply."[25] In our opinion, this type of situation should be differentiated from a power relationship, because B is likely to attach more value to an object, Y, which it already possesses and which it regards as rightfully belonging to itself, than to the same object Y if Y is not and has not been possessed by B. In the latter case there is no reason for B to assume rightful ownership nor can A threaten to deprive B of what it does not have. This is true even if B's expectations have shifted to anticipate receiving a large reward. More importantly, there is reason to believe that individuals react differently to behavior that is rewarding as opposed to that which is threatening.[26]

The focus of this study is on the behavior of nation-states. Meaningful sanctions in relations between states are those that deprive a state of things it possesses or will possess in the future, assuming no external interference, and which it deems valuable to its well-being. Things deemed valuable may include access to natural resources in the international environment, freedom of navigation on international waterways, participation in international organizations. As a bare minimum, any state values its ability to govern and regulate its internal affairs and its external relations with other states, since these are a *sine qua non* of statehood.

Military force is the most drastic sanction that states impose upon one another. The outbreak of war between two states represents the extreme manifestation of a breakdown in a power relationship (or the attempt to assert a power relationship) and the extreme manifestation of a force relationship. States employ military force as a last resort to compel other nations to follow their dictates, and under some circumstances use military force to annihilate other states as a penalty for their failure to do as bidden. Consequently, in this study, the concept of power capabilities will refer to a state's general ability to employ military force against another state. The emphasis is on military force because it is the ultimate sanction and because the principal goal of this study is to determine if power capabilities are significantly related to whether states employ military force in the course of conflict with one another and, if such force is applied, whether it is significantly related to certain outcomes of such conflicts.

Military Hostilities and War Defined

Military hostilities occur when both sides to a conflict resort to the use of military force with resulting casualties and fatalities. At what point does a conflict involving military hostilities become a war? Are all military hostilities wars? Unfortunately, there is a current lack of consensus within the discipline about what is a war and what is something less. Scholars who have sought to define systematically inventories of war events have tended to agree that a minimum threshold of involvement by the participants must be present if a conflict is to qualify as a war, but there is less than complete agreement as to what that threshold might be.

Lewis Richardson largely restricted his study of war to conflicts in which the number killed on both sides equalled 317 or more.[27] Richardson declared that there did not appear to be any scientific reason for terminating the list of fatal quarrels at any level less than 317, but observed that many of these conflicts were insurrections, revolts, or riots and thus "distinct in their causation from international war."[28] Quincy Wright, in identifying international conflicts that involved military hostilities during the 1945-1965 period, adopted the same threshold, arguing that it represented "sufficient size and organization to justify the designation 'war' in the material sense," and that there were so many revolutions, border incidents, and interventions of a magnitude less than 317 deaths that "the list would have been unduly long if they had been included."[29] More recently, J. David Singer and Melvin Small have proposed a somewhat larger threshold, defining as interstate war only those conflicts that lead to a minimum of one thousand battle-connected fatalities among all the participants. In addition, they insist that a state sustain a minimum of one hundred fatalities or have a minimum of one thousand of its armed forces personnel engaged in active combat within the war theater in order to qualify as a war participant, and a conflict qualifies as an interstate war only if at least one entity on each side qualifies as a member nation of the international system.[30]

Hence, there are pragmatic and theoretical grounds for establishing some minimum threshold as a qualifying criterion for specifying war events. Other criteria than number of fatalities have, of course, been proposed and used by investigators to delineate war events. In *A Study of War*, Quincy Wright employed a variable mixture of standards to identify war events for the

1480-1940 time period, including whether a conflict was legally recognized as a war, level of troop involvement, and political consequences flowing from the event. The fatalities indicator, however, has become the most commonly applied index. As noted above, Wright himself used it to specify war events for the 1945-1965 years. In terms of the time frame of the present study, inventories based on the fatalities threshold provide the most complete identification of war events.

At the same time, there is a degree of arbitrariness inherent in the choice of particular thresholds. There does not appear to be any a priori reason for supposing that a level of one thousand fatalities is inherently a better threshold than nine hundred fatalities, or that 317 fatalities is a better threshold than 316. It is also a moot question whether or not there is something intrinsically different between conflicts involving 317 and one thousand fatalities which necessarily makes one a more valid criterion for delineating war events.[31] Most students of the subject, however, would probably agree that both thresholds are intuitively more reasonable than twenty-five or fifty fatalities.

The present study does not propose to offer an alternative standard, since any definitive resolution of the problem is probably not possible, would require a level of effort beyond the limit of feasibility for the present endeavor, and in any case may not be at all necessary. Military hostilities involving from 317 to 999 fatalities do represent an important level of material sacrifice and hence of involvement on the part of participant states, which is attested to by the fact that not many conflicts between nation-states attain such a level.[32] Moreover, reliance on the lower threshold permits use of a somewhat enlarged set of observations, and this is important for statistical testing of hypotheses when the total number of events under consideration is small. This was an important consideration for using the smaller threshold in testing some of the hypotheses in the present study that focus on the 1919-1965 time period.

Furthermore, a not inconsiderable amount of effort has already been expended for generating existing data bases. Given the extent of our current imperfect understanding of war, it now seems most reasonable to work with those data banks at hand. If there is something qualitatively different about a threshold involving only 317 fatalities and another comprising one thousand, then that should become apparent in the form of disparate findings that result from the use of the two different thresholds. Such findings would be sufficient reason for further inquiry into the matter and might themselves proffer clues or evidence as to possible reasons for such differences.

For the purpose of this study, therefore, both thresholds have been used. The validity of some of the hypotheses formulated in the course of the inquiry is tested by the use of the one-thousand-threshold criterion, while certain other hypotheses are tested according to the more modest threshold of 317. As previously noted, this study requires that at least one participant to each side of a conflict qualify for membership in the international system of sovereign states, and the criteria for membership are largely those used by Singer and Small. Hence, the principal differences distinguishing conflicts that qualify as wars according to the one thousand level as opposed to the 317 threshold, aside from the size of the threshold, are that conflicts that qualify as wars according to the 317 criterion do not necessarily meet the standard for individual participation of either one hundred fatalities or one thousand armed forces personnel engaged in the war theater. And the tabulation of fatalities for the 317 criterion is not restricted to military battle-connected deaths.

In order that the reader may always be aware of which operational definition is in use, the concept "military hostilities" will be used in those hypotheses that rely upon the lower limit, and the concept "war" will be applied in those hypotheses operationalized according to the higher standard. Apart from the hypotheses themselves and specific reference to them, "war" will be used in a more general sense to designate either condition.

2

Theoretical Overview: Power Capabilities and War

Power and war are phenomena central to the study of politics in general and international politics in particular. Our purpose in this chapter is not to review all that has been written about power and war, since that alone would require a volume or more. Our focus is much more restricted, arising from the overall purpose that has guided the framing of this study, namely, a theoretical and empirical examination of relationships between power capabilities, on the one hand, and the occurrence of military hostilities, on the other. To this end we will review in this chapter some of the principal works that have asserted the existence of relationships between the variables or that have adduced empirical support or opposition to such relationships.

In the process we shall at times find it necessary to use the concept "power" in a more inclusive fashion than was outlined in Chapter 1. Concepts of authority, force, influence, control, and power capabilities have all been used interchangeably with the concept of power. As already noted, this problem is compounded by the fact that investigators often fail to specify explicitly their intended meaning. Consequently, one must frequently infer what the concept of power connotes in a particular context. In speaking of "power" in this chapter, therefore, we are reporting on its usage by other theorists. We do so when the concept appears to designate the notion of power capabilities. We do not, however, substitute the concept "power capabilities" for their usage, since in at least some cases the theorists have meant more than just power capabilities.

Are Power Capabilities Relevant to the Causation of War?

Systematic inquiry into the causes of war is of recent origin. By systematic inquiry is meant that which includes the structuring of hypotheses for testing, the operationalization of key concepts within the hypotheses, and the testing of the hypotheses against a respectable sample of events.

It was not until the 1940s and 1950s that the results of efforts by Quincy Wright[1] and Lewis Richardson[2] to provide theoretical criteria and empirical identification of past wars became available. In the 1960s, J. David Singer and Melvin Small,[3] not fully satisfied with the efforts of Wright and Richardson, launched their own study for defining and identifying a universe of war events.[4] Since it is only with the identification of a representative sample of events that one can begin to compile data on independent variables that one might suspect to be causally related to the occurrence of war, it is perhaps not surprising that there is a paucity of evidence, in terms of systematic inquiry, about the causes of war. Studies that focus on a relatively large number of wars, that identify independent variables possibly related to the outbreak of war, and that are based on empirical observation of variation in the independent and dependent variables are few and far between.[5] Consequently, knowledge of the causes of war remains vague and ill defined. This is true with respect to hypotheses about the relation of power capabilities to the onset of war, as well as for other important variables. Rummel observes that although it is the central thesis of international relations that power relationships determine the policy and behavior of states, it has yet to be shown that power is a concept leading to testable propositions of nation behavior.[6]

Two of the classical studies on the causes of war, *Statistics of Deadly Quarrels*[7] and *A Study of War,*[8] differ significantly in coverage of, importance attributed to, and findings about relationships between power and the occurrence of war. In the former, Lewis Richardson identified a large number of conflicts (between independent nation-states, between independent and dependent states, and between various groups within individual states) that resulted in hostilities.[9] He set forth some sixty background conditions of variables possibly related to the outbreak of hostilities and classified each according to whether it was judged likely to promote amity, ambivalence, or hostility with respect to the occurrence of conflict. The classification scheme was derived from the ideas of certain other scholars and especially from a review of histories relevant to each of the conflicts. Of the many variables listed by Richardson, only a few seem to be classifiable as power-related variables. Two, in particular, are the "tail-group felt itself stronger than the tip-group" and the "tail-group had been making exceptional preparations for war."[10] In view of the importance many theorists in international relations have attached to power-related variables, it is surprising that Richardson's long list of independent variables includes so few. As already noted, it was largely constructed from historical reviews of particular conflicts, not from theoretical works; so that if he included in his study all the factors cited, power-type variables were seldom adduced as a cause of international conflicts.

Equally interesting is that Richardson hypothesized in his classificatory scheme that both of the above-quoted "tip-tail-group" variables were "ambivalent" with respect to the occurrence of "deadly quarrels."[11] This is curious, since Richardson did not offer a rationale in justification of his reasoning and since alternative explanations, equally if not more plausible, would readily come to mind. For example, one might argue that conflicts are likely to escalate to hostilities when one of the two sides perceives itself to be stronger than the other. In such circumstances the stronger may conclude that it has little to lose and much to gain by going to war and hence go out of its way to provoke hostilities or even initiate hostilities in pursuit of its objectives. It is likewise reasonable to hypothesize that exceptional preparations for war by one side will provoke hostilities. Neighboring states may undertake counter-preparations as a defensive measure, which in turn may unleash an arms race that eventually leads to hostilities. Or a neighboring party might find the preparations for war so threatening as to launch a preventive war.

A third point of import is inherent in Richardson's findings. No mention is made of the two power-type variables. It would appear that he either did not calculate the results for these two variables or, if he did, that he found them to be unimportant for the purpose of citing. An examination of Richardson's raw data has disclosed that thirty-six of his conflicts are classified elsewhere, by Singer and Small, as interstate wars.[12] Of these only three are coded by Richardson as being conflicts where the tail-group's exceptional preparations for war were a contributing factor to the conflict: the War of the Italian Union and the First and Second World Wars. None of the thirty-six is coded as being a conflict in which one side's feeling itself to be stronger than the other precipitated the conflict. The data thus supports Richardson's presumption of a null relationship between the power-type variables on the one hand, and the occurrence of military hostilities on the other.[13] Theorists who have heretofore asserted the importance of power-type factors should be especially interested in these results.

In direct contrast to Richardson's work is Quincy Wright's *A Study of War*. In this volume Wright introduced original data on warfare among primitive peoples and on war between independent states of "modern" civilization. In his theoretical discussion of the causes of war, Wright appears to have commented on nearly every conceivable factor that might be related to its occurrence. His discussion included extensive coverage of power-type variables and incorporated a comparative analysis of the extent to which great powers have participated in war as opposed to lesser powers. As to the causes of war, Wright concluded that the concept of balance of power provided the most general explanation (although other factors are also said to be important) for the occurrence of war in Europe since the early seventeenth century.[14]

His analysis, however, rests upon historical interpretation of who the great and lesser powers were, rather than a rigorous empirical effort to identify greater and lesser powers by quantification of the power capabilities of states over time. Overall, Wright's examination of and generalizations about independent variables related to the occurrence of war appears to rest largely on a review of six major wars that transpired during the 1480-1945 time frame. In a later study Wright did undertake a more systematic analysis of relationships between power capabilities and the occurrence of military hostilities, about which more will be said shortly.

Theorists who have held power-type factors to be important to the occurrence of war have argued over whether an equilibrated or unequilibrated distribution of power capabilities is more likely to contribute to the outbreak of war. This debate has been conducted around the notion of balance of power.

The concept balance of power has been subjected to criticism in recent years,[15] but international theorists have not abandoned its usage.[16] A principal reason for criticism is found in the multiple meanings various theorists have attached to the concept and in their frequent failure to specify which meaning or meanings they have in mind in the context of their discourse.[17] Critical commentary by others of such usage is likely to persist until theorists are regularly explicit as to the verbal meaning attached to usage of the concept and until valid empirical reference terms are established for operationalizing the concept.

The meaning of balance of power used here is that adopted by Inis Claude to designate one type of international system, namely, a system of states organized so that the various states operate autonomously, without the controlling direction of a superior agency, and most if not all states compete with one another in an effort to aggrandize power, so as to protect as best as possible their individual interests.[18] States seek to prevent other states from securing a preponderance of power which would threaten seriously their individual security and frequently try to increase their strength so as to match, if not exceed, that of other members in the system.[19]

The concepts of equilibrated and unequilibrated refer to the amount of power capabilities possessed by various actors in the system and specifically to whether capabilities are distributed equally or not. Theoretically, power capabilities can be so distributed so that all states have an approximately equal amount or some actors may possess greater capabilities than others.

In *Politics Among Nations*, Hans Morgenthau equated the notion of equilibrium with that of balance, declaring that he would use the term "balance of power," unless otherwise qualified, to mean "an actual state of affairs in which power is distributed among several nations with approximate equality."[20] However, this characterization is perhaps overly restrictive, since it is questionable whether power capabilities of states have frequently, if ever, been distributed equally. The power capabilities scores derived in the course of this study and covering all independent states in the international system for the 1850-1966 period are a case in point.

It appears that the notion of equilibrium as more generally used designates a system in which power can be distributed unequally among states but in which no single state or group of actors in combination is allowed to overwhelm the other actors.[21] As Morton Kaplan has said, it is an essential rule for the behavior of states who would preserve a balance of power system to "act to oppose any coalition or single actor which tends to assume a position of predominance with respect to the rest of the system."[22]

In employing the concepts of equilibrium and disequilibrium, theorists frequently fail to state explicitly whether their generalizations designate all states in the international system or only one or more subsets of states.[23] At times the usage appears to apply only to the major actors in the system; at other times to all states; and at still other times to any conceivable subset of actors, such as any dyad or tryad.[24] In this study equilibrium and disequilibrium will designate the latter, the only exception possibly being when the ideas of other theorists are cited. There we will try to indicate which usage a theorist seems to have in mind. (It is not always possible to be definitive, however, because of obscure language used by theorists. When that occurs, a theorist's writing can be considered only suggestive with respect to hypothesizing relationships between power capabilities and the occurrence of war.)

Does a condition of approximately equilibrated power capabilities promote peace? Inis Claude surveyed usage of the concepts of equilibrium and disequilibrium and reported that theorists and statesmen were divided over the question. He pointed out some of the pitfalls of drawing a conclusion one way or the other:

The notion that confrontation with approximately equal power will deter a state from undertaking aggressive adventures is often stated as a commonsense proposition. [Claude seems to refer to any combination of opposing states.] This assumes that statesmen will be guided by common sense, or rational prudence. War is begun with the expectation of winning; if the opposing power is equal to that of the disturber of the peace, the latter can have no reasonably confident expectation of victory. Indeed, it is traditionally assumed that equality gives the defender an edge over the attacker. Hence, the reasonable statesman will refrain from starting trouble in an equilibrium situation.

However, one may argue that if an equilibrium means that either side may lose, it also means that either side may win. The advantage of the equal power of the defender may be offset by the advantage which surprise attack may give the offensive state. Statesmen may not require more than a fair chance of victory; while they may be unwilling to gamble against heavy odds, they may not regard it as reckless to attack when the odds appear substantially even. In those terms, equilibrium may present a feeble deterrent.

After noting other pros and cons, including the apparent motives, morals, and purposes of the superior state, Claude concludes that equilibrium is a condition more favorable to the preservation of peace. Equilibrium, Claude declares, fails to provide any group of states with a *marginal* sense of security against attack, but it is less threatening than a preponderance of power in favor of one state. The latter "sets in motion the dynamic urge to challenge the champion, an urge which is postponed only until the challenger feels reasonably well equipped." The sense of insecurity experienced by the state in a position of decided inferiority is sufficiently intense to impel it to close the gap and, as the gap is narrowed, to embark upon war. A condition of marked disequilibrium, therefore, may not be directly associated with war, but it "looses the drives that lead to war."[25]

The idea that an equilibrated distribution of power promotes peace is supported by Morgenthau, but on different grounds. In his judgment, without a state of equilibrium one element in the system "will gain ascendancy over the others, encroach upon their interests and rights, and may ultimately destroy them."[26] The notion is also supported by Wright, who argues that stability in the international system increases as parity in the power of member states increases. The ability of each state to defend itself is enhanced when power is distributed equally, even if the system is characterized by a large number of states acting independently of one another. Great instability would occur if the system were comprised of only two states and one of the two possessed superior capabilities, and the same is said to result if the system is polarized into two rival camps.[27]

As noted above, Wright concluded that the concept of balance of power provided the most general explanation for the occurrence of war in Europe since the early seventeenth century, but his account is unclear as to whether most of these wars were due to an imbalance in the system as a whole or to an imbalance within a subset of states. The discussion seems to stress the role of major powers, suggesting that war usually resulted when one of the principal powers became so strong as to threaten the other major actors.

The notion that an equilibrated distribution of power capabilities furthers peace is opposed by Organski:

The relationship between peace and the balance of power appears to be exactly the opposite of what has been claimed. The periods of balance [Organski may be talking about the system as a whole], real or imagined, are periods of warfare, while the periods of known preponderance are periods of peace.

The claim that a balance of power is conducive to peace does not stand up. Indeed, it is not even logical. It stands to reason that nations will not fight unless they believe they have a good chance of winning but this is true for both sides only when the two are fairly evenly matched, or at least when they believe they are. [Organski seems to be referring to any possible subset of opposing states.] Thus a balance of power increases the chances of war. A preponderance of power on one side, on the other hand, increases the chances for peace, for the greatly stronger side need not fight at all to get what it wants, while the weaker side would be plainly foolish to attempt to battle for what it wants.[28]

It might be objected that Organski overlooks the likelihood that a more powerful state may drive its neighbor to war by making demands so outrageous as to require the neighbor's resort to war, or by actually attacking the neighboring state in pursuit of its objectives, irrespective of the possibility of securing its goals by the mere threat to resort to force. While Organski does not categorically rule out the former, he is emphatic in absolving preponderant states of blame for initiating major wars:

There is one last point that must be raised about the balance of power. According to the theory, the danger of aggression is to be expected from the stronger nation. A peaceful nation intent on maximizing its power is expected to press its advantage and make war upon its neighbors if it ever succeeds in achieving a clear preponderance of power. Here again, the facts do not back up the theory. Nations with preponderant power have indeed dominated their neighbors, but they have not been the ones to start the major wars that have marked recent history. This role has fallen almost without exception to the weaker side.[29]

Organski's position receives some support from Rudolph J. Rummel, who argues that a power disparity is necessary in order for peace to prevail between two states. A situation of preponderance is characterized by intimidation. The weaker side recognizes, implicitly or otherwise, the threat of the stronger side's using force and gives in to avoid such a consequence. In a condition of approximate parity, however, ambiguity prevails, with neither side being able to judge accurately which has greater capabilities. The temptation arises, therefore, to engage in battle, presumably to eliminate the ambiguity and determine which of the two is the stronger.[30]

Evidence

The position that weak states would be foolish to fight against formidable opponents has enjoyed considerable support among theorists of international relations and served as a basic premise of the deterrence school. Empirical evidence to the contrary, however, has been provided in a cross-historical study conducted by Raoul Naroll.[31] His study drew a sample of twenty cases, covering a period of two thousand years and focusing on several major world civilizations. He selected, for each specified time period and given civilization, the state that was most conspicuously involved in conflicts with other states and paired it with the state with which it was most frequently involved in diplomatic or military rivalry. Naroll's hypothesis that war would be less frequent when the conspicuous state maintained a defensive stance and enjoyed military advantages of numerically larger, more mobile, and better quality armed forces, along with extensive fortifications, was not upheld. On the contrary, superior military power apparently made war more likely.

Evidence contrary to Naroll's is found in a study by Wright that focused on forty-five nation-state conflicts that occurred during the 1920-1965 period.[32] Of these, nine involved no military action, twenty escalated to the level of military hostilities, and the remainder resulted in military hostilities that escalated beyond a year's duration or above a level of one thousand casualties.[33] Among the findings to emerge from the analysis: relative equality in forces immediately available to participants promoted escalation when each side believed it could amass superior forces, either on its own or via support from allies; comparative equality in forces available and great capability for destruction militated against escalation; and a marked imbalance in forces immediately available to the parties, or anticipated to develop in the course of further conflict, militated against escalation. The results are only suggestive, however, since operationalization of the independent variables was based on subjective evaluations. By Wright's own admission, the findings are "educated guesses," requiring more precise measurement of the variables.[34]

A recent study by Singer and Small, restricted to major powers and covering the period between 1815 and 1965, found some evidence that strength is more conducive to peace.[35] Of sixty-five nations involved in war, 60 percent had power capabilities below the average for all major powers, whereas only 40 percent had capabilities above the average. On the other hand, when the relative capabilities of the sides to specific wars were examined, seven of the nine wars studied were characterized by a marked disparity in capabilities.

Yet another study by Singer, along with Stuart Bremer and John Stuckey, outlined and applied to a subsystem of the international system two alternative models that incorporate many of the basic notions discussed in this study. One model predicts that there will be less war in the subsystem comprised of the major powers when there is approximate parity among them, change toward parity, and a relatively fluid power hierarchy. The second model predicts the opposite, namely, that there will be less war when there is a preponderance of power capabilities concentrated in the hands of a few states, change toward greater concentration, and a relatively stable rank order among the major nations. The models are tested against the subsystem of major powers for the 1820-1965 period. The findings show that predictions of the parity-fluidity model are closer to historical reality for the nineteenth century, whereas the preponderance and stability explanation better describes the twentieth century, although not nearly as well.[36]

Evidence on the preponderance versus equilibrium controversy has also been forthcoming from experimental inquiry. An internation simulation at Northwestern University predicted that when one state, OMNE, acquired invulnerability in nuclear forces, the probability of strategic war would decrease. In fact, the exact opposite resulted. OMNE became more belligerent and aggressive, which in turn led to a significant increase in the number of nuclear wars.[37]

In an experimental study undertaken by Swingle and MacLean, the investigators created conditions of unilateral power, bilateral power, and no power in conjunction with a Prisoner's Dilemma Game and a Chicken Game.[38] Bilateral and no-power dyads demonstrated less conflict or competition than unilateral power, and bilateral-power dyads were least conflictual in both games.

While it is not certain to what degree one can generalize from experimental situations to the real world, the findings suggest that states having a preponderance of power may act more aggressively and hence contribute to an increase in the frequency of war.

Rank-Disequilibrium and Power Capabilities

Johan Galtung has outlined a theory of aggression that includes equilibrium-preponderance notions, but which assesses the importance of these in terms of the concept of rank-disequilibrium.[39] In any system, whether of individuals, groups, or nations, there is said to be a division of labor. Actors in the system are evaluated and ranked according to a number of criteria. Actors who score either high or low on all criteria are said to be in equilibrium. Actors who score in-between are said to be in rank-disequilibrium. Aggression, Galtung argues, is most likely to be associated with positions of rank-disequilibrium.

The theory assumes that an actor in a disequilibrated position will be more dissatisfied than an actor ranked low on all criteria, on the grounds that with one foot in at the top and one foot in at the bottom the actor is constantly reminded of its disequilibrium. Moreover, in an achievement world such as we presently find ourselves, actors are thought to be more likely to raise claims for compensation on the basis of achievement than lack of achievement. Finally, rank-disequilibrated actors, by virtue of their position, have better access to resources than lower-ranked actors and hence are more capable of initiating aggression to improve their position.[40]

As applied to the system of nation-states, then, aggression is more likely to occur between states that share differentially in the ranking criteria of the system; states that lie between the lowest- and top-ranked actors are most likely to aggress. Galtung stands apart from Organski, since implicit in his model is the idea that aggression will no longer be necessary once a rank-disequilibrated actor begins to approach closely the top-ranked actors. Galtung sides with Claude in regarding an equilibrium situation as more conducive to peace, but his notion of equilibrium is qualitatively different and more complex. His model, unlike Claude's, allows for a peaceful world in which there can be a wide disparity in the extent to which states share in power capabilities, provided that the disparity exists across the broad spectrum of criteria on which the actors are evaluated. At the same time, two (or more) states within the system may enjoy preponderant capabilities relevant to other actors but approximately equivalent capabilities relative to one another, and still be unlikely to engage in armed conflict with one another—if they are ranked about the same on other criteria of the system.

Several empirical analyses aimed at evaluating the validity of the rank-disequilibrium model have been completed. One, by Michael Wallace,[41] focused on the dimension of power capabilities. Wallace hypothesized that rank-disequilibrium or status inconsistency would correlate significantly with the amount of international war. Status inconsistency was measured as the difference between national rankings on achieved and ascribed status dimensions. Five indicators of power capabilities were selected to represent *achieved* status, and one indicator of diplomatic importance was chosen to represent ascribed status. The hypothesis was tested for the 1820-1964 time frame (as well as subsets of the 144-year period). A subset of the international system comprising the more active and influential state members was utilized. Significant associations were found between status inconsistency and the amount of international war when time lags of ten and fifteen years were employed.[42] In a subsequent study, Wallace probed the relation further by incorporating additional variables into the equation and applying causal modeling techniques to the analysis.[43] The consequence was a significant reduction in correlation coefficients, with the highest coefficient explaining no more than 9 percent of the variance for status inconsistency.

Overview

Few concepts are as basic and central to an understanding of international politics as those of power and power capabilities, yet theoreticians and practitioners remain divided as to whether an equilibrated distribution of power capabilities, or its converse, is more conducive to the maintenance of peace. Systematic theoretical and empirical inquiry aimed at shedding light on, if not fully resolving, the problem is only now beginning to get underway. What little evidence is presently available is contradictory and ranges across the broad spectrum, from that indicating little or no relationship, to evidence in favor of the preponderance school of thought, to that in favor of the equilibrium viewpoint.

Resolving the matter will in all likelihood be no easy affair and may require many studies employing a variety of perspectives and empirical tools of analysis. Results may vary considerably, depending upon whether an investigator's focal point is systemic, a smaller subset of states such as the major actors, or interactions among any subset of system members. Equally important to the outcome may be whether the focus of attention is on potential power, forces in being available for immediate use, or some combination of the two. The meaningfulness of the overall results, of course, will hinge critically upon the reliability and validity of the measures chosen to operationalize key concepts, and whether or not results from similar and divergent theoretical perspectives can be fitted together so as to embody a harmonious and logical whole.

3

Power Capabilities Related to the Occurrence and Resolution of War: A Theoretical Model

Introduction

This chapter outlines an elementary model relating the power capabilities of nation-states to the occurrence of war and to certain aspects of the resolution of such conflicts. Three principal distinctions will differentiate the propositions set forth from those examined in Chapter 2. First, the hypotheses will focus on power capabilities as independent variables. Power, in the sense of the control of the behavior of other states and as defined in greater deail in Chapter 1, is outside the present theoretical focus. While it would be an easy task to alter the propositions so as to accommodate the more inclusive concept of power, empirical testing of the resulting hypotheses would require data far beyond the scope of this inquiry.

A second principal distinction concerns the notions of equilibrium and disequilibrium discussed in the last chapter. Our hypotheses predicting the outbreak of war will center on power capabilities relationships between states involved in specific conflicts. We shall not seek to generalize about whether or not an equilibrated or disequilibrated distribution of capabilities in the international system as a whole is significantly related to the outbreak of war. Our preference is to examine particular interstate relationships rather than the system of states as a whole, since the former may be somewhat more important in explaining the involvement of nation-states in conflict. The distribution of capabilities in the system as a whole might change considerably, either away from or toward a state of equilibrium, yet have little effect on many members in the system. For example, change in the capabilities of certain European actors may affect the degree to which capabilities are distributed equally throughout the system, but register little or no impact on states in other regions of the world, such as Latin America or Asia. Conversely, important change in power capabilities relationships among a few states in Latin America may not be of sufficient magnitude to produce significant alteration in the degree to which capabilities at the systemic level are equilibrated, but may be sufficiently important to trigger an outbreak of hostilities among the affected Latin American states.

A third principal distinction is that we will devote more attention to change in relative power capabilities over time. A notion touched upon in the previous chapter, change will be treated more extensively in this chapter. In our judgment change may be an important intervening variable affecting relationships between power capabilities and the occurrence of military hostilities.

Table 3-1 lists the hypotheses formulated for testing, all of which are *a priori*. In the subsequent discourse of this chapter we will briefly outline the rationale and certain underlying assumptions upon which the hypotheses rest. In Chapter 4 procedures for operationalizing the key concepts in the hypotheses will be outlined.

**Perception of Interests at Stake
and Probability of Winning War**

Recognizing that it is possible to conceive of war as the product of a wide variety of causal forces, we propose to view it as primarily a function of two factors: the value or importance which each party to a conflict attaches to a conflicting interest, and the probability that one party to the conflict can secure

Table 3-1

Hypotheses Relating Power Capabilities Variables to Occurrence and Resolution of International Conflicts

1. Given the occurrence of war, the side possessing the greater power capabilities prior to the initiation of war will almost always be victorious.
2. Given the occurrence of war, the greater the power capabilities disparity prior to the initiation of war, the lesser the devastation resulting from the war.
3. Given the occurrence of war, the greater the power capabilities disparity prior to the initiation of war, the shorter the duration of war.
4. Given an interstate conflict, the greater the disparity in the power capabilities relationship between the two sides to the conflict prior to the occurrence of the conflict, the greater the probability the conflict will escalate to the level of military hostilities.
5. Given an interstate conflict *involving the threat of or actual resort to force*, the greater the disparity in the power capabilities relationship between the two sides to the conflict prior to the occurrence of the conflict, the greater the probability the conflict will escalate to the level of military hostilities.
6. Most wars are characterized by a high level of disparity in the power capabilities relationship prevailing between the sides prior to the initiation of war.
7. The greater the change in the power capabilities of states, the greater the probability of involvement in military hostilities.
8. Given an interstate conflict, the greater the change in the power capabilities relationship between the two sides prior to the occurrence of the conflict, the greater the probability the conflict will escalate to the level of military hostilities.
9. Given an interstate conflict *involving the threat of or actual resort to force*, the greater the change in the power capabilities relationship between the two sides prior to the occurrence of the conflict, the greater the probability the conflict will escalate to the level of military hostilities.
10. Most wars are characterized by significant change in the power capabilities relationship between the two sides to the conflict prior to the outbreak of war.
11. Most wars are characterized by significant change toward an equality in power capabilities between the two sides to the conflict prior to the outbreak of war, rather than by insignificant change or change away from an equality in power capabilities.
12. The greater the change in the distribution of power capabilities within the international system, the greater the amount of war.

the interest at issue by resort to the use of military force. Other factors may be pertinent to an explanation of war, but only indirectly as antecedent variables that contribute to variation in these two primary variables.

States come into conflict over interests or desired goals that they deem important or necessary to their welfare and security. If two states desire the same interest, and if the interest cannot be enjoyed equally and fully by both parties, a conflict situation exists. The method of conflict resolution chosen by the two parties depends, in part, upon the value or importance each party attaches to the interest.[1] The importance attached to interests can vary from low to moderate to high. When high value is attached to the interests, "vital" or "national" interests are perceived to be at stake. In any conflict situation between two parties, there are six possible value-attachment outcomes. Party A, for example, may attach low, moderate, or high value to the conflicting interest; party B can do likewise. The six possible combinations are: low-low; low-moderate; low-high; moderate-moderate; moderate-high; and high-high. All other things being equal, war as a method of conflict resolution has a small probability of occurrence when each party to a conflict attaches low value to the desired interest. War has a high probability of occurrence if both sides attach high value to the conflicting interest. In general, the probability of war occurring increases as each party places greater value on the desired interest.

Given two sides to a conflict, the probability that one will win a war is 1 minus the probability that the other will win. As the win-probability of one party increases, the win-probability of the other necessarily diminishes. We assume that the probability of winning a war is primarily a function of the power capabilities each party to the conflict is able to bring to bear. Generally speaking, the side that musters the most capabilities will win the conflict. But more importantly than that, this study hypothesizes that the probability of war itself increases as does the probability that *one* side to the conflict can secure the interest in question through the use of military force. Expressed differently, the likelihood of war increases as does the power capabilities disparity between two sides to a conflict.[2] Relative parity in power capabilities, according to this line of reasoning, has deterrent value. The concept of deterrence places special emphasis upon one particular aspect of a power relationship: those factors requisite for one party to dissuade, tacitly or otherwise, another from either making a threat to employ sanctions or from carrying out such a threat if compliance with its demands is not forthcoming. As Glenn Snyder has said:

Conceived broadly, deterrence appears to be a species of "political power." Defining political power generally as the capacity to induce others to do things or not to do things which they would not otherwise do or refrain from doing, deterrence is simply its negative aspect. It is the power to dissuade another party from doing something which one believes to be against one's interests, achieved by the threat of applying some sanction.[3]

A state confronted with equal power capabilities is less likely to initiate war than if it is confronted with weak power capabilities. And it is more likely to wage war than it would be if confronted with preponderant power capabilities.

We assume that the leaders of states act rationally in making important decisions concerning the direction and well-being of the state, and that war itself is usually, if not always, a rational undertaking.[4] By a rational decision is meant one based on a careful and intelligent assessment of factors relevant to the goals of decision-makers. Goals unlikely to be achieved are usually not opted for, nor are means selected which are not likely to advance desired goals. If, after a careful weighing of pros and cons, a decision-maker concludes that resort to war will secure his objectives and simultaneously result in much loss of life and material devastation, and if he places greater value on the objectives than the costs estimated to accrue in terms of life and property, then his decision to wage war is a rational one. Needless to say, it may not be an accurate one; important decisions frequently must be made on the basis of imperfect knowledge. Moreover, the decision may not be at all "rational" in terms of the perspective of other individuals who attach far greater value to the lives and well-being of those who will bear the brunt of the war.

We assume that statesmen are capable of judging with a reasonable degree of accuracy the power capabilities that their own state and probable opponent states can bring to bear in a military confrontation, which is essential if rational decisions are to be made about whether war is likely to advance one's objectives.[5] The decision to go to war is made only if the probability of winning is fairly high or if one's objectives are held to be so important as not to be compromised without a war on their behalf.[6] In order for any particular war to be rational, it is not necessary that the probability of winning be high for each party. Obviously, if the probability is high for one, it necessarily is low for the other. A party that recognizes itself to be at a great disadvantage may still find it rational to wage war if it attaches great importance to the interest in conflict. One can also envisage a situation in which neither side to a conflict has a high probability of winning, yet both find war to be "rational" because each places high value on the interest in conflict.

More importantly, perhaps, the leaders of a disadvantaged state may find it perfectly rational to go to war, not to secure the interest in conflict or even to prevent the opponent from attaining that interest, but to promote different, and what are perceived to be higher, interests that might be jeopardized or sacrificed by letting the other state succeed and without having to fight a war. A state's leaders may reason that appeasement will whet the adversary's appetite for concessions in the future or undermine the morale of the citizenry at home, weakening national cohesion. They may perceive a threat to their personal positions of authority. Opposition elites could exploit the issue of appeasement to bring about their ouster. Finally, since war necessarily involves costs for both sides to a conflict, the weaker may conclude that the costs factor alone will dissuade the stronger from waging war, even if the latter has threatened to wage war in furtherance of its objectives. The weaker state may, given the stakes at question, find it rational to gamble that the stronger is bluffing. If wrong, it may become involved in a war that it would have avoided if it had had perfect knowledge as to the intentions of its opponent.

Hypotheses: Power Capabilities Related to War Outcome

The assumption that the probability of winning a war is primarily a function of the power capabilities each party to the conflict possesses will be tested. Our *first hypothesis* is: *Given the occurrence of war, the side possessing the greater power capabilities at the time of the initiation of war will almost always be victorious.* ("Side" rather than state is used, since some conflicts involve more than two states. We assume that the capabilities of two or more states to one side of a conflict are equal to the sum of their individual capabilities. Chatterjee, in a formal model of a balance of power system, makes a similar assumption.)[7]

The validity of this proposition is not as obvious as it perhaps appears on first glance. Superior strategy may enable a weaker state to defeat a stronger, especially if disparity in power capabilities separating the two is slight. A state on the defensive is likely to require less capabilities than a nation on the offensive, particularly if the latter has to stretch its supply lines over a great distance. Outcome hinges on the nature of the objectives of the parties to a conflict. If A's objective is to destroy B's military force and occupy B's territory, whereas B's goal is merely to prevent A from so doing, A will require more power capabilities to attain its objectives. Willingness on the part of a weaker side to endure greater sacrifice, in terms of material devastation, human losses, and the costs of supplying the fighting forces, may enable it to defeat a stronger foe. The validity of the hypothesis also depends on how power capabilities are measured. A state with superior military forces in being at the initiation of hostilities may be defeated by an opponent able to stave off defeat by translating greater resources into military force over an extended period of time. Consequently, a finding that most wars are won by the side with greater power capabilities, and without taking into consideration any other variables, would be an important one. It would tend to support two of our principal theoretical assumptions: the probability of war increases as power disparity grows, and weaker states frequently find rational reasons for waging war apart from the objective of winning.

If outcome is directly related to the power capabilities relationship between the belligerents, then the duration of the conflict and the resulting devastation may also hinge on the power capabilities relationship. Accordingly, our *second hypothesis* states: *Given the occurrence of war, the greater the power capabil-*

ities disparity prior to the initiation of war, the lesser the devastation resulting from the war.

A *third hypothesis* states: *Given the occurrence of war, the greater the power capabilities disparity prior to the initiation of war, the shorter the duration of war.* The logic of these and subsequent hypotheses may not conform, of course, to the reality of unconventional war. National liberation movements employ a strategy purposefully designed to achieve victory without directly confronting the complete strength of a much superior foe. Waging war against an opponent that either cannot bring its forces fully to bear (because guerillas seldom concentrate their armed forces and have few if any strategic points the loss of which would entail defeat) or will not because of moral or other restraints, does provide important advantages. As already stated, however, the focus of this study is on war between sovereign national states and not civil war or war between independent nation-states and dependent political entities.

These three hypotheses, therefore, will serve indirectly as a check upon the validity of our assumptions set forth above. If statesmen do act rationally with respect to the decision to go to war, if statesmen are capable of judging power capabilities accurately, and if the probability of winning a war is primarily a function of the power capabilities each party to the conflict is able to muster, then we would expect to find an association between power capabilities disparity, on the one hand, and victory, duration, and intensity of war, on the other hand.

Power Capabilities Related to
the Occurrence of War

According to our theory, the probability of the occurrence of war increases as the power capabilities disparity between the conflicting parties increases. Our *fourth hypothesis* states: *Given an interstate conflict, the greater the disparity in the power capabilities relationship between the two sides to the conflict, the greater the probability the conflict will escalate to the level of military hostilities.* As was previously discussed, in articulating our hypotheses the concept "military hostilities" is used to designate war events characterized by a minimum threshold of 317 fatalities and the concept "war" is used to identify war events involving a minimum threshold of one thousand battle-connected fatalities. This distinction is made because of the lack of consensus within the discipline about what is the best threshold to use, and so that the reader may easily be aware of which operational definition is employed for the testing of specific hypotheses. (See Chapter 1, pp. 8-10)

Our next hypothesis is very similar, but focuses only on interstate conflicts that have included a threat of or the actual use of military force. In short, the hypothesis is confined to conflicts where one or both sides to the conflict have actually attempted to assert a power relationship (by threat of sanctions) or employed military force as a result of the collapse of a formerly existing power relationship or as a means of establishing a power relationship. The difference between this hypothesis and the previous one, then, is that the former may include some conflicts in which neither side sought to effect a power relationship. This distinction is theoretically relevant. It is empirically possible to test both propositions because of the availability of two different inventories of interstate conflicts, one of which includes only conflicts that involved a threat of or resort to the use of force. We will return to this theme in Chapter 4.[8] The *fifth hypothesis* is: *Given an interstate conflict involving the threat or actual resort to force, the greater the disparity in the power capabilities relationship between the two sides to the conflict, the greater the probability the conflict will escalate to the level of military hostilities.*

The *sixth hypothesis* focuses exclusively on war events: *In most wars a high level of disparity characterizes the power capabilities relationship prevailing between the two sides prior to initiation of a war.* The focus is restricted so that a large number of war events can be examined. Available inventories of interstate conflicts, some of which do not result in war, are only available for the 1919-1965 time period, as will be discussed in greater detail in Chapter 4. War events are available back to 1850.

Intervening Variable: Change in Power Capabilities Relationships

Disagreement among international relations theorists about the relationship between equilibrated or disequilibrated power capabilities and the occurrence of war may be partially attributed to the importance of change in capabilities as an intervening variable. Change, especially rapid change, has frequently been held to be a destabilizing element in social-political relationships. It is an important causal factor cited by Wright: "Wars tend to increase both in frequency and severity in times of rapid technological and cultural changes because adjustment, which always involves habituation, is a function of time. The shorter the time within which such adjustments have to be made, the greater the probability that they will prove inadequate and that violence will result."[9] Morgenthau states that "most of the wars that have been fought since the beginning of the modern state system have their origin in the balance of power system" and suggests that change in the relative capabilities of states and accompanying change in the intentions of the decision-makers frequently account for such wars.[10]

According to the theory outlined earlier, it might seem that the prospect of war has diminished if the gap in power capabilities has narrowed rather than widened. If statesmen of the stronger state act rationally, they will perceive that war is less likely to be successful than it was formerly. However, this is not true for the weaker side. Compared to the past, it is in a better position to wage war. Its increase in power capabilities may be accompanied by a desire for commensurate change in political influence, power, and authority on the international level. Consequently, the value attached by the weaker side to any conflicting interest is likely to have increased. Hence, *change* in the power capabilities relationship is an intervening variable that causes variation in the other key variable of our theory, value-importance.

Another aspect of change could have a significant effect on what is regarded as rational behavior by the leaders of the stronger state. They are likely to be reluctant to relinquish political influence, authority, and power commensurate with their relative loss in power capabilities because of the satisfaction their state draws from such influence, authority, and power and because of a fear that relinquishing these attributes may further accelerate the downward trend.

Third, for the stronger states, the acceptance of a diminished role may be a sensitive issue with respect to the positions of authority held by the leaders. Opposition political elites could blame the leadership for the declining stature of the state, thereby hoping to discredit the leaders before the public and justify forced ouster of the leadership. Consequently, a political leadership will have important personal reasons for not readily or easily acquiescing to a diminished role for its state in the international system. These personal reasons could be conveniently served by refusing to accord an upcoming state commensurate influence, power, and authority and perhaps even by seeking to rebuild the power capabilities base to its former relative level. Leaders may deem it quite rational to risk war by refusing to accommodate the upcoming state, in spite of the fact that their state is no longer as capable of winning a war as it once was. Indeed, they may even consider it rational to initiate war for the purpose of reversing the deteriorating power capabilities situation, in the hope of improving the position of their state in the world arena and of enhancing their own position as rulers of the state. A passage from Wright supports this thesis:

If a government yields strategic territory, military resources, or other constituents of power to another without compensating advantage, it is quite likely to be preparing its own destruction. The theory which considers war a necessary instrument in the preservation of political power is relatively close to the facts. The most important technological cause of war in the modern world is its utility in the struggle for power.[11]

Finally, we should note that if change in the power capabilities relationship between the two states has been rapid, the leaders of the stronger state may be psychologically more prone to misperceiving the behavior of the upcoming state as being hostile in intention.

Hence, several reasons can be advanced for hypothesizing that change that narrows the power capabilities gap between states increases the prospects of war. This point of view has been articulated by John Herz, Quincy Wright, and

Theodore Abel.[12] A.F.K. Organski, as previously noted, argues that war is more likely when states are approximately equal in capabilities, and warns that the situation is particularly unstable with respect to those states that have been closing the gap. Inis Claude states that an equilibrated distribution of power capabilities is more conducive to peace, but partly on the grounds that a disadvantaged state would be motivated to close the gap and perhaps expedite the process by resorting to war. Change, then, would appear to be an important intervening variable with respect to the relationship between power capabilities and the occurrence of military hostilities, including war.

By the same token, it seems conceivable that under some circumstances change that widens the gap may be important. Imagine the situation of two states, A and B, which have for some time enjoyed more or less approximately equal power capabilities and which have frequently experienced important conflicts of interest. State A grows more rapidly than B in terms of relative capabilities. State B can accept the changing situation or seek to halt or reverse the trend. State B may conclude that the chances of reversing the trend by actions short of war are slim and, hence, opt for war as the most preferable course of action.[13]

In order to test these various notions of change, we shall formulate several hypotheses explicitly positing relationships between change in power capabilities and the occurrence of war, and rely on several different units of observation, including states, conflicts, wars, and the international system of states.

Since rationales can be evolved for hypothesizing that change toward or away from an equality in power capabilities may be causally related to the occurrence of military conflict, we shall begin by focusing only on the extent of change and not on the direction of change. *Hypothesis seven* states: *The greater the change in the power capabilities of states, the greater the probability of involvement in military hostilities.* Here our focus is on change for each individual state in the international system, without reference to any specified relationship between it and one or more other states in the system.

Hypothesis eight shifts our focus to particular conflicts: *Given an interstate conflict, the greater the previous change in the power capabilities relationship between the two sides to the conflict, the greater the probability the conflict will escalate to the level of military hostilities.*

Hypothesis nine centers on conflicts in which a threat to use force has been made: *Given an interstate conflict involving the threat of or actual resort to force, the greater the previous change in the power capabilities relationship between the two sides to the conflict, the greater the probability the conflict will escalate to the level of military hostilities.*

Hypothesis ten focuses exclusively on war conflicts: *Most wars are characterized by significant change in the power capabilities relationship between the two sides to the conflict prior to the outbreak of war.*

Hypothesis eleven is similar to ten but specifies the direction of the change:

Most wars are characterized by significant change toward an equality in power capabilities between the two sides to the conflict prior to the outbreak of war rather than by insignificant change or change away from an equality in power capabilities.

Our last hypothesis is the only one that adopts a systemic perspective: *The greater the change in the distribution of capabilities within the international system, the greater the amount of war.* It is aimed at determining whether change in the relative capabilities of states throughout the system is sufficiently important to affect the amount of war occurring in the system as a whole.

4 Operationalizing the Hypotheses

This chapter outlines the procedures used to operationalize each of the concepts of the various hypotheses. For the benefit of the reader unfamiliar with this terminology, "to operationalize a concept" is to specify the activities or "operations" used to measure a theoretical concept or variable. Operational definitions are a requisite for scientific research as a means of mediating between abstract theories and hypotheses, on the one hand, and the empirical world of observation, on the other. Science rests on observations, and observations are meaningless without clear rules of how and what is to be recorded.[1]

As Table 3-1 indicates, four concepts in particular are fundamental to the thrust of the entire set of propositions. They are international conflict, war, military hostilities, and power capabilities. All of these concepts were previously outlined in Chapter 1, including the specification of operational criteria for war and military hostilities (pp. 8-10). All participants to international conflicts need not be nation-states. However, the focus in this study is on conflicts in which at least one participant to each side of the conflict is both a sovereign state and a member of the international system. The operational criteria for designating sovereignty and membership in the international system are basically those of J. David Singer and Melvin Small,[2] with some modifications and refinements provided by the same authors in a later study,[3] and Arthur S. Banks,[4] supplemented by experience gained by the author in the course of this research endeavor. The essential criteria employed are: some measure of diplomatic recognition, effective control over foreign affairs and armed forces, and a minimum population threshold of 100,000. This matter is discussed more fully in Appendix A, which lists all states that meet the qualifications of sovereignty and membership in the international system for the 1850-1966 period and which specifies for what years each state qualified during the time frame.

International conflicts that escalate to the level of war are singled out for attention in this study. As previously discussed, in articulating our hypotheses, the concept "military hostilities" is used to designate warlike events character-ized by a minimum threshold of 317 fatalities, and the concept "war" is used to identify armed conflicts involving a minimum threshold of one thousand battle-connected fatalities. This distinction is made because of the lack of consensus within the discipline about what is the most appropriate threshold, and so that the reader may be aware of which operational definition is employed for the testing of specific hypotheses. War as a unit of analysis (hypotheses 1, 2, 3, 6, 10, 11) is operationalized by reference to the list of "interstate wars" identified by Singer and Small.[5] Military hostilities as a unit of analysis (hypotheses 4, 5, 7, 8, 9) is operationalized according to the criterion of 317 fatalities, and evidence on this score has been drawn with respect to two other inventories of international conflicts. One, compiled by Quincy Wright, is largely comprised of conflicts brought before the League of Nations or the United Nations, as well as some conflicts brought before neither organization but which involved military hostilities. The other is a set of conflicts provided by K.J. Holsti, which, according to the author, includes "most of the international conflicts which have occurred and ended since 1919 and which involved the threat or use of force."[6] Thus, Holsti's inventory can be characterized as embracing conflicts in which an attempt to establish a power relationship has been made. Of these, some were transformed to a force relationship because the threatened party refused to accede to the wishes of the threatening one. Holsti's list of conflicts differs from Wright's, then, in that it includes only conflicts involving a threat or actual use of force. As earlier noted, this distinction is theoretically important. The mere threat by a state to use military force against another may be sufficient to precipitate armed conflict. The reactions of a state's leadership to the attempt by another nation to effect a power relationship at its expense may differ significantly from efforts by the latter aimed only at creating an authority-type of relationship or at establishing an influence relationship. Moreover, in accordance with the theory outlined in Chapter 3, a threat to use force or the actual use of force is less likely to occur in a conflict situation characterized by an equilibrated distribution of power capabilities than in a situation characterized by an unequilibrated distribution.

Wright's inventory of conflicts presumably includes events that never reached the threat-to-use-force level, since it contains about twice as many conflicts as Holsti's inventory, and since Holsti claims that his listing incorporates most of the international conflicts involving the threat or use of force for the same time period as that surveyed by Wright. Hence, in hypothesizing relationships between power capabilities and occurrence of war, it is possible to differentiate between conflicts in general (hypotheses 4 and 8), and those which always involve the threat or actual use of force (hypotheses 5 and 9). In accordance with the theory set forth in this study, it is *expected* that the correlations between power capabilities and occurrence of hostilities will be higher for the Holsti set of conflicts than the Wright set, precisely because conflicts in the former always involve the threat of force.

However, because Wright's inventory does include some conflicts that involve the threat or actual use of force (many of the conflicts appearing in Holsti's inventory appear in Wright's), and because Wright did not code his conflicts so that one can separate conflicts that involve the threat of force from those that do not, the results arising from this exercise can only be suggestive. Significant differences between the results from the two inventories will occur only if a sizable number of conflicts in the Wright inventory did not involve the threat of force. If important differences do manifest and if they are in the predicted direction, our theoretical reasoning will have been supported. If the differences are not substantial, a careful examination of whether or not threat was an element central to most of the Wright conflicts would be required before one could satisfactorily conclude that the findings contradict the theory.

Appendixes C and D list all the conflicts drawn from the Holsti and Wright inventories for the purpose of operationalizing the concepts "interstate conflict" and "interstate conflict involving the threat to resort to force." Since both inventories contain conflicts that did not escalate to the level of military hostilities, as well as ones that did, they provide relevant units of analysis for testing hypotheses 4, 5, 8, and 9.

Power Capabilities Operationalized

The concept of power capabilities was previously defined in Chapter 1 as composed of those factors that enable one state to threaten sanctions vis-à-vis another. This book focuses on those factors that equate with or are capable of being translated into military force. The emphasis is on military force because it is the ultimate sanction and because a principal goal of this study is to determine whether power capabilities are significantly related to the use of force in the course of international conflict.

Elements that constitute power capabilities in this sense are numerous. They include armed forces personnel, morale of the fighting forces, material supplies, and land, naval and air armament. They also encompass transportation and communications facilities normally used for civilian purposes (railroads, motor vehicles, and civil aircraft) but which can be conscripted for military use. And they include population, raw materials, industrial capacities and skills.[7] Thus, we can differentiate between actual and potential power capabilities. The former refers to resources and military forces-in-being that are more or less ready for immediate use. The latter consists of factors that can be translated into effective military force through mobilization[8] and includes economic capacity for war, administrative capability for managing war, and morale or motivation of a state's citizenry in support of a war effort.[9]

Some theorists have carried the analysis of power capabilities to a higher level of abstraction. For example, Harold and Margaret Sprout point to the importance of intelligence functions, the "ability to collect, analyze, store, recall, and utilize information in defining policy objectives and in formulating strategies for action," and of decision-making functions, the "ability to define feasible objectives, and to combine instruments and techniques of statecraft into effective strategies for attaining objectives" as ingredients of power capabilities.[10]

In this study, however, the measurement of power capabilities focuses on indicators of strength of armed forces (both actual and potential), economic capacity, and administrative capacity. More abstruse indicators, such as motivation and intelligence and decision-making functions, are not operationalized because of the likely impossibility of so doing for all independent states of the world during the 1850-1966 time frame and because it would have required a level of effort far beyond that possible for the purpose of the study.

To secure data on the less abstruse indicators for all states during this time span was itself a formidable undertaking. There are few indicators for which complete data can be found, and the time element involved in collecting the information is disproportionately large.[11] In defense of this approach, it is to be recognized that more tangible indicators of power capabilities are themselves related to the more abstruse indicators, and in this sense can serve as an indirect measure of the latter. For example, as Klauss Knorr observes, "Ability and will to fight are not entirely independent factors. Up to a point, they support each other; and up to a point, the one can be substituted for the other."[12] Hence, tangible indicators of ability to fight will measure, albeit imperfectly, the will to fight.

Overall, the problem is to select indicators which validly measure the power capabilities of states and for which data can be found for most states throughout the research time frame. The strategy chosen in this study for measuring the power capabilities of states is that of multiple indicators to be combined into a single index.[13] It is unlikely that any one indicator will, by itself, accurately measure the relative power capabilities of all states, since power capabilities is a complex variable comprised of many elements, since error is undoubtedly inherent to some degree in virtually all indicators, and since missing data was certain to be a problem for any indicator selected, given the domain and time frame of the study. Consequently, the author deemed it important to select several indicators which, in combination, were more likely to tap accurately the power capabilities dimension. The assumption was that the effect of error inherent in individual indicators would be significantly reduced if not completely canceled out by a multiple-indicator approach.

Initially, six basic indicator-variables were chosen to measure power capabilities: armed forces personnel,[14] defense expenditure, population, government revenue, trade value, and area. A few words in justification of their choice are in order.

Army personnel and defense expenditure are, of course, measures of the strength of armed-forces-in-being. The former records the number of able-bodied individuals more or less immediately available for engaging in military hostilities, and the latter is reflective of the resources expended to train and equip the forces. The fighting ability of armed forces does depend importantly upon the training facilities, equipment, and armament available to it. As a rule, the more men enrolled by a state in its armed forces and the more resources allocated to them, the better the state's fighting capability relative to that of other states.

Armed forces and defense expenditures alone, however, are insufficient for describing power capabilities, since some states frequently keep minimal forces-in-being for immediate use. The potential of such states for mobilizing additional resources for a war purpose is necessarily greater—compared to other nations and all other things being equal—since they have in relative, if not absolute, terms a larger population and economic base to draw upon. Consequently, it is important to tap the dimension of potential capabilities. Hence, the other indicators in our research design.

Population is an indicator of the total human resource pool that a state can draw upon in the event of war. One might argue that population size is no longer an important determinant of power capabilities in a world of fission and fusion bombs. To the contrary, wars must still be fought with manpower. Territory must be physically taken and defended, and in the final analysis, only soldiers can do the job. A state without a large population cannot today attain the rank of a superpower, just as previous to the nuclear age states that qualified as the major actors in the international system invariably enjoyed a relatively large population base. A state with a population considerably greater than another should enjoy an advantage. It is likely to be capable of pouring more men into a war and to possess a greater capacity for diverting manpower to the task of supplying the armed forces.

Government revenue, which is largely equivalent to the amount of money a government expends in providing services for its people, reflects, if only indirectly, the wealth of a state's economy. The more productive an economy, the more resources potentially available for taxation by the government. Government revenue is also an indicator of administrative capacity. The more advanced an economy, the greater the likelihood it will rest upon well-developed administrative skills in the economic and political sectors of the society. The larger the government revenue, the more administrative capacity is required to collect and manage its disbursement.

Trade value, the sum of a state's annual imports and exports, is an indicator of economic capacity, since international trade enables states to acquire a larger national product than they would otherwise obtain. States produce goods and services for export in which they have a comparative advantage and, in turn, import those products and services that would require a greater outlay of indigenous resources.[15] Moreover, states with highly advanced economies are likely to engage in greater trade in order to supply the diversified materials, products, and services required in order to maintain an advanced economy. International trade is also a measure of administrative capacity, since skilled personnel are necessary to conduct trade efficiently and on a large scale. It is true that a nation's dependence on trade can be a weakness, if an enemy succeeds in curtailing the flow of goods. This, however, is a factor dependent on individual circumstances, and a state is likely to take this element into account before allowing itself to become involved in a war. Therefore, although trade can work to a state's disadvantage under certain circumstances, this should not disqualify it as a measure of the power capabilities of states in general, particularly if it is used in combination with other indicators of power capabilities.

Area is an indicator that usually remains constant for most states over time, yet it is a significant reflector of a state's capabilities. People, motivation, skills, resources, and military capabilities are required to govern territory and hold it intact under the rule of a single sovereign. In a period characterized by the relative absence of such factors, dissident political groups may be encouraged to break away and form a new state more conducive to their liking, and other nations may be tempted to attack in an attempt to augment their own interests. Area is important, furthermore, because in the event of war a state with a large area is more capable of conducting a defense in depth and thus more able to prevent an attacking state from achieving victory. Would-be aggressors may be dissuaded from initiating war against states that enjoy ample *Lebensraum*, and in this sense area can serve as a deterrent to war.

Standardizing the Monetary Variables

Simultaneously with the collection of data on the six indicator-variables, information was compiled on free exchange rates for all countries in the system and all years.[16] This was required for converting monetary indicator data into a standard currency so as to achieve comparability of figures. Free exchange rates were necessary, since official exchange rates are not a valid measure of the purchasing power of a country's currency. Governments exercise arbitrary control over their respective currencies, and information on monetary variables is frequently expressed in terms of paper currency, which is especially susceptible to manipulation. For example, a government may declare that a number of units of its paper currency is equivalent to one ounce of gold, but place restrictions on the redemption of its paper currency or even refuse altogether to redeem paper for gold. In such instances, an official exchange rate is likely to exaggerate the real purchasing power of the currency. Moreover, when the economy of any country is subject to significant inflation, the scores of that country on monetary indicators would thereby be inflated relative to the scores for other states in the system (assuming that official exchange rates were used to convert to a standard currency). This condition would persist unless and until the government of the country officially devalued its currency and to a degree comparable with the amount of inflation that has been registered. Consequently, it is necessary to know the value attached to a given currency by peoples of other countries. Free exchange rates provide such a measure, since they represent the demand for a country's money on the free market. Hence, they reflect more accurately the real purchasing power of a given currency.

Free exchange rates are themselves a less than perfect measure of the true purchasing power of currencies, because they are based considerably on the extent and type of international trade which countries engage in. The computation of more accurate purchasing power parities has begun to be applied in recent years to a few select states of the world, but requires detailed quantitative and qualitative information about the gross national product of states, and hence probably cannot be applied successfully to most states of the world and as far back in time as the 1850s.[17] For many countries much of the requisite information was undoubtedly never compiled; for others it has long since been lost. Even if the basic information were potentially available, millions of dollars would undoubtedly be required to assemble the data. Consequently, for the purpose of this study free exchange rate information was used whenever possible. Since free exchange rates are a less than perfect measure, this is an additional reason for adopting a multiple-indicator approach to operationalize the power capabilities of nation states.

Evaluating the Validity of the Indicator-Variables

It was necessary to test the validity of our theoretical assumption that all six indicator-variables represent different and important facets of power capabilities. While studies by other investigators of this type of indicator-variable data for the 1950s and 1960s supported the assumption, there was no empirical proof at hand to demonstrate its generality over more than a century. Principal components analysis,[18] which extracts the maximum of variance from the data in the first component (successive factors extract the maximum of remaining variance) and yields a mathematically unique solution, was selected as a convenient tool for determining the extent to which the six indicators are interrelated over the 117-year span between 1850 and 1966.[19] If the indicators do in fact represent power capabilities, then they should intercorrelate substantially, and in a principal components analysis they should correlate or "load high" on a single component.

Table 4-1 presents the loadings of the six variables on the first principal component[20] for selected years. It will be observed that all of the variables consistently load from moderate to high throughout the entire period, which itself is an important finding. But in spite of the high degree of interrelatedness, an examination of the factor scores derived from the first component suggested that the variables were inadequate, of themselves, for measuring power capabilities. When factor scores are computed, the six indicators tap a dimension that might more accurately be characterized as size. Countries with large populations but low levels of economic development, such as India and China, necessarily score high, relative to other states, on indicators of government revenue, defense

Table 4-1
Loadings of Six Variables on First Principal Component: 1850-1960

Variable						Loadings						
	1850	1860	1870	1880	1890	1900	1910	1920	1930	1940	1950	1960
AREA	.622	.586	.629	.572	.601	.685	.720	.493	.580	.777	.837	.814
POPULA	.963	.527	.485	.469	.521	.512	.588	.492	.690	.721	.647	.665
GOVREV	.924	.969	.920	.899	.923	.944	.918	.925	.892	.930	.937	.927
DEFEXP	.973	.974	.978	.971	.974	.932	.944	.898	.872	.872	.877	.801
TRDVAL	.763	.773	.761	.804	.765	.746	.716	.941	.847	.533	.663	.729
ARMFCS	.909	.873	.844	.854	.899	.866	.876	.463	.557	.809	.795	.797

POPULA = Population
GOVREV = Government revenue
DEFEXP = Defense expenditure
TRDVAL = Trade value
ARMFCS = Armed forces

expenditure, armed forces, and trade value, because of their numerically larger populations. Such states obtain high factor scores relative to other states even if their peoples are existing at or near a subsistence level.

But power capabilities are reflected by more than absolute size. This is certainly evident in the performance of a number of developing states in the 1950s and 1960s, and also in China's experience during the latter half of the nineteenth century. The degree of technological achievement which characterizes a state's level of advancement is also important. Superior technologies applied to weapons systems, communications facilities, and transportation capabilities can enable one state to defeat another state that enjoys higher levels of government revenue, defense expenditure, and a larger population base. Moreover, the further beyond the level of subsistence that a country progresses, the more resources it has available for transforming "butter" into "guns," and hence the better its capacity for outfighting and outlasting an opponent at a lower level of development. Consequently, an adequate index for measuring the power capabilities of states should reflect level of technological development as well as absolute size.

Two methods were selected to further this objective. First, the gross effects of size were reduced by "logging" (taking the logarithm of) the variable population. The distribution for the raw data on population is highly skewed; it is best described by a reverse-shaped *J*-curve. When the variable is logged, outlier cases are drawn in toward the center of the distribution. Thus, the scores for countries with very large populations are reduced in importance relative to countries with moderate or small populations. By including the log of population in the research design, we retained a respectable measure of its contribution to the power capabilities of states, while reducing its salience when population is very large and unaccompanied by commensurate development.

This technique discriminated against those states with large populations which have achieved a credible level of development. To balance out this side of the equation, we sought to supplement our original six variables with indicators that reflect level of technological development. It is relatively easy to find suitable indicators of technological sophistication for the 1950s and 1960s, but as one goes farther back in time it becomes quite difficult to find indicators that are relevant and for which adequate data can be found. Consequently, for the purpose of this study, three indicators were selected as proxy measures of technological development. They are government revenue per capita (GRPCAP), defense expenditure per capita (DEPCAP), and trade value per capita (TVPCAP). (When the three indicators were correlated with gross national product for most states of the world during the post-World War II period, extremely high coefficients resulted.) States that score high on such per capita measures should have more resources available, relative to other nations, to allocate for administration of the country in general and provision for a defense establishment in particular. It is likely that the peoples of such states will be more efficiently administered and the armed forces better equipped, fed, and trained.

Table 4-2 presents the factor loadings that result when the three per capita indicators and the log of population (LOGPOP) are incorporated, along with the six original indicator-variables, into a principal components analysis. Two of the three per capita indicators, GRPCAP and DEPCAP, do in fact load substantially throughout the entire time period, with typically at least 25 percent and at times 50 percent or more of their variation explained by the first component. TVPCAP, however, registers low in explanatory value. At best only 16 percent of its variation and at times 4 percent or less is accounted for. As such, it is not suitable for inclusion in a power capabilities index. It seems likely that less developed countries scored considerably higher on per capita trade value, relative to more developed states, than they did on the other indicator-variables. Trade apparently accounts for a relatively larger share of the economic wealth of underdeveloped states than it does for the more developed states.

Table 4-3 presents and compares factor scores and rankings based on the nine-variable and six-variable models for the ten highest-scoring states in the international system, and covering five select years from the 1850-1950 time frame. The scores and rankings illustrate that the six-variable model represents a size dimension to a greater extent than the nine-variable model and that countries with large populations score considerably higher in the six-variable model because of its emphasis on the size dimension.

Returning to Tables 4-1 and 4-2, it will be observed that AREA's loadings, when employed in the nine-variable model, have diminished considerably. Even

Table 4-2

Loadings on First Principal Component of Five Basic and Four Derived Variables: 1850-1965

Variable	Loadings										
	1850	1855	1860	1865	1870	1875	1880	1885	1890	1895	1900
AREA	.545	.477	.469	.516	.499	.517	.391	.394	.443	.440	.488
LOGPOP	.809	.755	.713	.711	.730	.753	.678	.696	.713	.701	.700
GOVREV	.945	.950	.967	.955	.927	.930	.913	.905	.937	.925	.936
DEFEXP	.972	.966	.951	.958	.959	.965	.948	.937	.959	.954	.947
TRDVAL	.816	.859	.833	.784	.824	.825	.868	.866	.835	.840	.861
ARMFCS	.863	.790	.849	.846	.787	.855	.782	.773	.858	.854	.771
GRPCAP	.297	.520	.521	.552	.532	.362	.528	.511	.433	.544	.542
DEPCAP	.232	.399	.480	.578	.522	.517	.645	.676	.605	.747	.804
TVPCAP	−.007	.155	.214	.200	.266	.228	.355	.307	.251	.272	.296

LOGPOP = Population logged
GOVREV = Government revenue
DEFEXP = Defense expenditure
TRDVAL = Trade value

so, 20 percent or more of the variation in AREA is usually accounted for by the first principal component. Further examination of Table 4-2 discloses that both AREA and ARMFCS experience substantially reduced loadings between 1920 and 1930 and to a degree that is neither consistent with the trend performance of the loadings on these variables nor in accord with the higher magnitudes obtained for nearly all other sample years. As the table indicates, the loadings of AREA also drop sharply in 1880, 1885 and 1915. GRPCAP exhibits unusually low loadings in 1850 and 1875.

In an effort to account for this unusual finding, we examined correlation coefficients and scatterplots for the bivariate relationships of AREA and ARMFCS with the other indicator-variables. The evidence demonstrated that a few extreme outliers were causing the reduced loadings. The years on which ARMFCS loads high are when it correlates substantially with GOVREV and DEFEXP. In 1920, 1925, and 1930, ARMFCS correlates poorly with these two variables and largely because of three extreme outliers: the United Kingdom, the United States, and China. Between 1920 and 1930, the United States and United Kingdom maintained levels of armed forces which, relative to government revenue and defense expenditure, were markedly below the average performance of most other states. China, in contrast, supported an army that was disproportionately large relative to its government revenue and defense outlays and that of other states.

Similarly, AREA's moderate to substantial loadings on the first principal

1905	1910	1915	1920	1925	1930	1935	1940	1945	1950	1955	1960	1965
.575	.550	.293	.290	.328	.364	.460	.655	.701	.746	.730	.693	.708
.744	.771	.650	.525	.648	.658	.735	.672	.565	.521	.518	.520	.536
.936	.910	.923	.930	.926	.933	.925	.903	.932	.940	.923	.916	.926
.938	.944	.834	.942	.906	.897	.928	.892	.885	.908	.876	.853	.862
.818	.822	.916	.966	.945	.944	.776	.681	.866	.822	.856	.870	.849
.853	.820	.603	.323	.424	.269	.523	.626	.636	.608	.616	.609	.699
.595	.437	.700	.769	.639	.633	.656	.731	.690	.690	.661	.741	.565
.800	.713	.806	.876	.761	.765	.784	.656	.853	.870	.870	.868	.819
.234	.219	.409	.389	.428	.362	.338	.419	.165	.199	.182	.272	.234

ARMFCS= Armed forces
GRPCAP= Government revenue per capita
DEPCAP= Defense expenditure per capita
TVPCAP= Trade value per capita

Table 4-3
Factor Scores and Rankings Based on Six-Variable and Nine-Variable Model Compared for Ten Highest Scoring States: 1850-1950[a]

1850 Six Variables	1850 Nine Variables	1880 Six Variables	1880 Nine Variables	1900 Six Variables	1900 Nine Variables
Russia 4.12	Russia 3.50	Russia 3.48	France 3.31	Russia 4.13	United Kingdom 3.36
United Kingdom 2.86	United Kingdom 3.23	United Kingdom 2.97	United Kingdom 3.16	United Kingdom 2.62	Russia 3.02
France 2.83	France 2.97	France 2.38	Russia 2.58	France 2.03	France 2.41
Austria-Hungary 1.91	Germany 1.81	Germany 1.51	Germany 1.61	United States 2.03	United States 1.85
United States 1.00	United States 1.00	United States 1.29	United States 1.46	Germany 1.84	Germany 1.81
Turkey .79	China .93	Austria-Hungary 1.09	Austria-Hungary 1.30	Austria-Hungary 1.08	Austria-Hungary 1.21
Prussia .79	Austria-Hungary .70	China .90	Italy 1.08	Italy 1.03	Italy .74
Spain .42	Italy .55	Italy .69	Netherlands .77	Netherlands .55	Netherlands .74
Brazil .11	Spain .23	Turkey .43	Spain .23	Belgium .20	Belgium .30
Netherlands -.07	Turkey .17	Brazil .41	Belgium .14	Argentina .09	Argentina .14

1930 Six Variables	1930 Nine Variables	1950 Six Variables	1950 Nine Variables
United States 4.41	United Kingdom 4.30	United States 5.21	United States 5.86
United Kingdom 3.29	United States 3.95	Russia/USSR 5.09	Russia/USSR 4.20
France 2.86	France 2.27	Comm. China 2.78	United Kingdom 2.14
Germany 2.44	Germany 1.68	United Kingdom 1.40	Canada 1.40
Russia/USSR 1.80	Russia 1.26	India .85	Comm. China 1.18
Italy 1.68	Italy 1.12	Canada .76	France 1.13
Japan .86	Canada .73	France .57	Australia .75
Canada .71	Japan .66	Brazil .51	Belgium .39
Australia .51	Australia .58	Australia .36	Brazil .32
China .25	China .53	Indonesia .15	Sweden .31

aFactor scores are for the first principal component. The six-variable model included area, population, government revenue, defense expenditure, trade value, and armed forces. The nine-variable model included all of the above (population now being logged), along with government revenue per capita, defense expenditure per capita, and trade value per capita.

component are largely based on its correlations with GOVREV, DEFEXP, and ARMFCS. In 1920, 1925, and 1930, government revenue and defense expenditure for the United Kingdom attained levels, relative to its area, that far exceeded the average performance of other nations. In 1930, the USSR maintained armed forces, relative to area, considerably beyond the levels supported by other states. As a result of these outliers, the bivariate correlations of AREA with GOVREV, DEFEXP, and ARMFCS fall. Consequently, AREA's loadings on the first principal component also fall.

Are we to conclude, then, that ARMFCS and AREA are poor indicators of power capabilities during this period of time? In our judgment the answer is "No." Both variables load moderately or substantially high throughout most of the century, including prior to 1920 and subsequent to 1930. The most reasonable interpretation seems to be that a few countries, for exceptional reasons, departed from a level of performance that was more in accord with their previous behavior, as well as that of other states. For instance, in 1920, Russia was beset by civil war, which in turn resulted in rampant inflation, accompanied by a dramatic plunge in the value of the Russian ruble on foreign-exchange markets. Consequently, when Soviet government revenue and defense expenditure figures were converted to US dollars, they exhibited unusually low values. There seems little reason to conclude, however, on the basis of a few deviant cases, that ARMFCS or AREA are any less a measure of the strength of nations during this period of time. That the low loadings of ARMFCS and AREA are principally the result of a few extreme outliers is demonstrated by logging all of the indicator-variables and resubjecting them to a principal components analysis. The results for five sample years, at decade intervals, are presented in Table 4-4 and compared to the loadings that resulted from the previous (nonlogged) principal components analysis. In the logged solution, the loadings for AREA and ARMFCS rise significantly to a level that accords with the trend of these variables across the half-century interval.

Overall, what is most important, as evidenced in Tables 4-1, 4-2, and 4-4, is the high degree of interrelatedness that characterizes eight of the indicator-variables throughout the 117 years of the study. The six-variable model consistently explains approximately 62 percent of the variance in the data on the first principal component, while the nine-variable model explains about 50 percent of the variance. Thus, eight of the nine indicator-variables appear to be eminently suited for utilization in an index for measuring the power capabilities of states over time.

Index Formation: Rescaling the Data
and Weighting the Variables

Having selected eight indicators to measure the power capabilities of nation-states, it remained to devise a suitable technique for aggregating the scores on the indicator-variables to produce a single index for each point in time.

Table 4-4

Loadings on Nine Variables, Nonlogged[a] and Logged, on the First Principal Component: 1900-1950

Variables	1900		1910		1920		1930		1940		1950	
	NL	L	NL	L	NL	L	NL	L	NL	L	NL	L
AREA	.488	.447	.550	.505	.290	.480	.364	.487	.655	.572	.746	.596
LOGPOP	.700	.786	.771	.849	.525	.793	.658	.823	.672	.803	.521	.788
GOVREV	.936	.984	.910	.976	.930	.965	.933	.972	.903	.979	.940	.958
DEFEXP	.947	.966	.944	.981	.942	.958	.897	.974	.892	.977	.908	.979
TRDVAL	.861	.967	.822	.962	.966	.937	.944	.952	.681	.946	.822	.905
ARMFCS	.771	.870	.820	.895	.323	.722	.269	.779	.626	.794	.608	.801
GRPCAP	.542	.609	.437	.536	.769	.541	.633	.474	.731	.716	.690	.450
DEPCAP	.804	.795	.713	.744	.876	.689	.765	.671	.656	.848	.870	.769
TVPCAP	.296	.511	.219	.409	.389	.426	.362	.371	.419	.375	.199	.105

[a]Population is logged in both solutions.

NL = Nonlogged solution	L = Logged solution
LOGPOP = Population logged	GOVREV = Government revenue
DEFEXP = Defense expenditure	TRDVAL = Trade value
ARMFCS = Armed forces	GRPCAP = Government revenue per capita
DEFEXP = Defense expenditure per capita	TVPCAP = Trade value per capita

As a preliminary step, all eight variables were first rescaled into percentage form. Each country's score on a particular variable was expressed as a percent of the sum of the scores on that variable for all states. It was necessary to rescale the data in order to redress a problem resulting from uneven inflationary growth across the entire system of states (which occurs in spite of the conversion of different currencies to a standard medium of exchange). If the standard currency to which all monetary variables are converted fluctuates over time and if the standard currency happens to be the US dollar (which is the case in this study), then $100 in 1950 may not be equivalent to $100 in 1955. This creates a problem because of the hypotheses that include the variable of change in the power capabilities of states over time—individually, in relation to one another, and in the system as a whole. Inflation across the entire system results in greater or lesser percent change figures than would otherwise be warranted, unless inflationary growth is constant for all years (an untenable assumption). As an example, suppose inflation between 1950 and 1955 had reduced the value of the dollar by 50 percent. An absolute government revenue figure of $200 in 1955 is then equivalent to a figure of $100 in 1950. However, if we ignore the factor of inflation in computing change rates, we will conclude that a country whose government revenue has gone from $100 to $200 has registered a change of 100 percent, whereas in fact real growth is 0 percent. Now suppose, additionally, that between 1955 and 1960 inflation caused the value of the dollar to depreciate 25 percent. A change in absolute values from $200 to $400 for the 1955-1960 period would again be interpreted as a change of 100 percent, when in fact the real change would be less than 100 percent (in fact 50 percent) but more than the change that occurred between 1950 and 1955 (0 percent).

Rescaling the data into percentage form solves the problem of systemic inflation, since the indicator-variable values that result are relative scores of how all states stand in comparison to one another at any one point in time and regardless of inflation in the international system compared to the near or more distant past. Thus, if the value of government revenue for Brazil as a percent of the rest of the international system remains constant from 1950 to 1960, it makes no difference if the dollar is fluctuating unevenly across those years. Since the scale for the international system remains constant over time (100 percent), Brazil will receive the same percent score for each year. Hence, for each point in time states receive an "honest" score of their standing relative to the rest of the states in the international system. If Brazil experiences rapid growth in an indicator-variable during a given time interval, its indicator score will automatically reflect the importance of that growth relative to other states. If certain other nations achieve comparable or greater growth during the same time period, Brazil's score will remain the same or drop in value, respectively, compared to those states.

This conception of power capabilities, as should be apparent, is a relative one. Power capabilities of states are deemed to be most important in terms of how states stand and change proportional to one another. The model does not provide a measure of absolute growth over time. This did not present a problem for the purpose of this study, however, since none of the hypotheses focuses on absolute change.

With the variable data rescaled, it was then possible to combine the indicators into a single index. The easiest way to accomplish such an objective is a straightforward summation of the percentage scores on each of the variables. Theoretically speaking, however, this method leaves something to be desired, since implicit in the solution is the assumption that all variables are equally important as determinants of power capabilities. Common sense suggests that it is unlikely that the real world conforms to such a model. In a war between two states, armed forces and defense expenditures are likely to be better predictors of outcome than area or trade value. On the other hand, neither common sense nor logic provides clearly defined principles for arriving at weights which precisely represent the relative importance of the variables. Are armed forces twice or only one and a half times as important as area? On what grounds? Merely to raise the question is to appreciate the difficulty of rationally assigning exact weights to the various indicator-variables. The problem is compounded by the fact that the importance of a particular variable may itself vary over time depending upon the magnitude of one or more of the other variables. One solution to the problem, albeit again less than perfect, is to assign weights according to the extent to which each of the variables is related to an overall dimension of power capabilities. One can assume that those variables that correlate highest with such a dimension are more important as determinants of the phenomenon in question. The validity of this assumption depends, of course, upon the representativeness of the variables selected to measure power capabilities. If many of the variables more accurately stand for a dimension other than power capabilities, then this will not be the case.

The factor loadings that resulted from the principal components analyses of the nine indicator-variables provided a basis for such an interpretation. If the factor loading of a variable on a component is squared and multiplied by 100, the result equals the percent variation that the variable has in common with that component. It can be interpreted as the percent of data on a variable that can be predicted from the values of a state on the pattern.

Table 4-5 presents the squared factor loadings (times 100) for the twenty-four sample years, along with the mean for each variable across all years. Examination of the table shows that approximately 85 percent of the variation in government revenue and defense expenditure are explained by the first principal component. About 72 percent of the variation in trade value is accounted for. Armed forces, defense expenditure per capita, and population

Table 4-5

Percent Variation Explained by Nine Variables on First Principal Component: 1850-1965

	Percent Variation										
Variable	1850	1855	1860	1865	1870	1875	1880	1885	1890	1895	1900
AREA	30	23	22	27	25	27	15	16	20	19	24
LOGPOP	65	57	51	51	53	57	46	48	51	49	49
GOVREV	89	90	94	91	86	87	83	82	88	86	88
DEFEXP	95	93	90	92	92	93	90	88	92	91	90
TRDVAL	67	74	69	62	68	68	75	75	70	71	74
ARMFCS	75	62	72	72	62	73	61	60	74	73	59
GRPCAP	9	27	27	31	28	13	28	26	19	30	29
DEPCAP	5	16	23	33	27	27	42	46	37	56	65
TVPCAP	0	2	5	4	7	5	13	9	6	7	9

LOGPOP = Population logged
GOVREV = Government revenue
DEFEXP = Defense expenditure
TRDVAL = Trade value

logged have about 50 percent of their variation explained. Lowest of all in explanatory value are government revenue per capita (35 percent) and area (28 percent).

To a considerable extent, the squared factor loadings appear reasonable in terms of reflecting the relative importance of each variable as a representative of power capabilities. Defense expenditure represents the amount of resources earmarked for military purposes, and government revenue is indicative of the extent to which additional resources might be freed for war purposes. Both indicators are measures of absolute size, which is important in terms of evaluating the power capabilities relationship between two sides to a conflict. Trade value's high ranking is anomalous, since there does not appear to be any reason why it should score above all of the remaining indicator-variables as a determinant of power capabilities. The other rankings, however, appear plausible.

Armed forces, which scores fourth highest as a weighting factor, is a measure of size and, of course, more directly represents military forces-in-being than any of the other indicator-variables. However, its validity as a measure of power capabilities hinges upon the quality of the armament and training available to military personnel. Consequently, the greater importance that the weights attribute to defense expenditure and government revenue serves a useful function, since armed forces is an indicator of only the *number* of armed forces personnel. Defense expenditure and government revenue reflect the amount of resources directly and potentially available for use by the armed forces.

1905	1910	1915	1920	1925	1930	1935	1940	1945	1950	1955	1960	1965	Mean
33	30	9	8	11	13	21	43	49	55	53	48	50	28
55	59	42	28	42	43	54	45	32	27	27	27	29	45
88	83	85	87	86	87	86	82	87	88	85	84	86	86
88	89	70	89	82	81	86	80	78	82	77	73	74	85
67	68	84	93	89	89	60	46	75	68	73	76	72	72
73	67	36	10	18	7	27	39	40	37	38	37	49	51
35	19	49	59	41	40	43	53	48	48	44	55	32	35
64	51	65	77	58	59	62	43	73	76	76	75	67	51
6	5	17	15	18	13	11	18	3	4	3	7	6	8

ARMFCS = Armed forces
GRPCAP = Government revenue per capita
DEPCAP = Defense expenditure per capita
TVPCAP = Trade value per capita

48

Defense expenditure per capita and population (logged), which are weighted approximately the same as armed forces, further qualify the importance of armed forces. Defense expenditure per capita is another indicator of the amount of resources, relative to other states, made available to the armed forces. Population is a measure of the extent to which the armed forces can be supplied with additional manpower, if necessary.

Government revenue per capita and area are the indicator-variables that one might well expect to weight lowest as measures of power capabilities. Government revenue per capita, unlike defense expenditure and defense expenditure per capita, does not directly measure the amount of resources made available for the military purpose. Nor is it a measure of absolute size. Area is an indicator of size, but it reflects less directly than any of the other indicators the amount of resources available, directly or indirectly, for use by the armed forces. Moreover, for most countries and most years, area remains constant. Consequently, it is the poorest measure of variation in the power capabilities of states over time.

Use of the squared factor loadings as weighting factors may not be an ideal measure of the importance of the eight indicator-variables. As previously noted, such weights cannot be fully justified on a priori grounds. But any alternative set devised on purely logical grounds would be equally if not more difficult to rationalize. Consequently, the strategy selected for this study is to weight the indicator-variables according to the *mean* (for the twenty-four sample years) amount of percent variation accounted for by each indicator-variable on the first principal component.

An additional justification of this choice may be in order. As Tables 4-3 and 4-5 demonstrate, the indicators fluctuate over time in terms of the amount of variation each has in common with the power capabilities dimension. In many cases the change from one sample year to the next is minimal. In a few cases, namely, for AREA and ARMFCS between 1920 and 1930, this fluctuation is substantial and, as previously discussed, irregular in terms of the trend performance of the variables. Several of the variables exhibit a pattern of increasing or diminishing importance over a considerable stretch of time. GRPCAP shows increased importance after 1910; AREA after 1930. ARMFCS diminishes in significance after 1910. DEPCAP increases in importance from 1850 to 1900.

This raised the question whether to assign weights that are constant over the entire time frame or to utilize weights that are time specific, i.e., that fluctuate from one time interval to the next, such as from one year to another. Our decision was to utilize a constant weight for each variable, namely, the mean percent of variation each variable has in common with the power capabilities dimension, and as computed for the twenty-four sample years set forth in Table 4-5. In our judgment an element of error is inherent in either approach. By using a constant weight based on the mean, one disregards possible diminishing or increasing importance of a variable as a determinant of power capabilities over time. On the other hand, as previously discussed, a degree of arbitrariness characterizes the use of squared factor loadings as weights. One cannot completely justify the exact magnitude of these weights on the basis of a priori reasoning. This being the case, it is not possible to conclude that precise shifts that occur in these loadings from one year to the next represent equivalent change in the importance of a variable as a measure of power capabilities. Since principal components analysis fits a linear model to the data, extreme outliers can cause substantial change in the loadings, as was demonstrated for AREA and ARMFCS between 1920 and 1930. One cannot conclude that the irregular appearance of such outliers and the change that results necessarily represent corresponding change in the importance of the variables as measures of power capabilities. If anything, the change resulting from this type of phenomenon is more accurately characterized as spurious. To adopt a time-specific model, then, is to permit a degree of statistical noise to enter into the results. This being the case, and since the constant weights approach is a somewhat less complex and hence more parsimonious model, it seemed more appropriate to present the constant weights model in this book. In a later study results for both approaches will be presented and compared.

To recapitulate, then, the weight selected for each variable represents the mean percent of variation it has in common with the first component or power capabilities dimension that results from principal components analysis of the nine indicator-variables. Analyses were made at half-decade intervals, beginning in 1850 and concluding in 1965. For each year the loading of each variable on the first principal component was squared and multiplied by 100 to yield the variable's percent of variation in common with that component. The *mean* of each variable's percent of variation scores over the twenty-four sample years was computed.

In order to simplify evaluation, interpretation, and, later presentation of the findings, the resulting weighting factors were set equal to unity, and the total number of units of power capabilities in the international system was set at 100 million. Table 4-6 presents the adjusted weighting factors, along with the original mean percent of variation weighting factors. Thus, a state's power capabilities score for any given year was computed by multiplying its score[a] on each variable by the relevant weighting factor for the variable, and summing the resultant figures for the variables and multiplying the new result by 100 million. Since the raw data for all variables was previously rescaled into percentage form, the units of power capabilities held by all states in the international system necessarily sum to 100 million units for every year, regardless of the number of states holding membership in the system. (Owing to round-off error, the figures do not exactly equal 100 million.)

---

[a]It will be remembered that the variables were previously rescaled into percentage form. For example, each state's government revenue score was expressed as a percentage of the sum of government revenue scores for all states. These original "percentage" scores are not to be confused with the "percent" of variation scores, which were derived for use as weighting factors and discussed immediately above.

Table 4-6
Weighting Factors for Eight Variables Selected to Measure Power Capabilities

Variable	Mean Percent of Variation Weighting Factors	Adjusted Weighting Factors (Set Equal to Unity)
AREA	27.9	.0615
LOGPOP	45.3	.0998
GOVREV	86.4	.1905
DEFEXP	85.5	.1885
TRDVAL	72.1	.1589
ARMFCS	50.9	.1122
GRPCAP	34.6	.0762
DEPCAP	50.8	.1120

LOGPOP = Population logged
GOVREV = Government revenue
DEFEXP = Defense expenditure
TRDVAL = Trade value
ARMFCS = Armed forces
GRPCAP = Government revenue per capita
DEPCAP = Defense expenditure per capita

Operationalizing the Remaining Indicator-Variables

Having specified criteria for operationalizing international conflict, war, military hostilities, and power capabilities, several other terms in the hypotheses presented in Table 3-1 remain to be defined. They are the victorious side to a war (hypothesis 1), almost always (hypothesis 1), war devastation (hypothesis 2), duration of war (hypothesis 3), power capabilities disparity (hypotheses 4 and 5), high level of power capabilities disparity (hypothesis 6), most wars (hypotheses 6, 10, and 11), prior to the initiation of hostilities (hypotheses 1, 2, 3, 4, 5, and 6), prior to the occurrence of the conflict (hypotheses 4, 5, 8, and 9), change in the power capabilities of states (hypothesis 7), change in power capabilities relationship between two sides to a conflict (hypotheses 8 and 9), significant change in the power capabilities relationship between two sides to a war (hypotheses 10 and 11), change in the distribution of power capabilities within the international system (hypothesis 12), amount of war in the international system (hypothesis 12). We will now present operational criteria for each of these concepts.

The *victorious* side to a war has previously been operationalized by Singer and Small on the basis of historical consensus.[21] Their findings have been utilized for the purpose of this analysis.

Almost always is defined as 85 percent of the war events examined in this study.

War devastation is operationalized as the total number of battle-connected fatalities among military personnel incurred by all independent states participating in the conflict, divided by the total population for the participant states.[22]

Duration of war is operationalized as the total number of nation-state-months-at-war for the states participating in the conflict divided by the number of states. If two states are at war with each other for a year, the duration of the war is twelve nation-state-months-at-war.[23]

Power capabilities disparity (ratio) is defined as the ratio of the side possessing greater power capabilities prior to the initiation of hostilities to the side possessing lesser power capabilities.

A *high level of power capabilities* is operationalized as a power capabilities disparity ratio of 2.0 or greater, meaning that one side has a power capabilities score two times greater than the other side.

Most wars is defined as 85 percent of the war events examined.

Prior to the initiation of hostilities is defined as the year preceding the year of the outbreak of military hostilities.

Prior to the occurrence of conflict is defined as the year preceding the year of the outbreak of the conflict (used with the list of international conflicts drawn from K.J. Holsti) or as one year before the conflict was brought before the League of Nations or the United Nations (used with the list of conflicts drawn from Quincy Wright). It is important to take the preceding year, for this variable as well as that immediately above, since statistics for some of the power capabilities indicators during the year in which a conflict originates may register an increase as a direct result of the occurrence of the conflict. For example, in the event of a conflict, a state may increase its defense expenditures and armed forces personnel as a contingency against, or because of, the outbreak of hostilities.[26]

Change in the power capabilities of states is defined as the power capabilities score of a state at time x (the more recent year) minus its power capabilities score at time y (the earlier year), divided by the power capabilities score at time y. For this indicator, and other change rate indicators, time lags of three, five, ten, fifteen, and twenty years are computed. These time lags are somewhat arbitrary (there is no reason to suppose that a lag of fifteen years is any more important than a lag of thirteen years), but are conveniently spaced to permit evaluation of short-, medium-, and long-term change. Needless to say, if a state was not a member in the international system for a lagged year, it was excluded from the data base; hence, no change rate could be computed. If a state was not a member of the system fifteen years previous to a given year, there is no meaning to examining a relationship between change in its power capabilities over a fifteen-year interval and involvement in hostilities. If change in power capabilities over a moderate length of time is related to the involvement of states in hostilities, then a lag of ten years would probably register the effect of such change for a state that was a member of the system thirteen but not fifteen years previously.

One lag, however, requires special consideration. That is the three-year lag, which is aimed at determining whether or not change over the short term is significant. By virtue of their very nature, variables selected to measure power capabilities tend to be characterized by stability over the very short run. In many cases the onset of substantial change over the short run may not be fully manifest for a period of a few years, and hence a three-year lag will more accurately register the occurrence of this change than a one- or two-year lag.

But there is a special set of cases that a three-year lag completely misses. That is change resulting from the entry of new members into the international system. Such states go from nonmembership to membership in the international community in a very short time. Such events represent a dramatic moment in the "life" of a state and may be associated with the culmination of significant structural changes within a regional subsystem or the international system as a whole. The citizens of new member states may be imbued with exaggerated pride. Neighboring states may feel threatened by a new entrant, particularly if it has considerable strength in power capabilities. Consequently, it is reasonable to suppose that change in the relative power capabilities of states, arising from the entry of new members to the international system, may be associated with the occurrence of military hostilities. For this reason it was deemed desirable to estimate, if only roughly, the importance of such change.

Accordingly, in computing change rates for the three-year time lag, new entrants to the international system were assigned a change rate of 100 percent if they were not a member of the system the previous year; 50 percent if they entered the system one year previously; and 25 percent if they entered two years previously.

Change in the power capabilities relationship between two sides to a conflict is defined as the power capabilities disparity ratio between the two sides at time x minus the power capabilities disparity ratio between the two sides at time y, divided by the power capabilities disparity ratio at time y. Time lags of three, five, ten, fifteen, and twenty years were computed. If a given side to a conflict included only one state and if, for the three-year time lag, that state was not a member of the international system, the change rate was computed by dividing the power capabilities score of the state by the power capabilities score of the opposing side and assigning a negative sign to the result. If the new state's power capabilities score is very small compared to the score of other side, the resulting figure will be minimal. But if the new state's power capabilities score is large relative to the other, the resulting figure will be substantial. The change is coded negative, since the power capabilities position of the latter has deteriorated as a result of the entry of the newcomer. We thus have a measure of the destabilizing effect of the new state's entry relative to the state it has come into conflict with. If the states on both sides of a conflict are new entrants and if they entered the system during the same year, the change rate for the three-year lag is computed by taking the side with lesser power capabilities as a percent of the side with greater power capabilities and assigning a negative sign to the result.

Significant change in the power capabilities relationship between two sides to a war is defined as change in the power capabilities relationship between the two sides to the conflict that is greater than 20 percent.

Change in the distribution of power capabilities within the international system is defined as the mean change in the power capabilities of all states in the system for any given year. Time lags of three, five, ten, fifteen, and twenty years are computed. No special allowance is made for the time lag of three years in cases in which a state did not previously exist. The entry of a state into the system in a particular year automatically causes an immediate change in the power capabilities scores for all other states, because these scores are based on each state's standing relative to all other states in the system. If a new entrant to the system has a large power capabilities score, change in the distribution of capabilities in the system as a whole will be considerable. If the state's power capabilities score is small, change will be minimal.

Amount of war in the international system is defined in terms of four indicators: number of states in war underway; number of nation-months-war underway; number of nation-months-war begun; and number of war entrants.[27] Each indicator is computed on an annual basis and normalized according to the number of states in the international system. The third indicator is derived by summing the total number of nation-months-war resulting from all interstate wars begun in a given year and normalizing. For example, if only one war was begun in 1939 and if it lasted five years, the number of nation-months-war resulting from that war for the half-decade is summed and then normalized (according to the number of states in the international system in 1939); the result is entered as the score for 1939. If no wars were begun in 1940, the entry for that year will be "0," even though war was underway as a consequence of the one war begun in 1939. The fourth indicator is derived by taking the number of states that enter a war in any year and dividing by the number of states in the system for that year.

Thus, the first two variables are measures of the amount of war *underway* in the system at any given period in time, whereas the latter two tap the dimension of war *begun.* There is a rationale for utilizing both kinds of indicators. Interstate war in the international system is a relatively infrequent occurrence. As a result, when amount of war is operationalized on an annual basis according to the war begun, many years are scored as zero entries. When amount of war is measured in terms of number of nation-months-war begun, some years, such as that when the First or Second World War began, score inordinately high. Assuming that there really is a relationship between change in the distribution of capabilities within the international system and amount of war, we may fail to confirm it if we measure amount of war in terms of war begun, unless that relationship happens to be very tightly determined.

For example, assume that change over a generational period is related to the occurrence of war. In the approximately twenty-year period preceding the outbreak of the First World War, the international system *may* (this is a hypothetical example) experience substantial change in the distribution of capabilities. However, values of the amount-of-war-begun indicators reflecting that particular war will be concentrated exclusively in the year 1914. But change in the distribution of capabilities over the twenty-year time frame is likely to be spread over several years, such as, for example, 1892, 1893, 1894, 1895, 1896. When the two variables are correlated, then, the values for 1894 and 1914 will both be high and correlate as predicted. But those for 1892 to 1912, 1893 to 1913, 1895 to 1915, and 1896 to 1916 will not correlate (assuming that amount of war was negligible in 1912, 1913, 1915, and 1916); the values for change will be high and those for amount of war low. Hence, unless the relationship between change and amount of war follows a precise twenty-year interval, so that change achieves low values in 1912, 1913, 1915, and 1916, the relationship between the two variables will be masked.

Use of the amount-of-war-underway indicators is aimed at finessing this problem. A sizable war such as the First World War will register substantial scores for five years running, namely, 1914 to 1918. In that sense, chances for detecting lagged relationships are improved.

War-underway variables, however, also contain a built-in bias. When a major war actually occurs, the distribution of capabilities in the system is likely to be affected by the war itself. States involved in a war can be expected to augment defense expenditures and armed forces, and other states in close proximity to the belligerent states may do likewise as a contingency against becoming involved. As a result, the distribution of capabilities in the system will shift significantly. Hence, a high change rate based on a twenty-year time lag for the year 1915 may principally reflect change that occurred between 1914 and 1915 rather than change that transpired between 1895 and 1915.

Each of the two types of indicators selected is aimed at dealing with the problem inherent in the other. Even so, they do not necessarily represent a foolproof approach. If the four indicators all correlate with amount of war or, conversely, if all four correlate not at all, we can have considerable confidence in the results. If, however, the correlation coefficients arising from use of the two types of indicators differ importantly, interpretation of the results will be clouded. In the latter case, more sophisticated techniques may be required to determine the true relationship between the two variables.

5

Findings: The Empirical Evidence Regarding Relationships Between Power Capabilities and Conflict

In this chapter we shall present the empirical evidence regarding the hypotheses outlined in Chapter 3. In the process we shall briefly supplement our presentation with some of the descriptive findings that have been forthcoming in the operationalization and testing of the various hypotheses. Although the descriptive results do not provide answers to the hypotheses, they may nonetheless be of interest to the reader who has not previously seen the world of power capabilities empirically defined for all independent states over more than a century.

Table 5-1 presents the power capabilities scores of the ten highest- and ten lowest-scoring states in the international system for five select years of the 1850-1965 time frame. Table 5-2 rank orders the ten states that score highest on power capabilities for twelve select years, at decade intervals from 1855 to 1965. In general, the results do not contradict what one might expect on the basis of general historical knowledge of the strength of various states of the world. A few cases may appear to rank somewhat higher or lower than would otherwise be expected. A number of considerations are relevant to such cases.

First, any measuring instrument designed to tap variation in a complex variable is likely to contain an element of error. It would indeed be surprising if the index proposed for this study did not contain some error. The critical question is not whether error is inherent in the measuring tool, but whether it is appreciable enough to obscure the relationships it was designed to detect. In our opinion, the latter does not apply here. For reasons previously discussed, the indicator-variables included in the index are judged to be relevant and important indicators of power capabilities. Since the present study is statistical in nature, by observing relationships between variables across many cases, we expect to detect relationships that actually prevail. Error that distorts relationships for a few cases should not be large enough to mask the underlying relationships. Moreover, to the extent that error inherent in the index scores is random, the results will underestimate rather than overestimate the strength of relationships, since the effect of random error is to diminish correlation coefficients.[1]

Second, it is important to recognize that previous judgment by historians and statesmen of the capabilities of particular states in the international system may have been wrong. Power capabilities scores resulting from this index could shed important light on such cases.

Third, it is equally important to note that this index is not a measure of gross national product. Previous studies in the fields of economics and political science

Table 5-1
Power Capabilities Scores for Ten Highest-Scoring and Ten Lowest-Scoring States in the International System: 1850-1960 (In Thousands of Units)

1850		1875		1900		1930		1960	
United Kingdom	12728	Russia/U.S.S.R.	11343	Russia/U.S.S.R.	12651	United States	11755	United States	21942
Russia/U.S.S.R.	12306	France	10897	United Kingdom	12515	United Kingdom	10524	Russia/U.S.S.R.	12709
France	11737	United Kingdom	10730	France	9473	France	6710	United Kingdom	5024
Austria-Hungary	7379	Germany	7228	United States	8387	Russia/U.S.S.R.	5755	Communist China	4476
United States	4668	United States	6487	Germany	8062	China	5510	France	4019
Prussia	4523	Austria-Hungary	5859	Austria-Hungary	5792	Germany	5345	West Germany	3034
Turkey	3528	Italy	4974	Italy	4180	Italy	4184	Canada	2871
Spain	3314	China	4203	Netherlands	2940	Japan	3269	Italy	1660
Netherlands	2626	Spain	3755	Turkey	2391	Canada	2473	Sweden	1620
Uruguay	2545	Turkey	2932	Belgium	2234	Spain	2038	Australia	1582
Bolivia	633	Venezuela	627	Colombia	422	Afghanistan	326	Cameroun	144
Parma	539	Bolivia	583	Honduras	422	Costa Rica	325	Liberia	139
Guatemala	516	El Salvador	526	El Salvador	398	Guatemala	323	Congo (Braz.)	138
Haiti	487	Luxembourg	507	Haiti	392	Nicaragua	322	Honduras	137
Colombia	473	Ecuador	458	Morocco	374	Ecuador	306	Guinea	135
Luxembourg	442	Colombia	455	Guatemala	355	Dominican Rep.	289	Cen. African Rep.	132
El Salvador	309	Morocco	424	Korea	310	Honduras	286	Haiti	119
Honduras	289	Nicaragua	422	Paraguay	293	Panama	257	Upper Volta	116
Nicaragua	269	Honduras	345	Montenegro	213	Haiti	234	Dahomey	114
Liberia	220	Liberia	229	Liberia	208	Liberia	165	Togo	98

Table 5-2
Ten Highest-Scoring States on Power Capabilities Rank-Ordered: 1855-1965

Rank	1855	1865	1875	1885	1895	1905
1.	United Kingdom	United Kingdom	Russia/U.S.S.R.	United Kingdom	Russia/U.S.S.R.	Russia/U.S.S.R.
2.	France	Russia/U.S.S.R.	France	France	France	United Kingdom
3.	Russia/U.S.S.R.	France	United Kingdom	Russia/U.S.S.R.	United Kingdom	France
4.	Austria-Hungary	United States	Germany	Germany	Germany	Germany
5.	United States	Austria-Hungary	United States	United States	United States	United States
6.	Prussia	Italy	Austria-Hungary	Austria-Hungary	Austria-Hungary	Austria-Hungary
7.	Spain	Prussia	Italy	Italy	Italy	Italy
8.	Turkey	China	China	China	Netherlands	Netherlands
9.	Netherlands	Spain	Spain	Spain	China	Japan
10.	Uruguay	Turkey	Turkey	Netherlands	Spain	China

Rank	1915	1925	1935	1945	1955	1965
1.	United Kingdom	United States	Russia/U.S.S.R.	United States	United States	United States
2.	Russia/U.S.S.R.	United Kingdom	United Kingdom	Russia/U.S.S.R.	Russia/U.S.S.R.	Russia/U.S.S.R.
3.	France	France	France	United Kingdom	United Kingdom	Communist China
4.	United States	China	United States	Canada	Communist China	United Kingdom
5.	Germany	Germany	Germany	China	France	West Germany
6.	Austria-Hungary	Russia/U.S.S.R.	Italy	Australia	Canada	France
7.	Italy	Japan	China	Belgium	West Germany	Canada
8.	China	Italy	Japan	Brazil	Australia	Italy
9.	Japan	Australia	Poland	Netherlands	Sweden	Sweden
10.	Netherlands	Spain	Netherlands	Italy	Belgium	India

have sometimes compared the relative strength of states on the basis of the GNP index.[2] While we would expect GNP to correlate significantly with power capabilities, we are interested in more than GNP. For example, countries that score very high on GNP but relatively low on armed forces personnel and defense expenditure will necessarily score lower on power capabilities relative to other states than they would on GNP alone.

Finally, it cannot be denied that other indicator-variables could be selected to measure power capabilities and alternative methods could be used for weighting the variables in the equation. The index utilized in this study should be evaluated, in part, in terms of its long-term contribution to the delineation of the power capabilities phenomenon. If other investigators conclude that the index is wanting in one or more respects, they may wish to experiment with alternative means of index formation. In fact, specific cases in this study deemed to be "deviant" may, if probed in depth, yield clues to other variables which might be equally, if not more, important in the calculation of power capabilities scores. The results generated by future endeavors, which incorporate other variables or weight variables differently, when compared systematically to the results forthcoming from this index, may be one of the more useful means for evaluating the validity of the technique.

The index developed and utilized in the course of this study does provide information on the power capabilities scores for virtually all sovereign states in the international system for the 1850-1966 years. To date, no comparable set of scores on power capabilities has been available for use in the field.[3] The utility of the proposed index is that it provides scores on the capabilities of nearly *all* states in the system *relative* to nearly all other states. It would be a difficult, perhaps even impossible, task to find evaluations by historians of the capabilities of all states in the world for the time frame of this study. Moreover, the scores provided by the index allow for the computation of change rates in the power capabilities of states, as well as other derivative-type variables. Without power capabilities scores it would be an impossible undertaking to evaluate changes in the power capabilities of all or even many states of the system for any sizable length of time and taking into account different time lags.

Table 5-3 presents mean change rates in the distribution of power capabilities of all states in the international system. The mean change rates were computed by summing the changes rates for the individual power capabilities scores of all states in the system and dividing by the number of states. Rates of change had previously been computed for five different time lags, ranging from three to twenty years. Accordingly, the mean rate of change for each of the five time lags is reported. Table 5-4 is similar to Table 5-3, but change rates of all states are averaged on a half-decade rather than on an annual basis. For example, the change rates of all states on the three-year lag are averaged for the period of 1856 to 1860, and all successive half-decade intervals through 1961 to 1965.

By examining change rates that have been averaged on a half-decade basis,

Table 5-3
Mean Change Rates in the Distribution of Power Capabilities in the International System: 1853-1966

	Mean Percent Change[a]				
Year	Lag 3	Lag 5	Lag 10	Lag 15	Lag 20
1853	6.7				
1854	6.5				
1855	8.3	7.9			
1856	6.1	8.0			
1857	6.8	10.1			
1858	7.1	7.7			
1859	6.4	7.8			
1860	7.6	8.6	12.5		
1861	9.7	9.9	11.4		
1862	8.6	9.4	10.6		
1863	12.5	10.0	10.8		
1864	7.8	9.9	11.0		
1865	10.0	15.5	15.6	15.0	
1866	10.5	11.6	14.1	15.6	
1867	16.2	19.6	23.0	23.7	
1868	11.4	17.3	20.1	20.8	
1869	11.9	16.2	21.5	22.8	
1870	11.1	16.5	28.1	30.2	25.2
1871	11.1	16.3	22.4	25.1	24.4
1872	13.8	12.7	23.1	25.8	25.1
1873	13.9	16.6	26.7	32.8	30.2
1874	14.1	17.5	23.1	29.3	30.9
1875	13.4	15.3	17.3	27.7	30.3
1876	16.9	18.1	23.6	24.0	32.2
1877	11.5	17.6	22.1	26.7	33.6
1878	13.0	12.7	19.1	25.1	30.0
1879	11.2	12.9	22.3	26.7	31.2
1880	12.4	17.6	19.3	24.5	37.0
1881	10.9	15.3	19.6	26.4	29.7
1882	11.0	14.1	19.1	22.6	33.1
1883	8.0	13.6	18.7	20.0	31.2
1884	11.2	14.3	18.4	23.2	32.3
1885	10.6	12.7	18.8	17.4	25.0
1886	9.7	12.6	18.0	18.2	23.1
1887	10.3	13.1	17.2	19.3	20.0
1888	12.2	13.0	16.0	19.6	18.9
1889	10.2	12.8	15.8	18.2	22.6

Table 5-3 (cont.)

			Mean Percent Change[a]		
Year	Lag 3	Lag 5	Lag 10	Lag 15	Lag 20
1890	12.3	15.7	16.0	17.8	22.1
1891	7.7	9.9	14.9	16.5	20.5
1892	9.8	11.4	15.4	17.9	19.7
1893	9.3	9.6	16.0	18.0	17.1
1894	8.6	11.2	15.3	17.9	18.3
1895	6.6	11.4	13.0	15.9	17.6
1896	8.3	10.6	13.9	16.4	18.2
1897	9.8	12.0	14.7	16.7	19.4
1898	9.0	13.3	15.5	18.6	22.8
1899	9.7	13.3	16.4	19.2	22.3
1900	9.8	11.5	17.9	16.9	20.8
1901	10.4	12.7	17.6	18.6	21.0
1902	11.3	12.0	16.2	20.5	22.9
1903	8.1	11.7	17.0	20.2	22.6
1904	8.4	10.5	16.1	19.1	21.7
1905	9.9	10.7	15.1	20.9	21.1
1906	10.8	13.4	15.4	17.8	21.3
1907	8.8	12.5	14.2	16.2	21.2
1908	9.7	12.3	14.6	17.1	20.1
1909	8.5	10.6	14.4	17.1	19.4
1910	8.7	10.4	12.1	14.8	20.2
1911	8.0	8.8	13.9	13.6	16.0
1912	9.8	9.6	15.6	14.9	16.1
1913	12.2	12.5	17.4	19.1	18.2
1914	14.0	16.7	15.7	20.8	23.4
1915	19.7	21.0	18.2	22.3	26.8
1916	23.6	24.8	23.5	24.2	30.6
1917	25.8	31.6	30.1	28.5	37.8
1918	26.0	36.5	37.2	31.3	38.1
1919	24.0	35.6	39.9	36.1	40.1
1920	15.3	22.6	31.2	28.8	32.4
1921	17.6	22.4	32.8	32.6	34.2
1922	23.3	19.4	31.6	32.0	32.5
1923	22.2	25.3	31.5	33.8	31.7
1924	19.9	32.1	25.9	32.5	28.1
1925	20.8	27.2	22.2	27.5	24.8
1926	19.7	23.0	20.4	26.6	26.6

Table 5-3 (cont.)

			Mean Percent Change[a]		
Year	Lag 3	Lag 5	Lag 10	Lag 15	Lag 20
1927	14.1	24.7	21.1	26.2	26.1
1928	9.9	23.3	32.1	25.8	26.1
1929	10.9	17.6	38.8	23.2	25.8
1930	10.4	12.3	30.1	21.2	24.8
1931	12.8	16.0	28.6	19.4	26.2
1932	16.3	18.1	32.9	22.3	29.3
1933	13.7	16.6	30.7	34.2	30.2
1934	13.7	16.9	23.4	38.3	28.6
1935	12.4	16.4	20.6	38.2	25.5
1936	12.0	15.1	20.8	32.5	23.3
1937	15.0	16.7	20.7	34.7	25.9
1938	11.9	16.9	22.0	36.0	33.4
1939	18.7	21.4	29.8	33.3	41.5
1940	23.7	28.8	35.9	39.3	56.4
1941	27.0	29.4	35.1	36.8	42.9
1942	19.6	28.0	36.9	37.3	44.2
1943	14.2	28.2	36.2	37.3	41.4
1944	15.2	21.4	35.3	39.6	38.6
1945	15.0	20.9	32.1	34.5	37.8
1946	17.8	21.9	29.7	33.8	38.9
1947	15.5	21.3	24.9	31.0	37.6
1948	17.5	21.9	22.2	28.8	33.5
1949	20.2	20.5	21.8	28.9	31.8
1950	15.9	22.2	27.1	26.2	30.4
1951	14.2	22.8	25.7	24.7	29.7
1952	14.1	18.6	23.9	23.4	31.8
1953	14.1	21.8	24.1	23.5	33.8
1954	13.5	19.5	22.2	24.3	34.0
1955	11.2	17.6	26.7	29.5	32.7
1956	9.2	15.3	27.6	28.1	28.8
1957	10.4	13.8	24.2	29.1	28.6
1958	10.3	14.7	26.4	30.4	27.6
1959	9.4	13.1	24.2	27.6	29.2
1960	10.1	15.1	26.2	32.4	37.3
1961	12.0	15.7	24.2	33.1	36.8
1962	13.7	15.6	22.8	32.1	36.6

Table 5-3 (cont.)

	Mean Percent Change[a]				
Year	Lag 3	Lag 5	Lag 10	Lag 15	Lag 20
1963	9.7	15.1	21.1	31.0	35.6
1964	8.8	15.4	21.0	27.9	32.1
1965	8.3	12.7	21.2	27.1	32.3
1966	8.2	11.5	20.1	24.8	33.2

[a]A blank space signifies change rate could not be computed because time lag extended farther back than data base.

one can more easily perceive trends of variation in the distribution of capabilities over time. As the figures demonstrate, there is considerable alteration over time. The different time lags manifest similar but not identical trends. As might be expected, longer time lags exhibit higher average rates of change. For all lags the 1916-1925 years represent a peak period of change. Other peak times are the late 1870s and the 1880s, the late 1930s and the 1940s. Thus, the effects of the two world wars show up unmistakably. Change in the international system was at minimum levels during the 1860s, the 1890s and 1900s, and the 1950s and early 1960s.

These results are suggestive of some important categories of summary information which can be derived from the power capabilities scores and which provide insight into the nature of the distribution of capabilities during the 1850-1966 period. Quite possibly, more refined and varied descriptive-analytical findings can be gleaned from the data generated for the purpose of this study. We now proceed to an examination of the validity of our hypotheses.

Power Capabilities and War Outcome

The first hypothesis stated: Given the occurrence of war, the side possessing the greater power capabilities prior to the initiation of war will amost always be victorious. Table 5-5 presents the results for this hypothesis. Of forty-two wars between 1850 and 1966, the side possessing the greater power capabilities was victorious in twenty-seven instances. The number noted in the upper left-hand corner of each of the two frequency cells is the expected frequency of occurrence if we define "almost always victorious" as 85 percent of the time.

Table 5-4

Mean Change Rates in the Distribution of Power Capabilities in the International System on a Half-Decade Basis: 1855-59 to 1955-59

Time Period	Mean Percent Change[a]				
	Lag 3	Lag 5	Lag 10	Lag 15	Lag 20
1855-59	6	8			
1860-64	9	10	12		
1865-69	12	16	19	20	
1870-74	12	15	24	28	27
1875-79	13	15	20	26	31
1880-84	10	14	19	23	32
1885-89	10	12	17	18	21
1890-94	9	11	15	17	19
1895-99	8	12	14	17	20
1900-04	9	11	16	19	21
1905-09	9	11	14	17	20
1910-14	10	11	15	16	18
1915-19	23	29	29	28	34
1920-24	19	24	30	31	31
1925-29	15	23	27	25	25
1930-34	13	16	29	27	27
1935-39	13	17	22	34	30
1940-44	20	27	35	38	44
1945-49	17	21	26	31	35
1950-54	14	20	24	24	32
1955-59	10	14	25	28	29

[a]A blank space signifies change rate could not be computed because time lag extended further back than data base.

Table 5-5

War Outcome and Power Capabilities Relationship: 1850-1965

	Side Possessing			
	Greater Power Capabilities		Lesser Power Capabilities	Total Wars
	35[a]	20.5[b]	6[a] 20.5[b]	
No. of Victories	27		14	41

[a]Expected frequency of occurrence when "most wars" is defined as 85 percent of all wars.

[b]Expected frequency of occurrence for null hypothesis that there is no relationship between power capabilities and victory.

Forty-one wars during the 1850-1965 time period are examined. Eighty-five percent of forty-one is thirty-five, the expected number of victories. Fifteen percent of forty-one is six, the expected number of losses. According to our yardstick, then, there were eight less victories by the side with greater capabilities than was expected and, consequently, eight more victories by the side with weaker capabilities than was anticipated.

Are the deviations statistically significant? Before replying to this question, one must first inquire as to whether tests of statistical significance are applicable to the data. In a real sense, they are not. We are looking at the *universe* of wars for the time frame under review (when war is operationalized according to the Singer-Small criteria). We have not randomly sampled our events from a larger set of war events occurring during the 1850-1965 years. In another sense, however, one can imagine that this set of war events is a representative sample from a hypothetical universe of all possible samples of wars between sovereign states that have occurred under similar conditions, but where chance factors result in random variation in different attributes. This interpretation acknowledges the dynamic and ever changing nature of the real world, while simultaneously assuming that patterns of regularity and stability are inherent in that world. The significance test, in this sense, can be employed as a standard for evaluating whether the variation in observations is likely to reflect chance variation alone.[4] Moreover, as Robert Winch and Donald Campbell note, tests of significance can be used as a nonsubjective and low-cost approximation of a model of literal randomization, which does not require the assumption of sampling from an infinite universe, and which one could construct for evaluating the likelihood that observed differences are due to chance variation.[5] For the purpose of this study, then, tests of statistical significance for this and other hypotheses will be reported so that readers who are inclined to accept the logic of these interpretations can more fully evaluate the import of the findings.[6]

Application of a X^2 One Sample Test[7] to the matrix in Table 5-5 results in rejection of the *affirmative* hypothesis at the .001 level of significance. A deviation of the above magnitude would occur less than one time in a thousand if the events were randomly selected from a larger universe of cases. "Most wars," when defined as 85 percent of all wars, are not won by the side with greater capabilities when power capabilities are operationally defined as in this study. Nonetheless, wars were won by the side with greater capabilities more often than not. Are the differences in the predicted direction sufficiently large to warrant rejection of the null hypothesis that there is no relationship between power capabilities and war outcome. If there was no relationship, we would expect to find approximately the same number of wars won by the side with lesser capabilities as by the side with greater capabilities. In terms of the above matrix, the expected frequency for the null relationship is 20.5, the number noted in the upper right-hand corner of each frequency cell. According to that criterion there were 6.5 more victories by the side with greater capabilities and

6.5 less by the side with weaker capabilities than would be anticipated.[8] Application of the X^2 One Sample Test (for the one-tail case) to the null hypothesis results in rejection of the hypothesis at the .05 level of significance. Overall, the evidence suggests that power capabilities are relevant to the outcome of war, but that other variables importantly affect outcome so that greater power capabilities do not "almost always" predict victory.

The second and third hypotheses framed for this inquiry were: Given the occurrence of war, the greater the power capabilities disparity prior to the initiation of war, (1) the less the devastation resulting from war, and (2) the shorter the duration of war. Devastation, it will be remembered, is defined as the total number of casualties incurred by all independent states participating in the conflict, divided by the total population of the participant states. Duration is defined as the mean number of nation-state-months-at-war for the states participating in the war. The Pearson Product-Moment Coefficient of Correlation formula was used to test the two hypotheses. Since observations for all three of the variables include extreme outliers (for example, see Table 5-6 which presents the power capabilities disparity ratios for the war events), correlation coefficients were computed for a logged version of the variable data, as well as for the raw data. Table 5-7 presents the results.

Interestingly, all of the coefficients are in the opposite direction of that predicted, suggesting that as power capabilities disparity increases, war devastation and war duration diminish. However, three of the four coefficients account for less than 3 percent of the variation in the data, and thus are so low as to evidence a null relationship. The highest coefficient, power capabilities disparity correlated with war devastation (logged), explains no more than 7 percent of the variance. (The correlation coefficient squared and multiplied by 100 equals the variance shared by the independent and dependent variables. Expressed differently, it indicates the proportion of the variance of the dependent variable determined by the variance of the independent variable.)

One might surmise that holding constant for duration would significantly improve the relationship between disparity and devastation. Some wars may be decided very quickly as a result of important military advantages accruing to the initiator, such as superior forces-in-being and the element of surprise. The opponent may not have sufficient time to mobilize his resources in the early stages of hostilities so as to stave off defeat. Holding constant for duration, however, does not result in any substantial change in the correlation between power capabilities disparity and devastation. In the unlogged solution, power capabilities disparity correlates $-.13$ with devastation when holding constant for duration; in the logged solution it correlates $-.23$. The net result, then, is a slight reduction in the correlation coefficients. Thus, while the side to a war with greater power capabilities is more often than not victorious, power capabilities disparity, as operationalized in this study, does not explain the length of war or the devastation the sides are willing to incur before agreeing to end the conflict.

Table 5-6
Power Capabilities Disparity Ratios and Change Rates in the Power Capabilities Relationship for War Inventory Events

Conflict I.D. #	Power Capabilities Disparity Ratio	Change Rates in Power Capabilities Disparity Relationship[a]				
		Lag 3	Lag 5	Lag 10	Lag 15	Lag 20
80	1.4675					
90	2.2672					
100	13.7739	−7				
110	2.1887	17	32			
130	2.7035	47	40			
140	2.8109	50	26			
150	11.3001	−3	7	26		
160	1.1357	−5	−3			
170	6.9847	−2	−11	−29		
180	1.1328	−2	−26	−11		
190	1.3345	0	−24	−61	−59	
200	1.0666	−73	−73	−78	−77	
210	4.0672	−1	4	5	−3	−9
220	2.4702	−2	25	8	−29	−13
230	3.5370	−9	26	20	41	22
240	1.4081	24	12	2	60	27
250	2.7506	15	13	−9	−27	−16
260	2.3615	−3	7	15	1	−35
270	2.0567	−20	−24	9	5	13
280	6.2815	−9	−14	−34	−7	−23
290	2.7574	35	19	66	40	74
300	1.6390	−27	−17	−25	4	−23
310	6.0522	22	17	−17	−6	−22
320	1.8977	5	−4	9	−9	−16
330	1.2884	26	10	67	16	15
340	6.3638	14	6	−6	−2	5
350	2.2734	8	4	−6	−1	8
360	4.3795	−23				
370	1.4836	11	12	−54	−33	−41
380	1.6854	39	16	129	55	132
390	1.2325	−16	−14	−20	−13	0
400	13.5019					
410	1.3809	−6	−15	11	12	16
420	5.6753	78	184	297	368	132
430	1.8849	−38	−64	−60	−89	−81

Table 5-6 (cont.)

Conflict I.D. #	Power Capabilities Disparity Ratio	Change Rates in Power Capabilities Disparity Relationship[a]				
		Lag 3	Lag 5	Lag 10	Lag 15	Lag 20
440	16.8713	32	80	185	237	
450	1.7455	−57				
460	7.9391	−42	−31	−4	10	−7
470	22.5458	−9	−181	−44	12	152
480	19.2742	6	11	−12	−30	−28
490	4.1925	6	10	21		
500	4.1017	61	56	91	88	

[a]A blank signifies that change rate could not be computed because data base did not extend far enough back in time, or because one or both sides to the conflict did not exist for a given time lag. Conflict I.D. 400 is a special case; complete data was unavailable for computing change rates.

Table 5-7
Correlation Coefficients for Power Capabilities Disparity with War Devastation and War Duration

	Unlogged Solution		Logged Solution	
	War Devastation	War Duration	War Devastation	War Duration
Power Capabilities Disparity	−.17	−.12	−.28	−.17

Power Capabilities and Occurrence of Military Hostilities

Our review of findings now shifts to hypothesized relationships between the level of power capabilities disparity, on the one hand, and whether or not conflict escalates to the level of military hostilities on the other. Hypothesis four of the study asserts: Given an interstate conflict, the greater the disparity in the power capabilities relationship between the two sides to the conflict prior to its occurrence, the greater the probability the conflict will escalate to the level of military hostilities. Quincy Wright's inventory of international conflicts was selected for the purpose of testing the hypothesis. (Table 5-8 presents the power capabilities disparity ratios for the conflicts in the Wright inventory.) The Pearson Product-Moment Correlation Coefficient for the two variables in question was computed.[9] Once again, power capabilities was logged because of outliers and tested separately. The results are a correlation coefficient of .10 for

Table 5-8

Power Capabilities Disparity Ratios and Change Rates in the Power Capabilities Relationship for Wright Inventory of Conflict Events

Conflict I.D. #	Power Capabilities Disparity Ratio	Change Rates in Power Capabilities Disparity Relationship[a]				
		Lag 3	Lag 5	Lag 10	Lag 15	Lag 20
1	1.3142	−46	−60	−69	−62	−62
2	11.1823	−24	−42	−47	−53	−44
3	1.9750	−51				
4	5.0484	−505				
5	1.3629	43	52	115	78	82
6	1.4840	36	17	16	6	
7	5.9305	−17				
8	2.2916	−229				
9	1.7001	−170				
10	5.6620	−18				
11	6.5193	308	429	573	529	455
12	1.2099	−14				
13	9.0507	139	152	242	321	221
14	1.9631	−196				
15	2.7656	−36				
16	5.8055	126				
17	2.0815	−51	−51	75	69	21
18	1.9616					
19	1.9593	270				
20	3.3035	−60	−50	8	−31	−24
21	2.6581	−38				
22	8.7190	20	40	45	92	70
23	12.1898	−41	−45	121	163	81
24	1.6781	45	126	94	397	249
25	3.0318	−8	44	51	263	164
26	1.0755	−8	8	44	129	128
27	4.1746	−25				
28	2.5557	−43	−30			
29	19.1720	−47	−23	−39	10	−13
30	4.0842	−24				
31	5.1886	338	133	2	−35	−51
32	19.9190	−27	−43	−63	24	17
33	4.7859	−37	−52			
34	7.3209	11	−15	−60	−30	−51
35	1.5352	5	18	8	7	37
36	2.0240	3	−33	−4	1	142

Table 5-8 (cont.)

Conflict I.D. #	Power Capabilities Disparity Ratio	Change Rates in Power Capabilities Disparity Relationships[a]				
		Lag 3	Lag 5	Lag 10	Lag 15	Lag 20
37	15.2642	−25	−29	−73		
38	2.6109	41	49	−14	73	135
39	1.5683	−11	−14	−52	−57	40
40	13.0508	3	−7	−45		
41	1.6854	39	16	129	55	132
42	24.3528	−4				
43	19.4368	−2	−2	−45	−64	21
44	1.0187	−2	−6	−10	−17	−23
45	3.1054	−24	−37	−62		
46	22.6252	−10	−20	−11	−51	−27
47	1.1171	15	32	167		
48	1.1171	15	32	167		
49	3.0015	−27	−21	−34	−82	−35
50	13.5019					
51	1.5952	−63				
52	1.8171	−1	−22	−26	−80	−77
53	1.0944	−19	−7	−24	−55	0
54	10.6292	27	35	85	65	29
55	1.2155	−37	−23	−30	−80	−23
56	1.2028	8	−2	−2	69	28
57	8.4956	−5	14	9	36	74
58	7.9512	57	136	130	745	
59	1.3809	−6	−15	11	12	16
60	1.8059	−9	1	6	24	
61	19.0283	2	47	60	114	
62	16.8713	32	80	185	237	
63	24.2448	7	10	54	122	214
64	3.3325	−30	13	28	116	121
65	2.4804	−40		172	138	104
66	2.2757	−44		−52	−46	−12
67	40.0614	−2		13	64	−5
68	16.2727	−16	−28	10	22	7
69	1.7455	−59				
70	2.0167	25	122	181	20	−18
71	2.9912	−33				
72	15.2432	−7		44	213	370
73	24.5829	−27	−7	47	125	531
74	2.1667	11	−1	19	−41	−63

Table 5-8 (cont.)

Conflict I.D. #	Power Capabilities Disparity Ratio	Change Rates in Power Capabilities Disparity Relationships[a]				
		Lag 3	Lag 5	Lag 10	Lag 15	Lag 20
75	2.7353	−19		−2	9	28
76	20.4083	−27	21	126	128	107
77	1.9443	−33	−20	19	−46	−67
78	2.3822	8	3			
79	23.0951	−4				
80	24.4402	−4				
81	7.9391	−42	−31	−4	10	−7
82	1.0971	−46	−12	93	−20	−48
83	4.2616	−41	−27	122	133	67
84	1.7530	−40	−10	7	−56	−67
85	17.3230	−1	−21	−37	−36	−18
86	19.3437	−33	−27	52	107	291
87	2.1487	−1	−26	27	−22	−57
88	1.4290	1	−27	143	61	−30
89	1.5415	23	−24	70	115	−8
90	9.1403	30	171	316	243	319
91	1.4724	1	20	125	331	557
92	1.5544	1	13	92	278	452
93	1.4894	22	−26	64	108	−11
94	1.5415	23	−24	70	115	−8
95	2.6932	15				
96	1.6295	14	30	1	142	35
97	5.0180	7	2	−10	166	206
98	1.7781	15	62	42	213	30
99	19.2742	6	11	−12	−30	−28
100	22.5458	−9	−18			
101	2.4427	−2	72			
102	1.8962	−36	−47	−70	−86	−79
103	9.6415	−17	−12	−71		−35
104	1.7531	7	12	24	30	146
105	1.5604	−3	−5	−10	−13	−66
106	2.6412	20	32	15		
107	1.3530	15	17			
108	1.0714	2	10	12	54	50
109	19.8137	−5				
110	3.9600	−10	−6	40		
111	4.0946	−24				
112	1.2700	65	163	65		

Table 5-8 (cont.)

Conflict I.D. #	Power Capabilities Disparity Ratio	Change Rates in Power Capabilities Disparity Relationships[a]				
		Lag 3	Lag 5	Lag 10	Lag 15	Lag 20
113	55.1150	3	2	47	11	210
114	29.4190	−12	−21			
115	68.8218	−24	−16	−24	−37	13
116	3.4234	−2	6	7		
117	6.1711	20	−5	−11	−63	−73
118	1.5987	−7	12	8	−18	82
119	4.1925	6	10	21		
120	2.3769	−42				
121	1.3608	−73				
122	1.4771	−68				

[a]A blank signifies that change rates could not be computed because one or both sides to the conflict did not exist for a given time lag. Conflict I.D. 00 is a special case; complete data was unavailable for computing change rates.

the unlogged solution and .08 for the logged version. The hypothesis is clearly disconfirmed.

Hypothesis five is very similar to four but is targeted exclusively on conflicts that involve the threat of or actual use of force: Given an interstate conflict involving the threat of or actual use of force, the greater the disparity in the power capabilities relationship between the two sides to the conflict prior to its occurrence, the greater the probability the conflict will escalate to the level of military hostilities. The inventory of international conflicts provided by K.J. Holsti has been used for the testing of this assertion. (Table 5-9 presents the power capabilities disparity ratios for the conflicts in the Holsti inventory.) The correlation coefficient for the two variables was computed. The result is a very low .10 and .04 when power capabilities is logged. Once again the hypothesis is disconfirmed.

To test this apparent absence of relationship between power capabilities disparity and military hostilities more systematically, we experimented with a few different mixes of the conflict events contained in our three international conflict inventories. Our goal was to further maximize the variance in the data. In our first pool we combined the conflict events from the Wright and Holsti inventories. In instances where each inventory contained the same conflict, one of the two observations was dropped. To this combination we added wars from the Singer-Small list of wars for the 1919-1966 time frame. Again, when duplication occurred, observations were omitted so that only one instance of each conflict appears in the pool. The result is a considerably expanded list of conflicts which ought to increase the variance in our independent and dependent

Table 5-9

Power Capabilities Disparity Ratios and Change Rates in the Power Capabilities Relationship for Holsti Inventory of Conflict Events

Conflict I.D. #	Power Capabilities Disparity Ratio	Change Rates in Power Capabilities Disparity Relationship[a]				
		Lag 3	Lag 5	Lag 10	Lag 15	Lag 20
1	8.3398	79	287	260	217	239
2	3.4019	−29				
3	4.5596	−455				
4	1.4836	11	12	−54	−33	−41
5	1.1016	−91				
6	6.4244	−16				
7	1.8901	−189				
8	2.8315	−35				
9	1.0626	−94				
10	1.1480	21	935	25	54	54
11	2.0068	18				
12	3.8545	57	141	257	291	250
13	3.3035	−60	−50	8	−31	−24
14	8.6197	−63	−26	67	54	35
15	16.1635	−6				
16	3.0318	−8	44	51	263	164
17	1.5352	5	18	8	7	37
18	1.6854	39	16	129	55	132
19	1.4096	1	16	10	15	32
20	1.0187	−2	−6	−10	−17	−23
21	1.7903	43	43	−62	−4	77
22	13.2075					
23	1.0303	25	88	176	330	199
24	1.0194	−35	−19	−25	−79	−17
25	1.2028	8	−2	−2	69	28
26	7.7791	76	69	20	86	
27	7.9512	57	136	130	745	
28	1.3873	1	15	15	172	
29	2.2701	59	33	28	−68	−15
30	6.1311	13	138	87	888	128
31	22.1105	28	114	92	734	196
32	19.0284	2	47	60	114	
33	25.9263	1	87	256	118	76
34	27.6063	42	81	158	243	52
35	27.8653	40	77	166	268	80
36	16.8713	32	80	185	237	

Table 5-9 (cont.)

Conflict I.D. #	Power Capabilities Disparity Ratio	Change Rates in Power Capabilities Disparity Relationships[a]				
		Lag 3	Lag 5	Lag 10	Lag 15	Lag 20
37	6.9374	70	194	111	522	
38	31.7272	39	29	181	195	270
39	2.7615	−36	−22	−48	−23	−10
40	1.9449	45	231	120	−5	−29
41	42.0827	−2		31	63	2
42	16.2727	−16	−28	10	22	7
43	1.7455	−57				
44	2.9912	−33				
45	2.9912	−33				
46	2.1667	11	−1	19	−41	−63
47	1.9443	−33	−20	19	−46	−67
48	1.0085	6	12	−28	30	28
49	21.8393	−18		68	193	386
50	7.9391	−42	−31	−4	10	−7
51	12.9260	−27	−33	−34	−16	−35
52	2.4927	89				
53	1.6926	4	−3	−10	4	−14
54	1.0556	−1	−8	11	33	13
55	19.2742	6	11	−12	−30	−28
56	22.5458	−9	−18	−44	12	152
57	38.0389	−13	8	−11	60	167
58	5.1340	−2	5	19	10	140
59	44.4472	−2				
60	2.7126	9	21	25	24	49
61	1.3916	14	14			
62	2.9088	−18	−14			
63	2.6769	−1	9	25	−8	59
64	55.1150	3	2	47	11	210
65	24.4492	15				
66	4.3016	24	40			
67	1.5987	−7	12	8	−18	82
68	1.6874	−168				
69	156.2149	15	20	34	73	169
70	3.3325	−30	−3	43	102	60
71	4.1746	−25				

[a]A blank space signifies that change rates could not be computed because one or both sides to the conflict did not exist for a given time lag. Conflict I.D. 22 is a special case; complete data was unavailable for computing change rates.

variables. The N for the Wright inventory was 122 conflict-events; for the Holsti inventory, 71. The set of pooled conflicts for the 1919-1966 time frame registers an N of 157 conflict-events.

In a second mix of pooled conflicts we supplemented the first pool by adding the remaining wars from the Singer-Small inventory for the 1850-1918 time period. This addition substantially increases the number of events that escalated to the level of military hostilities. Furthermore, the scope of the time interval for testing the relationship is more than doubled, from 47 years to 117 years. The principal limitation inherent in this pool of events is that it lacks a set of conflicts for the 1850-1918 years which did not escalate to the level of military hostilities. This might introduce distortion into the overall pool, as would be the case if intervening variables were systematically affecting the interaction between power capabilities disparity and occurrence of military hostilities in one of the two time segments. Since we have no a priori reason to believe this to be the case, we have added the wars to our first pool in order to maximize variance with respect to the military hostilities variable.

In a third pool of conflict events, we sought to maximize variance of conflicts involving the threat of or actual use of force. We began with Holsti's initial inventory of conflicts. To this we added the wars from the Singer-Small inventory for the 1850-1918 years. We also added conflicts from the Wright inventory which escalated to the level of military hostilities and which did not appear in the Holsti list of conflicts, and wars from the Singer-Small inventory for the 1919-1965 period which appeared in neither the Wright nor Holsti inventories.

Table 5-10 identifies the sets of conflict-events which we have utilized to test

Table 5-10
Correlation Coefficients of Power Capabilities Disparity with Involvement in Military Hostilities

	Power Capabilities Disparity	
Sets of Conflict Events	Not Logged	Logged
1. Wright Inventory of Conflicts, 1920-1965 (N = 122)	.10	.08
2. Pooled Conflicts, 1919-1965 (N = 157)	−.01	.03
3. Pooled Conflicts, 1850-1965 (N = 184)	−.09	−.07
4. Holsti Inventory of Conflicts, 1919-1965 (N = 71)	−.04	.04
5. Threat-Force Pooled Conflicts 1850-1965 (N = 108)	−.16	−.11

the hypotheses relating power capabilities disparity to involvement in military hostilities. The figures in parentheses refer to the number of conflict events contained in each inventory of conflicts.

It is immediately apparent that the international conflicts selected for review do not discriminate, on the basis of power capabilities disparity, between those that escalate to military hostilities and those that do not. This is true whether one focuses on conflicts in general or on conflicts all of which are known to involve the threat or actual use of military force.

The one remaining hypothesis to examine in this portion of our inquiry is restricted exclusively to war events: Most wars are characterized by a high level of disparity in the power capabilities relationship prevailing between the sides prior to the initiation of hostilities. "High level of disparity," it will be remembered, is defined as a power capabilities disparity ratio of 2.0 or greater, meaning that one side to the conflict has a power capabilities score twice that of the other side. Table 5-11 presents the summary results for this hypothesis.

The actual number of wars characterized by a power capabilities disparity ratio at 2.0 or above is greater, hence in the predicted direction. But defining "most wars" as 85 percent of all wars results in rejection of the affirmative hypothesis. A deviation of nine wars from the expected frequency would occur less than one time in a thousand if the events were randomly drawn from a larger universe of cases.

Following disconfirmation of the hypothesis we visually examined the power capabilities disparity ratios for all wars to determine if there was a more meaningful pattern inherent in the data. Such a threshold was discovered, with the discriminating point falling at the 1.45 level. Table 5-12 presents the results. Once again, the number in the upper left-hand corner of the frequency cells indicates the expected frequency if "most wars" is defined as 85 percent of all wars. The observed frequencies closely approximate the expected frequencies. The X^2 One Sample Test applied to the observed frequencies demonstrates that the deviations are not statistically significant at the .05 level. The affirmative hypothesis is now upheld.

Table 5-11
Power Capabilities Disparity Ratios Above and Below the 2.0 Level for War Events: 1850-1965

| | Power Capabilities Disparity Ratio | | Total Wars |
	High (2.0 or more)	Low (1.99 or less)	
	36[a]	6[a]	
No. of Wars	27	15	42

[a]Expected frequency if "most wars" is defined as 85 percent of all wars.

Table 5-12
Power Capabilities Disparity Ratios Above and Below the 1.45 Level for War Events: 1850-1965

| | Power Capabilities Disparity Ratio | | |
	High (1.45 or more)	Low (1.44 or less)	Total
	36[a]	6[a]	
No. of Wars	34	8	42

[a]Expected frequency if "most wars" is defined as 85 percent of all wars.

As a further and final check on the validity of the hypothesis we supplemented the war events examined, which are from the Singer-Small inventory, with wars which appear in the Holsti and Wright inventories but that do not qualify for the former because they did not involve a minimum of one thousand battle-connected fatalities or have one thousand of their armed forces personnel engaged in the war theater. This results in an additional fourteen war events. Of these, three had power capabilities disparity ratios below the 1.45 level; the remainder had disparity ratios well above the 2.0 level. Table 5-13 presents the results when "high level of disparity" is defined as a power capabilities disparity ratio of 1.45 or greater. The observed frequency of wars is forty-five, which closely approximates the expected frequency of forty-eight. The X^2 One Sample Test applied to the observed frequencies demonstrates that the deviations are not statistically significant at the .05 level. The affirmative hypothesis remains upheld. The data indicate that the power capabilities disparity relationship is relevant to the occurrence of war. Few wars are seen to occur when the two sides to the conflict approach equality in power capabilities below the ratio level of 1.45. Once that threshold is exceeded, however, the number of war events increases markedly.

How are these results to be interpreted in view of the low correlations found

Table 5-13
Power Capabilities Disparity Ratios Above and Below the 1.45 Level for Military Hostilities: 1850-1965

| | Power Capabilities Disparity Ratio | | Total Events |
	High (1.45 or more)	Low (1.44 or less)	
	48[a]	8[a]	
No. of Wars	45	11	56

[a]Expected frequency if "most military hostilities" is defined as 85 percent of all events.

between power capabilities disparity and the hypothesized escalation of international conflicts to the level of military hostitlities? One possible explanation comes to mind. It may be that most international conflicts examined, including those that did not result in military hostilities, are of such an intense nature as to be in a class by themselves, and hence distinct from less intense conflict situations as well as from nonconflict situations. The possibility that the absence of a relationship between disparity ratios and involvement in military hostilities is due to a qualitative difference between intense conflicts, on the one hand, and less intense or non-conflicts, on the other hand, is a theme to which we will return later in this chapter.

Change in Power Capabilities
and Occurrence of War

A number of the hypotheses framed in the course of this inquiry focus on change in the power capabilities of nation-states: on the individual state level of analysis, at the interstate level of analysis, and at the international system level of analysis. Hypothesis eight of the study asserts: Given an interstate conflict, the greater the change in the power capabilities relationship between the two sides prior to the occurrence of the conflict, the greater the probability that the conflict will escalate to the level of military hostilities. Hypothesis nine is identical, with the exception that it focuses on conflicts in which the threat or actual resort to force has been made.

As previously discussed in Chapter 3, plausible rationales can be advanced for surmising that both change in the direction of a narrowing of the power capabilities relationship between two sides to a conflict and change in the direction of a widening of the gap are related to the occurrence of military hostilities. We argued that the magnitude of change may be more important than direction in explaining the occurrence of hostilities. To test this notion, the direction of change rates is ignored. A negative rate of change, as earlier noted, represents a closing of the power capabilities gap separating two sides, whereas a positive rate of change signifies a broadening of the gap. By dropping all negative signs, variation in change is treated solely in terms of magnitude. A negative change rate of 35 percent is treated the same as a positive change rate of 35 percent. Since involvement in military hostilities is a dichotomous variable that was scored "0" for noninvolvement and "2" for involvement, in correlating the two variables, a high positive coefficient results if substantial change in either direction is associated with hostilities and if minimal or no change is associated with nonhostilities.

Table 5-14 presents the results. Correlation coefficients were computed for the five sets of conflict events. Immediately apparent is the virtual absence of relationship. Most of the coefficients (twenty-two out of twenty-five) explain

Table 5-14

Correlation Coefficients for Change in the Power Capabilities Relationship with Involvement in Military Hostilities, When Direction of Change is Ignored

Set of Conflict Events	Lag 3	Lag 5	Lag 10	Lag 15	Lag 20
Wright Inventory, 1920-1965	.05	−.15	−.12	−.12	−.06
Pooled Conflicts, 1919-1965	.05	.00	.01	−.02	−.03
Pooled Conflicts, 1850-1965	−.03	−.09	−.12	−.16	−.18
Holsti Inventory, 1919-1965	.12	−.06	.03	−.11	−.01
Threat-Force Pooled Conflicts, 1850-1965	−.01	−.16	−.11	−.22	−.20

less than 3 percent of the variation in the data. The second striking feature in the matrix is the direction of the correlations. Twenty of the twenty-five coefficients are negative or in a direction opposite that hypothesized. In other words, conflicts that escalate to the level of military hostilities are seemingly characterized by less change in the power capabilities relationship between the opposing sides. This conclusion is unwarranted, however, since the two highest coefficients in the other than predicted direction account for only 4 percent of the variance. What is important without exception, then, is the null relationship that describes the five different time lags, ranging from a short interval of three years to a generational interval of twenty years, and the absence of any noticeable difference between conflicts that always involve the threat or use of force and those that do not. The two hypotheses are clearly unsupported.

If magnitude of change is unimportant, perhaps direction is. To test this notion, signs for the negative change rates were restored. Theoretically, then, a positive correlation would result if negative change rates, or a narrowing of the gap, are associated with nonhostilities, and if positive change rates, or a widening of the gap, are associated with military hostilities. A negative correlation would result if these relationships were reversed.

Table 5-15 presents the results. It is evident that the direction of change is no more related to involvement in military hostilities than magnitude of change. Twenty-three of the twenty-five coefficients explain less than 3 percent of the

Table 5-15

Correlation Coefficients for Change in the Power Capabilities Relationship with Involvement in Military Hostilities, When Direction of Change is Accounted for

Set of Conflict Events	Lag 3	Lag 5	Lag 10	Lag 15	Lag 20
Wright Inventory, 1920-1965	−.15	−.05	−.03	−.03	.00
Pooled Conflicts, 1919-1965	−.05	.01	.02	.00	−.01
Pooled Conflicts, 1850-1965	−.01	−.06	−.10	−.13	−.13
Holsti Inventory, 1919-1965	−.08	−.05	−.01	−.06	−.02
Threat-Force Pooled Conflicts, 1850-1965	.00	−.17	−.17	−.21	−.20

variation in the data. The two highest coefficients explain no more than 4 percent. Twenty-two of the coefficients are negative, which, if the coefficients were larger, would indicate that a widening of the gap is associated with escalation to military hostilities. But this is not the case. Quite clearly the coefficients are so low as to demonstrate nothing other than a null relationship.

As a final test in search of a possible relationship, we logged the change rate variable data and once again ignored direction in favor of magnitude, the focus of our original hypothesis. As Tables 5-6, 5-8, and 5-9 demonstrate, some of the change rate observations are extreme outliers. It may be that change is in fact related to involvement in military hostilities, but that once a relatively high threshold is exceeded, further increases in magnitude are no longer relevant. Logging the variable pulls in the extreme outliers, permitting us to examine this notion.

Table 5-16 reports the findings. With few exceptions, this set of results differs little from those set forth in previous tables. Most of the coefficients have increased in size and, as might be expected, are still predominantly negative. But the size of the coefficients continues to indicate an absence of relationship. Twenty of the twenty-five coefficients account for 4 percent or less of the variance. Two account for 5 percent and two others for 8 to 9 percent. When viewed according to the perspective of twenty-five coefficients, the four highest coefficients could easily have resulted from chance variation. The chance

Table 5-16

Correlation Coefficients for Change in the Power Capabilities Relationship with Involvement in Military Hostilities, When Direction of Change is Ignored and Independent Variable is Logged

Set of Conflict Events	Lag 3	Lag 5	Lag 10	Lag 15	Lag 20
Wright Inventory 1920-1965	−.02	−.25[a]	−.22	−.19	−.03
Pooled Conflicts, 1919-1965	.06	−.08	−.04	−.05	.01
Pooled Conflicts, 1850-1965	−.05	−.18[a]	−.19[a]	−.30[b]	−.22[a]
Holsti Inventory, 1919-1965	.08	−.17	−.08	−.12	.01
Threat-Force Pooled Conflicts, 1850-1965	−.04	−.24[a]	−.21	−.29[a]	−.21

[a]Significant at .05 level or less for two-tailed test.

[b]Significant at .01 level or less for two-tailed test.

interpretation is supported on theoretical grounds by the location of the high coefficients within the correlation matrix. They are not concentrated in any one of the time lags. Nor are they concentrated in conflicts that always involve the threat or use of force as opposed to those that do not, or vice versa. Overall, then, the hypotheses are unsupported for five change rate intervals and all sets of conflict events.

If change in the power capabilities relationship between conflicting parties is not related to involvement in military hostilities, perhaps change in the power capabilities of states treated individually is. Hypothesis seven of the study asserts: The greater the change in the power capability of states, the greater the probability of involvement in military hostilities. The focus is on change in each state's respective power capabilities scores over time. A state's scores are, of course, relative in the sense that they are derived on the basis of each state's standing compared to other states in the system. But in computing change rates for the purpose of testing the seventh hypothesis, we do not focus on change in any nation's scores relative to the standing of one or more other specific states. Rather, we randomly select for each state of the international system a year from the total number of years that it was a member of the international system during the 1850-1966 time frame. To this group of states were added all states involved in military hostilities during the same period. For the latter group each state was selected for the year immediately prior to its involvement in hostilities. Change rates were then computed for all states in both groups and for the five typical time lags. The change rates were computed by: taking a state's score for the year in which it was sampled; subtracting from that its score at a previous point in time (three years previously for the three-year time lag); and dividing by the score for the lagged year. Thus, a given state's change rates represent most directly change in its position relative to its past standings.

The hypothesis was tested by pooling all states together (those that were involved in hostilities and those that were randomly selected) and correlating change rates with whether or not states were involved in hostilities. Table 5-17 presents the findings.

The first set of correlation coefficients (horizontally) is a result of allowing the direction of change to affect the outcome. The second set of coefficients results when direction of change is ignored, and the third set represents direction of change ignored and the independent variable logged. As the table demonstrates, all of the coefficients are in the predicted direction and several are statistically significant. But the magnitude of all the coefficients is so low as to prompt the conclusion that change in the power capabilities of states, treated severally, is not related to involvement in military hostilities.

Hypothesis ten of the study centers on change in the power capabilities relationship for war events only: Most wars are characterized by significant change in the power capabilities relationship between the two sides to the conflict prior to the outbreak of war. Significant change, it will be remembered, was defined as change equal to or greater than 20 percent, regardless of the direction of change. In testing this hypothesis we have once again worked with intervals of three, five, ten, fifteen, and twenty years. Table 5-18 presents the results. The hypothesis is clearly disconfirmed for all change-rate intervals. For each time lag except one, the number of wars for which change in the power

Table 5-17
Correlation Coefficients for Change in the Power Capabilities of States with Involvement in Military Hostilities: 1850-1966

Direction of Change	Lag 3	Lag 5	Lag 10	Lag 15	Lag 20
Accounted for	.13[b]	.05	.06	.10[a]	.07
Ignored	.20[c]	.09[a]	.05	.09	.11
Ignored and Independent Variable Logged	.18[c]	.05	.01	.04	.03

[a]Significant at .05 level.

[b]Significant at .01 level.

[c]Significant at .001 level.

Table 5-18

Number of Wars Characterized by Change Greater Than 20 Percent in the Power Capabilities Relationship Between the Two Sides, for Five Different Time Intervals

| | Change in the Power Capabilities Relationship for War Events | | | | | | | | |
| | Lag 3 | | Lag 5 | | Lag 10 | | Lag 15 | | Lag 20 | |
	Less than 20 Percent	More than 20 Percent	Less than 20 Percent	More than 20 Percent	Less than 20 Percent	More than 20 Percent	Less than 20 Percent	More than 20 Percent	Less than 20 Percent	More than 20 Percent
No. of Wars	23	17	22	14	16	16	14	14	11	13

capabilities relationship was *less* than 20 percent equals or exceeds the number of wars in which change was greater than 20 percent. For the twenty-year lag there were thirteen wars in which change was greater than 20 percent compared to eleven wars in which change was less than 20 percent. While one might expect this to be the case for a very short time lag, such as three years, the same cannot be said for intervals of a considerably longer duration, especially those of ten, fifteen, and twenty years. In and of itself, the evidence is not sufficient to disprove the assertion that substantial change in the power capabilities relationship between states is causally related to the occurrence of war. But it does demonstrate that change on the order of 20 percent or greater is not associated with the occurrence of war for time intervals ranging from three to twenty years.

Hypothesis eleven of the study focuses on the direction of change in the power capabilities relationship between the two sides to a war. It states that most wars are characterized by significant change toward an equality in power capabilities between the two sides to the conflict prior to the outbreak of war, rather than by insignificant change or change away from an equality in power capabilities. Since a relatively small number of the wars are characterized by change in the power capabilities relationship greater than 20 percent, it was decided to modify our definition of significant change in order to test the hypothesis. A more modest change rate of 15 percent was selected as a threshold for differentiating between significant and insignificant change. The choice of this threshold still does not yield a significant relationship between level of change in the power capabilities relationship and the occurrence of war. Table 5-19 presents the evidence with respect to the hypothesis.

The hypothesis is not supported for any of the time lag intervals. In fact, for three out of five time lags the number of wars characterized by change of 15 percent or more and in the direction of greater inequality exceeds the number of wars characterized by change of 15 percent or more in the direction of equality.

Table 5-19
Direction of Change in the Power Capabilities Relationship Between the Two Sides to Wars, Utilizing Different Change Rate Intervals

Change Interval	Number of Wars Characterized by:		
	Change of 15 Percent or Greater Toward Equality	Change of 15 Percent or Greater Away from Equality	Change of Less Than 15 Percent in Either Direction
Lag 3	8	11	20
Lag 5	8	11	17
Lag 10	10	9	13
Lag 15	7	8	13
Lag 20	9	7	8

This is the case without even taking into account the number of wars characterized by change of less than 15 percent in either direction. Is there, then, a significant relationship in the direction opposite of that hypothesized? Are most wars characterized by significant change in the direction of an increasing disparity in the power capabilities relationship between the two sides to the war? The evidence does not warrant this conclusion. Application of the X^2 One Sample Test to the null hypothesis for the three-, five-, and fifteen-year change rate intervals did not yield a level of statistical significance at or below the .05 level.

The last hypothesis on change in the power capabilities of states concerns the international system as a whole: The greater the change in the distribution of power capabilites within the international system, the greater the amount of war. Four indicators were chosen to operationalize amount of war: number of states engaged in war underway; number of nation-months-war underway; number of nation-months-war begun; and number of war entrants. All indicators are normalized according to the number of states in the international system. Table 5-20 presents the correlation coefficients that result when change rates and amount of war are measured on an annual basis. Change in the distribution of capabilities is significantly related to amount of war when the latter is measured in terms of *war underway*. Seven of the ten coefficients account for 17 to 27 percent of the variance in the data. But change in the distribution of capabilities in the system is not related when amount of war is measured in terms of *war begun*. For reasons discussed in Chapter 4, such divergent results are not easily interpretable. The amount-of-war-begun indicators may correlate poorly because of the relative infrequency of interstate war and because of the

Table 5-20

Correlation Coefficients for Change in the Distribution of Capabilities in the International System with Amount of War: 1853-1965

Change Rate Lag Intervals	Amount of War Indicator-Variables			
	War Underway		War Begun	
	Number of States in War	Number Nation-Months-War	Number War Entrants	Number Nation-Months-War
Lag 3	.44[c]	.49[c]	.14[a]	.10
Lag 5	.44[c]	.52[c]	.08	.07
Lag 10	.36[c]	.42[c]	.04	.03
Lag 15	.27[b]	.32[c]	.02	.05
Lag 20	.51[c]	.51[c]	.17[a]	.09

[a]Significant at .05 level.
[b]Significant at .01 level.
[c]Significant at .001 level.

degree to which variable values are concentrated in single years. On the other hand, amount-of-war-underway indicators may correlate highly because of change in the distribution of capabilities in the international system that is produced by war itself (i.e., amount of war correlating with the change in the distribution of capabilities that it causes).

In an effort to shed further light on this matter, amount of war indicator variables were averaged for half-decade periods, beginning with the 1855-1859 years and extending through the 1960-1964 years. Change rates in the distribution of capabilities were measured for the year preceding each of the five-year intervals for the amount of war variables. For example, change rates were lagged off the year 1959 to be correlated with the amount of war averaged over the 1960-1964 years. This technique leaves something to be desired in the sense that a five-year gap separates the amount of war occurring in 1964 from the year ending the periods from which change rates were computed, namely 1959. Moreover, the choice of 1855 as the initial year for measuring amount of war on a five-year interval basis is arbitrary. Conceivably different results might emerge if a different cutting point was made, such as 1852 or 1853.

Table 5-21 presents the results. It is at once apparent that the correlation coefficients for the amount-of-war-underway variables have dropped substantially. Seven of the ten coefficients now explain 5 percent or less of the variation. Two explain 8 or 9 percent, and one explains 11 percent. Regarding the war begun variables, most of the coefficients are now negative or in the direction opposite that predicted. Eight of the ten explain 4 percent or less of the variance. The two highest coefficients account for 8 to 9 percent. In sum, these results suggest that change in the distribution of capabilities in the international system as a whole is not importantly related to amount of war in the system.

Table 5-21
Correlation Coefficients for Change in the Distribution of Capabilities in the International System with Amount of War: 1854-1964

| | Amount of War Indicator-Variables | | | |
| Change Rate Lag Intervals | War Underway | | War Begun | |
	Number of States in War	Number Nation-Months-War	Number War Entrants	Number Nation-Months-War
Lag 3	.24	.34[a]	−.12	.00
Lag 5	.01	.11	−.31	−.14
Lag 10	.00	.06	−.29	−.14
Lag 15	.17	.15	.00	.12
Lag 20	.28	.29	−.02	−.22

[a]Significant at .05 level.

Further Analysis of the Relationship
Between Power Capabilities and the
Occurrence of Conflict

The hypotheses that focus exclusively on war events have yielded mixed results. In some cases hypotheses have been partly confirmed. In others no significant relationship was found.

The hypotheses that focus on differences between international conflicts that escalate to the level of military hostilities and those that do not have yielded more consistent, although generally nonsignificant, results, and in a manner inconsistent with the relationships initially hypothesized. It is to these events that we now redirect our attention in an effort to explain the unexpected absence of relationships. Virtually no difference was found between the level of power capabilities disparity and the escalation of conflict to the level of military hostilities. Similarly, little or no relationship was found between previous change in the power capabilities relationship of the two sides to a conflict and the escalation of conflict to the level of military hostilities. This was the case when we focused exclusively on conflicts that involved the threat of or actual use of force, and this was also the case when we focused on a wider set of conflicts, some of which may not have included a threat to resort to force. In the process of testing the hypotheses we have experimented with several different sets of conflict events in two time periods, the 1850-1965 years and the 1919-1965 years.

The fact that some evidence of a relationship between level of power capabilities disparity and involvement in war has been detected (hypotheses 1 and 6) leads us to suspect that the inventories of conflict events that include some conflicts that escalated to the level of military hostilities and some that did not may be somewhat biased. As was earlier intimated, the international conflicts gathered together for the purpose of this study are characterized by a high degree of intensity. All of the conflicts in the Holsti inventory involve the threat of or actual use of military force. Nearly all the conflicts in the Wright inventory were sufficiently serious to be brought before either the League of Nations or the United Nations. The few conflicts in the Wright list which did not meet this qualifying criterion were ones that involved the occurrence of military hostilites.

It may be that both the power capabilities of states and change in power capabilities are principally relevant to whether or not conflicts between states escalate to an intense level or whether conflict originates at all. Substantial change in the power capabilities of states may contribute to an awakening or heightening of fears and tensions between the peoples and leaders of two or more states. Existing disparities in power capabilities relationships between states may influence whether leaders counsel moderation or actively contribute to a further heightening of animosity and ill-will. Once a conflict reaches a stage of high intensity, other intervening variables may enter into the equation, determining whether the conflict escalates to the higher level of war. One possibly important factor that immediately comes to mind is the personality dispositions of the peoples and leaders of the conflicting parties and, more importantly, how different dispositions interact with one another. One way of partially testing this general proposition would be to operationalize our variables for a set of conflicts that are characterized by a low level of intensity and test the hypotheses by comparing differences across the two types of conflicts.

For the purpose of this study a control group of conflicts marked by a low level of intensity was not readily available. But an alternative solution did present itself. This was to create randomly a hypothetical set of nonconflict events which could serve as the control group. Index scores for the power capabilites of all independent states in the international system had already been generated. Similarly, change rates for the five different time intervals had been computed for all states. Since it was a relatively simple procedure to derive relevant secondary variables from this basic set of variable data already at hand, it was decided to create a set of hypothetical nonconflict events.

To this end, each state in the international system between 1850 and 1966 was selected at random for one of the total number of years during which it qualified for membership in the international community. Each state was then randomly paired with one of its adjacent neighbors. In each case, only adjacent states that were members of the international system for the point of time selected were considered as possible partners. States were paired with their neighbors, since most international conflicts involve neighboring states. A review of the conflict events set forth in Appendixes B, C, and D will bear out this point. Altogether 105 hypothetical nonconflicts were generated. Possible error associated with this method of generating nonconflict events should underestimate rather than overestimate relationships found in the data. The reason is that our random selection of events may pair some states together at or near a point in time in which they actually were involved in an intense conflict. (Appendix E presents the states randomly paired, along with the year randomly selected for pairing. Table 5-22 presents the power capabilities disparity ratios and change rates for the power capabilities disparity relationship for the hypothetical nonconflicts.)

Before proceeding to a review of findings resulting from the inclusion of this new set of nonconflicts, it is appropriate to express our original hypotheses in their reformulated form and enter them into the lineup of hypotheses as numbers 13 and 14.

Hypothesis 13: *The greater the disparity in the power capabilities relationship between states, the greater the probability that the states will become involved in an intense conflict.*

Hypothesis 14: *The greater the change in the power capabilities relationship between states, the greater the probability the states will become involved in an intense conflict.*

Table 5-22
Power Capabilities Disparity Ratios and Change Rates in the Power Capabilities Relationship for Hypothetical Nonconflicts

Conflict I.D. #	Power Capabilities Disparity Ratio	Change Rates in Power Capabilities Disparity Relationship[a]				
		Lag 3	Lag 5	Lag 10	Lag 15	Lag 20
10	1.3346	2	−1	4	−2	
20	2.5971	24	54	−40	−29	
40	1.1366	−91	−7	3	0	−2
50	1.8313	2	−20	−39	−27	−5
60	2.3036	5	5	2	11	27
61	1.0015	−3	20	6		
62	1.9171	6	5	80	48	35
80	4.9080	−4	−9	−18	−20	−17
100	2.2930	2	4	−22	−18	−23
120	4.6407	15	47	17	33	19
130	1.3321	−10	−8	13		
140	1.2768	−6				
160	1.0628	−16	−17			
180	6.7912	8	7	−7	30	52
200	10.4897	36	81	123	118	
220	1.8929	−10	−9	−22	−33	−5
230	2.6803	21	−20	48		
231	9.1309	1	13	43		
240	4.0157	10	−26	0	−21	−13
270	1.6866	5				
280	2.7109	15	−14	−1	−16	−24
300	1.4056	−19	−44	−42		
320	1.3147	−6	−6	19	9	0
330	1.3069	0	10	0	6	0
340	1.1780	8	7	4	8	28
350	1.0492	7	5	25	17	4
360	13.8718	41	91	17	−6	
370	2.3383	0	1			
380	1.2672	−2	5	1	13	27
390	2.2119	1	1	15	−9	−14
420	1.2917	2	−15	5	−4	0
421	1.1720	−1	0			
422	2.1175	2	−1	−7		
423	1.8112	15	8			
424	1.7326	−2	3	−2		
425	6.2788	6	−10	0	−5	

Table 5-22 (cont.)

Conflict I.D. #	Power Capabilities Disparity Ratio	Change Rates in Power Capabilities Disparity Relationships[a]				
		Lag 3	Lag 5	Lag 10	Lag 15	Lag 20
426	1.7172	1	1			
427	5.0172	−5	−4	−5		
428	5.3602	6	1	9	8	
429	7.2251	15	18	2		
430	1.3742	−41	−37	−51		
431	2.3981	−5	8			
450	3.4417	−11	−21	−8	−13	
460	1.1879	102	75	93	58	83
490	1.1840	18	15	41	176	189
500	1.1950	12	7	20	−27	3
510	16.5172	11	19	51		
520	3.9600	−10	−6	40		
530	1.3939	−10	−4	−20		
540	23.0198	4	4	100	153	138
550	1.3035	−5	-9	14	−18	−19
560	1.1653	−22	−42			
570	4.3635	−15	−32	−4	2	
572	1.1744	6				
573	1.5654	2	12			
574	4.3462	−13	4			
575	1.5682	−5	2			
576	1.0094	−15	−10			
600	2.3909	−5	−11	−17	−32	−44
610	1.3807	5	51	−35	21	
630	7.2539	−21				
631	1.4829	20	−4			
632	1.3534	−2	−7	−30		
650	1.2795	2				
660	1.1878	6	56	10	44	−3
670	1.2887	3	13			
700	2.1836	64				
710	1.0094	−2	−2	3	8	19
720	4.6246	4	13	13	11	18
750	1.6161	1	20			
810	1.4602	−23	−3	−27	−38	−36
830	1.6891	−4				
850	1.3113	5	5	−5	2	1
860	1.8970	−1	4	−17	−37	−24

Table 5-22 (cont.)

Conflict I.D. #	Power Capabilities Disparity Ratio	Change Rates in Power Capabilities Disparity Relationships[a]				
		Lag 3	Lag 5	Lag 10	Lag 15	Lag 20
870	1.0295	−6	−20	−13	−10	−20
900	1.5906	22	−11	−7	−29	
910	1.4944	13	13	25	−22	−4
920	3.7423	−31	−51	−49	−52	−20
930	3.1368	−22	−11	33	183	98
940	1.6304	−21	−44			
950	2.9012	−12	−12	93		
960	1.6440	−7	12	8	−14	−29
970	1.7081	16	19	21	8	52
990	1.0193	3				
1060	2.3003	−11	−11	−16	−35	−4
1070	1.4072	2				
1090	7.0016	9	0	0	−11	−10
1091	1.8919	67	50	19	49	
1092	1.2339	−18	−17	−15		
1100	1.7453	−7				
1110	1.2968	4		1	13	
1160	1.4276	7				
1170	5.2900	8	7	20	23	25
1190	4.2931	−3	1	11	12	2
1200	1.6607	−60				
1210	10.5392	65	22			
1212	12.1604	−18	−6	−26	11	19
1220	5.3050	13	20			
1240	2.2199	21	31	36	98	136
1250	1.3848	10	3	18	15	25
1261	4.3841	9	33			
1262	2.0367	29	39			
1290	1.0559	−9	12	−5	19	−24
1291	10.0724	−7	−5	−16		
1292	1.1132	4	−19			

[a]A blank space signifies that change rate could not be computed because data base did not extend far enough back in time, or because one or both sides to the conflict did not exist for a given time lag.

For the purpose of this analysis an "intense conflict" is defined as any one of the conflicts included in the Holsti and Wright conflict inventories and any of the wars appearing in the Singer-Small inventory of wars. Note that in the two hypotheses set forth above we have not distinguished between sets of conflicts which exclusively involve the threat or actual resort to force and those that do not. However, in the actual testing of the hypotheses we will continue to rely on the five different sets of conflict events used earlier in the study. Two of these sets of conflicts, it will be remembered, are comprised only of conflicts involving the threat of or actual use of force. They are the Holsti list of conflicts and the Threat-Force Pool of conflicts. (See pp. 71-74.) The former spans the 1919-1965 time period; the latter the 1850-1965 years. In combining the nonconflict events with each of the conflict inventories, inventories covering the 1919-1965 and 1920-1965 period were only combined with nonconflict events applicable to those years.

Table 5-23 presents the results relevant to our first modified hypothesis, and in terms of a logged and unlogged solution. All of the coefficients are in the predicted direction, and all are significant at the .01 level or less. The reader might suppose that the randomly generated set of nonconflicts meets, at least partially, the assumption of randomness required in terms of the conventional use of tests of significance. However, the element of randomness is for the most part lost, since we have combined the same set of nonconflict events with several different inventories of conflict events. The correlation coefficients are considerably higher when the power capabilities disparity variable is logged. For the logged solution, two of the coefficients explain from 9 to 11 percent of the variation in the data. There seems to be little doubt as to existence of a relationship, although admittedly the coefficients explain only a small percent of the variance. As disparity in power capabilities increases, the probability of

Table 5-23

Correlation Coefficients for Power Capabilities Disparity with Involvement in Intense Conflict

When Nonconflict Events Were Combined With:	Power Capabilities Variable	
	Not Logged	Logged
Wright Inventory, 1920-1965	.20[a]	.27[b]
Pooled Conflicts, 1919-1965	.17[a]	.28[b]
Pooled Conflicts, 1850-1965	.20[a]	.28[b]
Holsti Inventory, 1919-1965	.23[a]	.34[b]
Threat-Force Pooled Conflicts, 1850-1965	.22[a]	.30[b]

[a]Significant at .01 level or less.

[b]Significant at .001 level or less.

involvement in intense conflict likewise increases. Of perhaps added importance is the fact that somewhat higher correlations are registered for the two inventories of conflicts restricted exclusively to conflicts involving the threat or actual use of force. And each of these two coefficients covers one of the two different *over all* time periods. Hence, the relationship is not time-bound to the 1919-1966 years. It appears to hold across the entire span of 117 years. The fact that the correlations are highest for conflicts involving the threat or actual use of force is consonant with the theory outlined in Chapter 3 of this study: Force is more likely to be threatened and more likely to be used as disparity increases.

Table 5-24 presents in a different format the relationship that has been discovered. Scores on power capabilities disparity have been collapsed into four categories and cross-tabulated with involvement in intense conflict. As disparity increases, the number of intense conflicts increases, while the number of nonconflict events diminishes.

Table 5-25 presents evidence regarding the fourteenth hypothesis, which concerns change in the power capabilities relationship between states. The direction of change rates is ignored; negative change rates are treated the same as positive rates of change. All of the correlation coefficients are positive or in the predicted direction, and all are significant at the .05 level or less. Nine of the twenty-five coefficients account for 7 to 11 percent of the variance in the data. Five account for less than 4 percent and the remaining eleven account for 4 to 6 percent of the variance. In terms of time lags, the ten-, fifteen-, and twenty-year lags account for considerably more variance than the three- and five-year lags. In terms of type of conflict events, the inventories that consist solely of conflicts involving the threat or use of force usually account for somewhat more variance than those that do not. Overall, our theoretical reasoning is supported, but admittedly at a low level of explanatory value. The two highest coefficients explain only 9 to 11 percent of the variance in the dependent variable.

Table 5-24

Number of Nonconflicts and Intense Conflicts for Varying Levels of Power Capabilities Disparities: 1850-1966

Power Capabilities Disparity Ratio[a]	Number of	
	Nonconflicts	Intense Conflicts[b]
1.0 to 1.50	42	34
1.51 to 2.50	30	44
2.51 to 6.00	20	45
6.01 and higher	13	61

[a]Ratios have not been logged.

[b]Data are from Pooled Conflicts, 1850-1965

Table 5-25

Correlation Coefficients for Change in the Power Capabilities Relationship with Involvement in Intense Conflict, When Direction of Change is Ignored

Set of Conflict Events	Lag 3	Lag 5	Lag 10	Lag 15	Lag 20
Wright Inventory, 1920-1965	.17[b]	.15[a]	.21[b]	.27[b]	.24[b]
Pooled Conflicts, 1919-1965	.17[b]	.15[a]	.22[b]	.24[b]	.23[b]
Pooled Conflicts, 1850-1965	.21[c]	.19[c]	.28[c]	.27[c]	.26[c]
Holsti Inventory, 1919-1965	.22[b]	.21[a]	.29[b]	.29[b]	.34[b]
Threat-Force Pooled Conflicts, 1850-1965	.23[c]	.21[b]	.31[c]	.27[c]	.30[c]

[a]Significant at .05 level.

[b]Significant at .01 level.

[c]Significant at .001 level.

Perhaps direction of change is more important in explaining involvement in intense conflict. To test this notion, our working hypothesis is that negative change rates, or a narrowing of the power capabilities gap, are associated with noninvolvement, and positive change rates, or a widening of the gap, are associated with involvement in intense conflict. Table 5-26 presents the results. With the exception of the three-year time lag, all of the coefficients are positive or in the predicted direction. The coefficients for the three-year lag are all in the opposite direction but so low as to indicate virtually no relationship. Once again, the highest coefficients in the matrix are registered for time lags of ten, fifteen, and twenty years, and conflicts that always involve the threat or use of force obtain higher coefficients than those that do not.

A comparison of the coefficients to those that resulted when direction of change was ignored demonstrates that nearly all of the coefficients have dropped, and often considerably. Table 5-27 juxtaposes the coefficients for the two different hypotheses. The most significant differences occur for the three-year time lag. When direction of change is ignored, all of the coefficients are positive and in the predicted direction. When direction is taken into account, the coefficients for the three-year lag are negative and opposite that predicted.

Table 5-26

Correlation Coefficients for Change in the Power Capabilities Relationship with Involvement in Intense Conflict, When Direction of Change Is Accounted For

Set of Conflict Events	Lag 3	Lag 5	Lag 10	Lag 15	Lag 20
Wright Inventory, 1920-1965	−.06	.04	.16[a]	.18[a]	.16[a]
Pooled Conflicts, 1919-1965	−.05	.11	.18[b]	.19[b]	.17[a]
Pooled Conflicts, 1850-1965	−.05	.13[b]	.19[c]	.22[c]	.19[b]
Holsti Inventory, 1919-1965	−.09	.21[b]	.29[b]	.25[b]	.29[b]
Threat-Force Pooled Conflicts, 1850-1965	−.08	.19[b]	.24[c]	.25[c]	.24[b]

[a]Significant at .05 level.
[b]Significant at .01 level.
[c]Significant at .001 level.

As a final test of the relationship between change in the power capabilities relationship and involvement in intense conflict, we examine the correlation coefficients that result when direction of change is ignored, which was the focus of our original hypothesis and which has yielded the highest coefficients, and when the change rate variable is logged. Table 5-28 reports the coefficients and Table 5-29 compares the coefficients to those that occurred when the change rate variable was not logged. In every instance, except one, the logged solution leads to higher coefficients, indicating that there is a threshold above which rate of change is no longer relevant to involvement in intense conflict. Thirteen of the twenty-five coefficients in the logged solution account for 10 to 20 percent of the variance in the data. Twenty-three of the coefficients explain approximately 7 percent of more the variance. All of the coefficients are in the hypothesized direction, and most are significant at the .001 level or less.

In general, time lags of ten, fifteen, and twenty years still account for more variance than lags of three and five years. This is plausible, since the importance of short-run gaps may not be immediately obvious to the governments of affected states or may be optimistically interpreted by such governments as transitory fluctuations unlikely to prevail over the long run. Or such govern-

Table 5-27

Correlation Coefficients for Change in the Power Capabilities Relationship with Involvement in Intense Conflict, Comparing when Direction of Change Is Accounted For and Ignored

Set of Conflict Events	Lag 3		Lag 5		Lag 10		Lag 15		Lag 20	
	Chg Direc Acct	Chg Direc Ignor	Chg Direc Acct	Chg Direc Ignor	Chg Direc Acct	Chg Direc Ignor	Chg Direc Acct	Chg Direc Ignor	Chg Direc Acct	Chg Direc Ignor
Wright Inventory, 1920-1965	-.06	.17[b]	.04	.15[a]	.16[a]	.21[b]	.18[a]	.27[b]	.16[a]	.24[b]
Pooled Conflicts, 1919-1965	-.05	.17[b]	.11	.15[a]	.18[b]	.22[b]	.19[b]	.24[b]	.17[a]	.23[b]
Pooled Conflicts, 1850-1965	-.05	.21[c]	.13[b]	.19[c]	.19[c]	.28[c]	.22[c]	.27[c]	.19[b]	.26[c]
Holsti Inventory, 1919-1965	-.09	.22[b]	.21[b]	.21[a]	.29[b]	.29[b]	.25[b]	.29[b]	.29[b]	.34[b]
Threat-Force Pooled Conflicts, 1850-1965	-.08	.23[c]	.19[b]	.21[b]	.24[c]	.31[c]	.25[c]	.27[c]	.24[b]	.30[c]

[a]Significant at .05 level.
[b]Significant at .01 level.
[c]Significant at .001 level.

Table 5-28

Correlation Coefficients for Change in the Power Capabilities Relationship with Involvement in Intense Conflict, When Direction of Change is Ignored and the Independent Variable is Logged

Set of Conflict Events	Lag 3	Lag 5	Lag 10	Lag 15	Lag 20
Wright Inventory, 1920-1965	.26[c]	.18[b]	.28[c]	.40[c]	.38[c]
Pooled Conflicts, 1919-1965	.26[c]	.22[b]	.30[c]	.35[c]	.40[c]
Pooled Conflicts, 1850-1965	.27[c]	.32[c]	.35[c]	.32[c]	.41[c]
Holsti Inventory, 1919-1965	.28[c]	.26[b]	.33[c]	.38[c]	.45[c]
Threat-Force Pooled Conflicts, 1850-1965	.27[c]	.31[c]	.33[c]	.27[c]	.38[c]

[a]Significant at .05 level.

[b]Significant at .01 level.

[c]Significant at .001 level.

ments may initially undertake to upgrade the capabilities of their own states as a means of offsetting the superior growth manifested by neighboring states. The persistence of a disadvantaging trend over the long run, and one that appears to be worsening, however, may prompt leaderships to instigate conflict and perhaps even armed hostilities as a means of sparking a period of national resurgence within their own state or cutting an opponent down to size.

How are we to interpret the importance of the direction of change with respect to involvement in intense conflict? Quite obviously, the fact that nearly all of the coefficients rise when direction is ignored indicates that both a narrowing and a widening in the power capabilities relationship are associated with the occurrence of intense conflict. Moreover, careful reflection indicates that positive change or change in the direction of a widening of the gap is more important in explaining the occurrence of intense conflict. The correlation coefficients, when the direction of change is allowed to effect the results, are generally substantial relative to the coefficients when change direction is ignored (Table 5-25). For the former case, this means that the positive change rates are associating with intense conflict, which was scored higher than nonconflict,

Table 5-29
Correlation Coefficients for Change in the Power Capabilities Relationship with Involvement in Intense Conflict, When Direction of Change Is Ignored, and When Independent Variable Is and Is Not Logged

Set of Conflict Events	Lag 3		Lag 5		Lag 10		Lag 15		Lag 20	
	Lŏg	Log	Lŏg	Log	Lŏg	Log	Lŏg	Log	Lŏg	Log
Wright Inventory, 1920-1965	.17[b]	.26[c]	.15[a]	.18[b]	.21[b]	.28[c]	.27[b]	.40[c]	.24[b]	.38[c]
Pooled Conflicts, 1919-1965	.17[b]	.26[c]	.15[a]	.22[b]	.22[b]	.30[c]	.24[b]	.35[c]	.23[b]	.40[c]
Pooled Conflicts, 1850-1965	.21[c]	.27[c]	.19[c]	.32[c]	.28[c]	.35[c]	.27[c]	.32[c]	.26[c]	.41[c]
Holsti Inventory, 1919-1965	.22[b]	.28[c]	.21[a]	.26[b]	.29[b]	.33[c]	.29[b]	.38[c]	.34[b]	.45[c]
Threat-Force Pooled Conflicts, 1850-1965	.23[c]	.27[c]	.21[b]	.31[c]	.31[c]	.33[c]	.27[c]	.27[c]	.30[c]	.38[c]

[a]Significant at .05 level.
[b]Significant at .01 level.
[c]Significant at .001 level.

while negative change rates are associating with nonconflict. The correlation coefficients are positive (the one group of exceptions is the change rates for the time lag of three years). When direction of change is ignored, virtually all of the coefficients rise but not to an extent comparable to the size of the original coefficients. Therefore, we conclude that a narrowing of the power capabilities relationship is associated with the occurrence of intense conflict, but not as much as change that widens the gap. The one exception to this generalization is the three-year time lag. When direction of change is taken into account, coefficients for the three-year lag are slightly negative. This indicates that for the short time-lag change that narrows the power capabilities gap is as important as, if not slightly more than, change that widens the gap.

It is important to note (Tables 5-28 and 5-29) that the coefficients for conflicts that always involve the threat or use of force no longer consistently outweigh those for conflicts that do not. Since the only alteration made was a logging of the change rate variable, it appears that the outliers for the conflicts that do not always involve the threat or use of force were slightly more extreme compared to those conflicts that always involve the threat or use of force.

Overall, the hypothesis that change in the power capabilities relationship is associated with intense conflict appears to be confirmed. Admittedly, most of the coefficients are not very high, but they are significant, and they are consistently in the anticipated direction. How is this confirmation of the importance of change rates to be explained in view of the disconfirmation of our seventh hypothesis, which supposed an association between change in the power capabilities of states and involvement in military hostilities? (Hypothesis seven, it will be remembered compares states involved in military hostilities to a randomly selected group of states not involved in hostilities.) The answer appears to lie in the factor of relationships between states. In the seventh hypothesis we examined change in the power capabilities of states as treated individually. But in the hypothesis examined immediately above (hypothesis 14) we were looking at change in the power capabilities of states relative to other specific states, usually neighboring states. The overall conclusion to be drawn from the results is that change in the power capabilities of states, even if sizable and irrespective of direction, is primarily important with respect to its effect on a given state's relation to other states in its immediate environment. If a dramatic increase in one state's capabilities is paralleled by similar increases in the capabilities of neighboring states, the change is less likely to provoke conflict than if one state's increase is to the detriment of adjacent states.

Significant correlation coefficients have been found, relating power capabilities disparity to involvement in intense conflict, and change in the power capabilities relationship to involvement in intense conflict. As originally conceived, the two variables were thought to be independently related to the occurrence of intense conflict. If so, the multiple correlation of the two variables with involvement in intense conflict should result in substantially increased correlation coefficients. Table 5-30 demonstrates that this is in fact the case. The bivariate correlation coefficients of power capabilities disparity with involvement in intense conflict and of change in the power capabilities relationship with involvement in intense conflict are juxtaposed and compared to the multiple-correlation coefficients that result when both independent variables are correlated with intense conflict and when direction of change is ignored and the independent variables are logged.

The findings show that power capabilities disparity explains somewhat more of the variance than change in the power capabilities relationship for the shorter time lags of three and five years, whereas the reverse is typically the case for the longer lags of ten, fifteen, and twenty years. For a lag of twenty years, change is clearly the more important of the two variables. When the multiple correlation is computed, the bivariate coefficients are higher in every case, with the largest increases registered for the three-year time lag. The lowest multiple correlation coefficient accounts for 10 percent of the variance. Fifteen of the twenty-five coefficients account for 15 percent or more of the variance, and three of the coefficients explain 20 to 23 percent of the variance. All of the coefficients are significant at the .05 level or less. In general, time lags of fifteen and twenty years account for more of the variance than lags of three, five, and ten years. Conflicts that always involve the threat or use of force do not correlate more highly than those that do not.

One additional relationship is of interest with respect to our two independent variables. As has been demonstrated, the two variables are independently and importantly related to the occurrence of intense conflict. But their most important explanatory significance may arise from their joint interaction. For example, if a high level of power capabilities disparity and appreciable change in the power capabilities relationship occur simultaneously, involvement in intense conflict may increase markedly. Table 5-31 presents evidence concerning the interactive effect of the two power capabilities variables. Multiple-correlation coefficients for involvement in intense conflict with power capabilities disparity, change in the power capabilities relationship, and the joint interaction of the two independent variables are reported[b] and juxtaposed to those that occurred prior to inclusion of the interactive variable (INTACT). Twelve of the twenty-five coefficients show no increase when INTACT is incorporated, and eight coefficients increase only .01. In general, then, the increase for most of the coefficients is minimal or nonexistent. We conclude, therefore, that the joint interaction of power capabilities disparity and change in the power capabilities relationship does not add appreciably to the amount of variance explained by the two variables when treated independently and additively.

[b]The multiple regression equation for this relationship is $Y = a + B_1 X_1 + B_2 X_2 + B_3 (X_1 * X_2)$.

Table 5-30
Bivariate and Multiple Correlation Coefficients of Intense Conflict with Power Capabilities Disparity and Change in the Power Capabilities Relationship, When Direction of Change is Ignored and Independent Variables are Logged

Set of Conflict Events	Lag 3			Lag 5			Lag 10			Lag 15			Lag 20		
	PCDISP	CHG	MULTP	PCDISP	CHG	MULTP	PCDISP	CHG	MULTP	PCDISP	CHG	MULTP	PCDISP	CHG	MULTP
Wright Inventory, 1920-1965	.27[c]	.26[c]	.37[b]	.27[c]	.18[b]	.32[a]	.27[c]	.28[c]	.35[b]	.27[c]	.40[c]	.45[b]	.27[c]	.38[c]	.43[b]
Pooled Conflicts, 1919-1965	.28[c]	.26[c]	.37[b]	.28[c]	.22[b]	.33[b]	.28[c]	.30[c]	.36[b]	.28[c]	.35[c]	.40[b]	.28[c]	.40[c]	.44[b]
Pooled Conflicts, 1850-1965	.28[c]	.27[c]	.38[b]	.28[c]	.32[c]	.39[b]	.28[c]	.35[c]	.40[b]	.28[c]	.32[c]	.38[b]	.28[c]	.41[c]	.45[b]
Holsti Inventory, 1919-1965	.34[c]	.28[c]	.43[b]	.34[c]	.26[b]	.39[b]	.34[c]	.33[c]	.40[b]	.34[c]	.38[c]	.44[b]	.34[c]	.45[c]	.48[b]
Threat-Force Pooled Conflicts, 1850-1965	.30[c]	.27[c]	.38[b]	.30[c]	.31[c]	.39[b]	.30[c]	.33[c]	.39[b]	.30[c]	.27[c]	.35[b]	.30[c]	.38[c]	.42[b]

[a]Significant at .05 level.
[b]Significant at .01 level.
[c]Significant at .001 level.

PCDISP = Power capabilities disparity
CHG = Change in power capabilities relationship.
MULTP = Multiple correlation

Table 5-31

Multiple Correlation Coefficients of Intense Conflict with Power Capabilities Disparity and Change in the Power Capabilities Relationship Compared to Multiple Correlation Coefficient of Intense Conflict with Power Capabilities Disparity, Change in the Power Capabilities Relationship, and Interaction of the Latter Two Variables (Direction of Change is Ignored and Independent Variables are Logged.)

Set of Conflict Events	Lag 3		Lag 5		Lag 10		Lag 15		Lag 20	
	Excl. Intr.	Incl. Intr.	Excl. Intr.	Incl. Intr.	Excl. Intr.	Incl. Intr.	Excl. Intr.	Incl. Intr.	Excl. Intr.	Incl. Intr.
Wright Inventory, 1920-1965	.37	.37	.32	.32	.35	.36	.45	.49	.43	.47
Pooled Conflicts, 1919-1965	.37	.37	.33	.33	.36	.37	.40	.43	.44	.48
Pooled Conflicts, 1850-1965	.38	.38	.39	.40	.40	.41	.38	.39	.45	.46
Holsti Inventory, 1919-1965	.43	.43	.39	.40	.40	.40	.44	.45	.48	.51
Threat-Force Pooled Conflicts, 1850-1965	.38	.38	.39	.39	.39	.39	.35	.35	.42	.42

Excl. Intr. = Excludes interaction variable.
Incl. Intr. = Includes interaction variable.

Controlling for the Number of
Conflict Participants

One final factor deserves attention before concluding our analysis. All of the randomly generated nonconflicts are comprised of only two states, whereas a considerable number of conflicts in the Wright, Holsti, and War inventories (and hence pooled sets of conflicts as well) are comprised of three or more states. In many of the latter one state confronts two or more other nations. A lesser number of these conflicts consist of two or more states on each side. It is possible that the number of state participants to a conflict is an intervening variable affecting relationships between power capabilities and intense conflict. When only one state is directly involved on either side of a conflict, the ability to calculate accurately power capabilities disparities may be enhanced. Moreover, if a state is appraising the pros and cons of going to war, its task will be less complicated, all other things being equal, if it does not have to assess whether or not one or more of its allies will remain committed in the event of escalation to the level of military hostilities, and if it does not have to evaluate alliance cohesion among two or more adversary states. In short, the element of uncertainty in judging outcomes is likely to increase as more states become participants to a conflict.

For these reasons, it seemed appropriate to control for the number of participants when testing those hypotheses in which involvement in intense possible to distinguish only between conflicts involving only two states and only possible to distinguish between conflicts involving only two states and those involving three or more. There was not a sufficient number of various combinations of three or more to differentiate among.

Table 5-32 presents the results when power capabilities disparity is correlated

Table 5-32
Correlation Coefficients for Power Capabilities Disparity With Involvement in Military Hostilities, Controlling for Number of State Participants

| | Power Capabilities Variable | | | |
| | Not Logged | | Logged | |
Sets of Conflict Events	2 States	More than 2 States	2 States	More than 2 States
Wright Inventory, 1920-1965	.14	.10	.08	.08
Pooled Conflicts, 1919-1965	.00	−.01	.04	.03
Pooled Conflicts, 1850-1965	−.05	−.09	.00	−.07
Holsti Inventory, 1919-1965	−.02	−.04	.05	.04
Threat-Force Pooled Conflicts, 1850-1965	−.13	−.16	−.08	−.11

with involvement in military hostilities and when the independent variable is logged and unlogged. As the coefficients demonstrate, whether the number of participants is two states only or three or more, there is virtually no evidence of a relationship between the two variables.

When we turn to change in the power capabilities relationship, Table 5-33 presents the findings when the variable is correlated with involvement in military hostilities and when direction of change is accounted for. As is readily apparent there is little or no difference in explanatory value when the number of conflict participants is controlled. Two state conflicts produce a few coefficients that are slightly higher, but these account at best for 5 to 6 percent of the variance. Twenty-three of the coefficients still explain less than 4 percent of the variance. Table 5-34, which reports the findings when direction of change is ignored, can be interpreted in much the same way. A few of the coefficients for two state conflicts are higher, but the overall results indicate little or no relationship between the variables. Twenty-one of the coefficients explain less than 4 percent of the variance.

Table 5-35 presents the correlation coefficients that result when direction of change is ignored and rates of change are logged. In this case some noticeable differences emerge. Six of the coefficients increase appreciably and to a level that accounts for 7 to 16 percent of the variance in the data. Even so, seventeen of the twenty-five coefficients explain 4 percent or less of the variation. Three of the time lags indicate virtually no relationship between change in the power capabilities relationship and involvement in military hostilities. Time lags of five and fifteen years exhibit several healthy coefficients, especially for conflicts that always involve the threat or use of force, and the relationship registered is opposite that hypothesized. But given the large majority of coefficients that indicate virtually no relationship, both in this and the previous two tables, the more plausible interpretation is that there is virtually no relationship between the two variables, irrespective of whether or not the number of participants is controlled for.

The last set of relationships to be examined focuses on power capabilities variables and intense conflict. Table 5-36 presents the results when power capabilities disparity is correlated with involvement in intense conflict, and when the independent variable is logged and unlogged. Some of the coefficients rise when the number of participants is restricted to two states. But several do not, and overall the explanatory value remains about the same.

Table 5-37 presents the results when change in the power capabilities relationship is correlated with involvement in intense conflict and when direction of change is taken into account. With the exception of a time lag of three years, the coefficients reflect somewhat improved explanatory value when the number of participants to a conflict includes only two states. Table 5-38 incorporates the correlation coefficients that result when direction of change is ignored and when change rates are logged. Nearly all of the coefficients register

Table 5-33

Correlation Coefficients for Change in the Power Capabilities Relationship with Involvement in Military Hostilities, When Direction of Change Is Accounted For, and Comparing Outcome When Number of Conflict Participants Is Controlled

Set of Conflict Events	Lag 3		Lag 5		Lag 10		Lag 15		Lag 20	
	Two or More States	Two States	Two or More States	Two States	Two or More States	Two States	Two or More States	Two States	Two or More States	Two States
Wright Inventory, 1920-1965	-.15	-.17	-.05	-.04	-.03	.05	-.03	-.08	.00	-.02
Pooled Conflicts, 1919-1965	-.05	-.05	.01	.09	.02	.05	-.00	-.01	-.01	-.02
Pooled Conflicts, 1850-1965	-.01	.00	-.06	-.01	-.10	-.08	-.13	-.13	-.13	-.18
Holsti Inventory, 1919-1965	-.08	-.11	-.05	-.06	-.01	-.09	-.06	-.11	-.02	-.03
Threat-Force Pooled Conflicts, 1850-1965	.00	.00	-.17	-.17	-.17	-.16	-.21	-.24	-.20	-.26

Table 5-34
Correlation Coefficients for Change in the Power Capabilities Relationship with Involvement in Military Hostilities, When Direction of Change Is Ignored, and Comparing Outcome When Number of Conflict Participants Is Controlled

Set of Conflict Events	Lag 3		Lag 5		Lag 10		Lag 15		Lag 20	
	Two or More States	Two States	Two or More States	Two States	Two or More States	Two States	Two or More States	Two States	Two or More States	Two States
Wright Inventory, 1920-1965	.05	.11	−.15	−.17	−.12	−.02	−.12	−.14	−.06	−.06
Pooled Conflicts, 1919-1965	.05	.07	.00	.01	.01	.06	−.02	−.04	−.03	−.04
Pooled Conflicts, 1850-1965	−.03	−.01	−.09	−.14	−.12	−.12	−.16	−.17	−.18	−.20
Holsti Inventory, 1919-1965	.12	.11	−.06	−.13	.03	−.04	−.11	−.16	−.01	.00
Threat-Force Pooled Conflicts, 1850-1965	−.01	−.01	−.16	−.25	−.11	−.18	−.22	−.27	−.20	−.24

Table 5-35
Correlation Coefficients for Change in the Power Capabilities Relationship with Involvement in Military Hostilities, When Direction of Change Is Ignored and Independent Variable Is Logged, and Comparing Outcome When Number of Conflict Participants Is Controlled

Set of Conflict Events	Lag 3		Lag 5		Lag 10		Lag 15		Lag 20	
	Two or More States	Two States	Two or More States	Two States	Two or More States	Two States	Two or More States	Two States	Two or More States	Two States
Wright Inventory, 1920-1965	-.02	-.02	-.25[a]	-.20	-.22	-.05	-.19	-.28	-.03	.00
Pooled Conflicts, 1919-1965	.06	.04	-.08	-.06	-.04	.04	-.05	-.14	.01	.03
Pooled Conflicts, 1850-1965	-.05	-.05	-.18[a]	.23	-.19[a]	-.18	-.30[b]	-.36[b]	-.22[a]	-.19
Holsti Inventory, 1919-1965	.08	-.00	-.17	-.30	-.08	-.02	-.12	-.26	.01	.12
Threat-Force Pooled Conflicts, 1850-1965	-.04	-.10	-.24[a]	-.41	-.21	-.29[b]	-.29[a]	-.41[b]	-.21	-.15

[a]Significant at .05 level or less for two-tailed test.
[b]Significant at .01 level or less for two-tailed test.

Table 5-36

Correlation Coefficients for Power Capabilities Disparity with Involvement in Intense Conflict, Controlling for Number of State Participants

| | Power Capabilities Variable | | | |
| | Not Logged | | Logged | |
When Set of Nonconflict Events Were Combined With:	More than 2 States	2 States	More than 2 States	2 States
Wright Inventory, 1920-1965	.20[b]	.22[b]	.27[c]	.27[c]
Pooled Conflicts, 1919-1965	.17[b]	.17[b]	.28[c]	.28[c]
Pooled Conflicts, 1850-1965	.20[c]	.21[c]	.28[c]	.28[c]
Holsti Inventory, 1919-1965	.23[c]	.25[c]	.34[c]	.36[c]
Threat-Force Pooled Conflicts, 1850-1965	.22[c]	.24[c]	.30[c]	.33[c]

[b]Significant at .01 level.

[c]Significant at .001 level.

increases, although many of these are quite minimal. Finally, Table 5-39 reports the multiple-correlation coefficients that occur when power capabilities disparity and change in the power capabilities relationship are correlated with involvement in intense conflict. The independent variables are logged and direction of change is ignored. Once again, virtually all of the coefficients register some increase when the number of conflict participants is restricted to two states.

Overall, then, our analysis controlling for the number of state participants to a conflict further supports our earlier finding of little or no relationship between the power capabilities variables, on the one hand, and involvement in military hostilities, on the other. And it confirms the existence of a relationship between the power capabilities variables and intense conflict, with a slight degree of evidence that the relationship is strengthened when only two states are involved in conflict.

Table 5-37

Correlation Coefficients for Change in the Power Capabilities Relationship with Involvement in Intense Conflict, When Direction of Change Is Accounted For, and Comparing Outcome When Number of Conflict Participants Is Controlled

Set of Conflict Events	Lag 3		Lag 5		Lag 10		Lag 15		Lag 20	
	Two or More States	Two States	Two or More States	Two States	Two or More States	Two States	Two or More States	Two States	Two or More States	Two States
Wright Inventory, 1920-1965	−.06	−.08	.04	.10	.16[b]	.26[b]	.18[a]	.25[b]	.16[a]	.25[a]
Pooled Conflicts, 1919-1965	−.05	−.06	.11	.20[b]	.18[b]	.27[c]	.19[b]	.27[b]	.17[a]	.24[b]
Pooled Conflicts, 1850-1965	−.05	−.06	.13[b]	.25[c]	.19[c]	.30[c]	.22[c]	.31[c]	.19[b]	.26[b]
Holsti Inventory, 1919-1965	−.09	−.10	.21[b]	.35[c]	.29[b]	.35[c]	.25[b]	.33[b]	.29[b]	.36[b]
Threat-Force Pooled Conflicts, 1850-1965	−.08	−.07	.19[b]	.35[c]	.24[c]	.35[c]	.25[c]	.35[c]	.24[b]	.29[b]

[a]Significant at .05 level.
[b]Significant at .01 level.
[c]Significant at .001 level.

Table 5-38

Correlation Coefficients for Change in the Power Capabilities Relationship with Involvement in Intense Conflict, When Direction of Change Is Ignored and Independent Variable Is Logged, and Comparing Outcome When Number of Conflict Participants Is Controlled

Set of Conflict Events	Lag 3		Lag 5		Lag 10		Lag 15		Lag 20	
	Two or More States	Two States	Two or More States	Two States	Two or More States	Two States	Two or More States	Two States	Two or More States	Two States
Wright Inventory, 1920–1965	.26[c]	.26[c]	.18[b]	.23[b]	.28[c]	.32[c]	.40[c]	.43[c]	.38[c]	.40[c]
Pooled Conflicts, 1919–1965	.26[c]	.28[c]	.22[b]	.31[c]	.30[c]	.36[c]	.35[c]	.41[c]	.40[c]	.44[c]
Pooled Conflicts, 1850–1965	.27[c]	.30[c]	.32[c]	.37[c]	.35[c]	.39[c]	.32[c]	.38[c]	.41[c]	.43[c]
Holsti Inventory, 1919–1965	.28[c]	.32[c]	.26[b]	.40[c]	.33[c]	.44[c]	.38[c]	.46[c]	.45[c]	.46[c]
Threat-Force Pooled Conflicts, 1850–1965	.27[c]	.31[c]	.31[c]	.38[c]	.33[c]	.39[c]	.27[c]	.34[c]	.38[c]	.38[c]

[a]Significant at .05 level.
[b]Significant at .01 level.
[c]Significant at .001 level.

Table 5-39

Multiple Correlation Coefficients of Intense Conflict with Power Capabilities Disparity and Change in the Power Capabilities Relationship, When Direction of Change Is Ignored and Independent Variables Logged, and Comparing Outcome When Number of Conflict Participants Is Controlled

Set of Conflict Events	Lag 3		Lag 5		Lag 10		Lag 15		Lag 20	
	Two or More States	Two States	Two or More States	Two States	Two or More States	Two States	Two or More States	Two States	Two or More States	Two States
Wright Inventory, 1920-1965	.37	.38	.32	.35	.35	.37	.45	.46	.43	.43
Pooled Conflicts, 1919-1965	.37	.39	.33	.38	.36	.40	.40	.44	.44	.46
Pooled Conflicts, 1850-1965	.38	.40	.39	.44	.40	.43	.38	.42	.45	.46
Holsti Inventory, 1919-1965	.43	.46	.39	.48	.40	.48	.44	.50	.48	.49
Threat-Force Pooled Conflicts, 1850-1965	.38	.43	.39	.46	.39	.44	.35	.40	.42	.43

6

Summary, Conclusions, and Suggestions for Further Research

Recapitulation of the Research

This book originated as an effort to contribute to a theoretical and empirical elucidation of the concept of power, a construct central to the study of political science and international relations. The objective was not to resolve in a definitive fashion ambiguity that continues to accompany usage of the concept in general, but rather to resolve partially, if not completely, uncertainty that characterizes one aspect of the notion of power, namely, the power capabilities of nation-states. The phenomena designated by the concept of power are so multifarious that it may be only through in-depth analysis of particular aspects denoted by the concept that such ambiguity will be eliminated.

To this end, we sought to differentiate theoretically between power in general and power capabilities in particular. At the same time, we reviewed previous thought and findings on relationships between power capabilities and the occurrence of war. Important theoretical differences of opinion were shown to exist. Inis Claude, Hans Morgenthau, Quincy Wright, and others have held that an equilibrated distribution of power promotes peace. Lewis Richardson hypothesized that power-type variables were ambivalent with respect to involvement in military hostilities. A.F.K. Organski has argued that an unequilibrated distribution of power promotes peace. Johan Galtung states that rank-disequilibrium promotes war providing that rank-disequilibrated actors have access to considerable resources.

Well-substantiated evidence of a relationship between power capabilities, on the one hand, and war, on the other hand, was found to be lacking. In part, the relative absence of evidence, confirmatory or otherwise, is a result of the paucity of systematic inquiry into the causes of war. Such inquiry has gotten underway only in recent years, and some of the pioneering inquiries that have been made have not differentiated between nonwar and war events, which is a prerequisite for the verification of such relationships.

Lewis Richardson's study of deadly quarrels incorporates a great many independent variables, but only a few are classifiable as power-type variables. Richardson did not report findings on these variables, but examination of his data indicates null relations. In an investigation conducted a considerable time after the appearance of *A Study of War*, Wright found that relative equality in forces immediately available to the participants to a conflict and a belief that superior forces would eventually be available promote the escalation of international conflict to the level of military hostilities. Great inequality of forces available or anticipated, or comparative equality and great capability for destruction militate against the escalation of conflicts.

Findings forthcoming from the Singer-Small et al. endeavors provide some evidence that strength is more conducive to peace and countervailing evidence that suggests disparity in capabilities promotes war. Raoul Naroll found that war was more likely when "conspicuous states" that were in a defensive stance enjoyed superiority in available military capabilities. Initial studies by Michael Wallace and Maurice East indicate that differentials in power capabilities are related to war involvement when associated with rank-disequilibrium, but more recent evidence forthcoming from Wallace indicates reduced importance for the rank-disequilibrium phenomenon. Finally, some experimental evidence suggests that a preponderance of power capabilities is likely to be associated with involvement in conflict and war.

Armed with the insights and results of previous studies, we outlined an elementary model in which relationships between power capabilities, on the one hand, and the occurrence and outcome of war, on the other hand, were postulated. The principal thrust of our hypotheses rested on the assumption that the decision by states to wage war is based upon an evaluation of the power capabilities relationship prevailing between both sides to the conflict, and upon the value attached by each side to the interests in conflict. We assumed that relative parity in power capabilities has deterrent value, in other words, that war is less likely to occur when conflicting states possess approximately equivalent capabilities and more likely to eventuate as disparity in the power capabilities available increases. On first reflection, this assumption perhaps appears somewhat nonsensical. As disparity increases, the prospects of the advantaged side winning improves; hence, its willingness to contemplate war as a method for resolving the conflict is likely to increase. But for the disadvantaged side, the very opposite would seem to be the case. It should be more interested in resolving the conflict peacefully, since its chances of winning are diminished.

This apparent contradiction is logically overcome in our theoretical model by incorporation into the equation of the other key variable, namely, value attached to the conflicting interest. (This variable was included in our model of the causes of war as presented in Chapter 3. However, it has not been included in the empirical interpretation of the theory's validity.) If the disadvantaged side attaches great value to the conflicting interest, its leaders may find it perfectly rational to wage war in defense of the interest. Or war may be regarded as a rational means for safeguarding other interests. Leaders may reason that appeasement beyond a certain minimum level will stimulate the adversary's appetite for future concessions or undermine the morale of their citizenry, possibly contributing to a weakening of the social fabric. The leaders may also perceive a threat to personal positions of authority. Elite individuals and groups waiting in the wings could exploit an issue of appeasement to bring about the downfall of the ruling hierarchy. Consequently, whereas the leaders of the side with less capabilities will have greater interest in resolving a conflict peacefully than they would in a situation of approximate equality, there is likely to be a point beyond which certain factors other than power capabilities will increasingly motivate them to fight.

One additional noteworthy aspect of value-importance: In a power capabilities situation characterized by approximate parity, the leaders of both sides will have good reason to favor a peaceful resolution of the conflict. But when one side has a decided advantage, its leaders may overestimate the ability to compel the other to yield by virtue of their superior capabilities. They may be more willing to bluff about their willingness to resort to force and, by such action, may convince the other side that war is inevitable.

The theoretical model outlined in Chapter 3 incorporated one intervening variable thought to be highly relevant to the two primary independent variables. The intervening variable is change in the power capabilities relationship, and it has been included in the empirical testing of the model. Change in the power capabilities relationship necessarily means an augmentation in capabilities for some states and a diminishment for others. To the degree that political authority, influence, and power are derived from power capabilities, adjustment is likely to be required when significant change in the distribution of capabilities occurs. A state that has substantially increased its capabilities is likely to seek increased power, influence, and authority. Because of its improved power capabilities position, it will be in a better position to contemplate waging war in pursuit of its objectives. Contrariwise, the state whose power capabilities have diminished will be less likely to contemplate war on the basis of power capabilities factors alone. But other considerations may lead the leaders of the latter to resist reductions in their power, influence, and authority. These considerations include the satisfaction derived from such attributes, fear that a trend leading to a further diminution of their capabilities will be set in motion, and concern that their leadership positions will be challenged by opposition elites. Overall, then, change is an intervening variable affecting value-importance.

The study goal of empirical elucidation was tackled by proposing a method for operationalizing the power capabilities of all independent states in the international system. The method proposed rests upon key assumptions about the elements that comprise the power capabilities of nation-states. The validity of these assumptions was tested, in part, by using principal components analysis to delineate patterned relationships among the indicator-variables that had been selected to represent power capabilities. Principal components analysis was applied to a sample of data drawn from the 1850-1960 time frame. The initial results of this analysis led us to modify the index via the incorporation of three additional indicator-variables. The index as finally proposed consists of eight key variables: area, population, government revenue, defense expenditure, trade value, armed forces personnel, government revenue per capita, and defense expenditure per capita.

The index was constructed via a series of steps. The eight variables were rescaled into percentage form so as to redress a problem presented by uneven inflationary growth across the entire system of states. Constant weights for the variables were derived on the basis of each variable's loading on the power capabilities dimension delineated in principal component analyses of twenty-four sample years of the nation-state data. The weight for each variable represents the mean percent of variation it has in common with the power capabilities dimension for the twenty-four sample years.

Power capabilities scores were computed for nearly all independent states in the international system between 1850 and 1966. We have thus mapped out an empirical world of the power capabilities of nation-states. The creation of derivative variables from the power capabilities scores, such as change rates for power capabilities scores, has further delineated the phenomena in an empirical manner. In the process, we have compiled data on government revenue, defense expenditures, trade value, exchange rates, and armed forces that is either original or that exceeds in completeness other published data sets that incorporate one or more of these variables for specific states of the world and specific time periods. This data may prove useful to other research endeavors conducted in the future in the fields of political science and international relations.

The index itself, as with all indices designed to measure a complex phenomenon, undoubtedly contains some degree of error. Its utility, in the long run, may derive from the role it plays in combination with the efforts of other investigators in the field who seek to nail down the operationalization of this concept as firmly as possible. Future research endeavors conceivably could lead to the addition of other indicator-variables to the index and the assignment of different weights to the various indicator-variables.

Having briefly reviewed the general purpose and thrust of the study, it remains to review the principal findings forthcoming from the inquiry, which are condensed in summary fashion in Table 6-1.

Hypotheses Focusing Exclusively
on War Events

Our first three hypotheses framed for testing centered on relationships between power capabilities and war outcome. As was hypothesized, superior power capabilities were found to be positively related with victory in war; but the strength of the relationship was not nearly as strong as originally thought. More often than not and more frequently than would be expected by random deviation associated with a null relationship, the side with superior power capabilities wins. Some 64 percent of the wars occurring between 1850 and 1966 and involving a minimum of one thousand battle-connected deaths were won by the side possessing greater capabilities. The substantial number of wars

Table 6-1
Summary Results of Principal Findings

Hypothesis	Finding
1. a. Given the occurrence of war, the side possessing the greater power capabilities at the time of the initiation of hostilities will *almost always* be victorious.	Unsupported
b. Given the occurrence of war, the side possessing the greater power capabilities at the time of the initiation of hostilities will be victorious more often than would be expected by chance.	Supported
2. Given the occurrence of war, the greater the power capabilities disparity at the time of the initiation of hostilities, the lesser the devastation resulting from the war.	Unsupported
3. Given the occurrence of war, the greater the power capabilities disparity at the time of the initiation of hostilities, the shorter the duration of war.	Unsupported
4. Given an interstate conflict, the greater the disparity in the power capabilities relationship between the two sides to the conflict, the greater the probability the conflict will escalate to the level of military hostilities.	Unsupported
5. Given an interstate conflict involving the threat of or actual use of force, the greater the disparity in the power capabilities relationship between the two sides to the conflict, the greater the probability the conflict will escalate to the level of military hostilities.	Unsupported
6. Most wars are wars in which a high level of disparity characterizes the power capabilities relationship prevailing between the belligerents at the initiation of hostilities.	Unsupported and Supported[a]
7. The greater the change in the power capabilities of states (treated severally), the greater the probability of involvement in military hostilities.	Unsupported
8. Given an interstate conflict, the greater the previous change in the power capabilities relationship between the two sides to the conflict, the greater the probability the conflict will escalate to the level of military hostilities.	Unsupported
9. Given an interstate conflict involving the threat of or actual use of force, the greater the previous change in the power capabilities relationship between the two sides to the conflict, the greater the probability the conflict will escalate to the level of military hostilities.	Unsupported
10. Most wars are characterized by significant change in the power capabilities relationship between the two sides to the conflict prior to the outbreak of war.	Unsupported
11. Most wars are characterized by significant change toward an equality in power capabilities between the two sides to the conflict prior to the outbreak of war rather than by insignificant change or change away from an equality in power capabilities.	Unsupported
12. The greater the change in the distribution of power capabilities within the international system, the greater the amount of war.	Supported and Unsupported[a]
13. The greater the disparity in the power capabilities relationship between states, the greater the probability	

Table 6-1 (cont.)

	Hypothesis	Finding
	that the states will become involved in an intense conflict.	Supported
14.	The greater the change in the power capabilities relationship between states, the greater the probability the states will become involved in an intense conflict.	Supported

ªDepending on the operational criteria employed.

which, however, were won by the side possessing weaker capabilities indicates that other important variables are required to explain fully this aspect of war outcome.

Two other aspects investigated were duration of war and devastation. The level of power capabilities disparity between the two sides to a war was found to be unrelated to either of these two variables. A high level of disparity does not predict to a shorter war or to a less destructive war. Overall, then, power capabilities are frequently efficacious with respect to winning a war, but do not seem to be immediately germane to the length of the conflict or the losses incurred by the combatants.

Moving on to our next set of hypotheses, it was postulated that war is more likely to be characterized by a high level of disparity in the power capabilities available to both sides to the conflict. This hypothesis was disconfirmed when a high level of disparity was operationalized as the stronger side having a power capabilities score twice that of the weaker side. But the hypothesis was supported when the threshold for a high level of disparity was set at 1.45. Nearly 85 percent of the wars examined for the 1850-1966 time frame were conflicts in which the stronger side had a power capabilities score 1.45 times or more greater than that of the weaker side. The evidence demonstrates that war is unlikely to occur when two rivals are more or less equally matched in power capabilities.

With respect to the relationship between change in the power capabilities of states as examined severally and the probability of involvement in military hostilities, virtually no relationship was found. This was the case when direction of change was taken into account and also when direction of change was ignored.

When change in the power capabilities relationship between the two sides to a war was examined, it was found, contrary to what had been hypothesized, that approximately half or less of the wars were characterized by a change rate of 20 percent or more. This was the case for five different time-lag intervals, ranging from three to twenty years. Utilizing a more modest threshold of 15 percent change in the power capabilities relationship also evidenced an absence of correlation.

Nor was direction of change found to be associated with war events. Contrary to our original hypothesis, more wars were found to be characterized by change in the direction of a greater inequality in the power capabilities relationship for three of the five time lags examined. The observed frequencies in the opposite direction, however, were not sufficiently large to warrant the conclusion that change in the direction of greater inequality is significantly related to the occurrence of war.

Our final hypothesis focusing on relationships between change and the occurrence of war concerned the international system as a whole. It was hypothesized that change in the distribution of power capabilities in the system as a whole is significantly related to the amount of war in the system. Conflicting evidence resulted in the course of testing this hypothesis, depending on whether the amount of war variables represented war *underway* or war *begun*. Our overall conclusion was that the results were best interpreted as not supporting the hypothesis, but that more sophisticated techniques would be required to resolve the question satisfactorily.

Hypotheses Focusing on Conflicts Escalating to the Level of Military Hostilities

Four hypotheses sought to explain why some international conflicts escalate to the level of military hostilities while others do not. In accord with the rationale underlying our other hypotheses, we hypothesized that conflicts are more likely to escalate to the level of military hostilities as the power capabilities disparity between the two sides to a conflict increases. We hypothesized that as change in the power capabilities relationship between the two sides to a conflict increases, the probability that the conflict will escalate to the level of military hostilities likewise increases.

In the course of formulating these hypotheses, we decided that the relationships might be more likely to hold true for conflicts that involved the threat of or actual use of force. A conflict-event characterized by a threat to resort to force is one in which the leaders on both sides are likely to have carefully calculated the prospects of winning a war should one eventuate and evaluated whether the goals at stake are worth the losses that could accompany a war, as well as worth risking loss of the war itself. Conceivably, a set of conflict-events in which the threat to resort to force was not necessarily made might include many conflicts in which neither side thought seriously of initiating war to secure its objectives, or seriously anticipated that the other side might resort to force in an effort to resolve the conflict to its favor. A set of conflict-events characterized by the threat or actual resort to force more or less guaranteed that at least one side to the conflict, and quite possibly both sides, attached considerable value to the interests at stake. Thus, the factor of power capabilities disparity was more likely to have been taken into account. Consequently, the first two hypotheses were supplemented by two modified versions that focused attention exclusively on conflict-events involving the threat of or actual use of force.

In testing the hypotheses, five sets of conflict-events were utilized, including three sets of pooled conflicts which were created by mixing together different combinations of the conflict-events comprising the Wright, Holsti, and Singer-Small inventories. Two of the sets spanned the 116-year period of time between 1950 and 1965. Three of the conflict sets applied to the 1919-1965 years.

All four of the hypotheses were disproven. Null relationships almost always resulted, including when the independent variables were logged so as to reduce the effect of extreme outliers. Null relationships manifested in the change rates variable when direction of change was ignored and when it was taken into account. Moreover, in a majority of instances coefficients were in a direction opposite to that hypothesized, but, as already noted, nearly always so low as to explain but a small portion of the variance in the data. Given the total number of coefficients computed, the very few that explained more than 4 percent of the variance are probably attributable to chance variation.

These unexpected findings led us to reassess the nature of the data selected for the purpose of testing the hypotheses. We concluded that most, if not all, of the conflicts under purview were intense conflicts in which both sides attached considerable value to the interests at stake. We reasoned, additionally, that once a conflict had reached a high level of intensity, considerations other than previous rates of change in the power capabilities relationship and level of power capabilities disparity might be crucial determinants of whether the conflict escalated to the level of military hostilities. In so doing, we considerably extended the scope of our explanation. Whereas previously we had restricted our attention to already existing conflicts, we now shifted our focus to relationships between power capabilities variables and the occurrence of intense conflicts.

Our attention shifted to the occurrence of international conflict in general. We now hypothesized that involvement in international conflict would vary with the level of disparity in the power capabilities relationship. Previously we had conceived of change in power capabilities as being an important dispositional factor determining whether conflicts escalate to the level of military hostilities. Now we conceived of the level of power capabilities disparity as being a dispositional factor affecting whether international conflicts escalate to a high level of intensity. And we hypothesized that change in power capabilities is related to involvement in intense conflict.

In order to test our two new hypotheses, a set of hypothetical nonconflicts was randomly generated. Power capabilities disparity ratios and change in the power capabilities relationship between the sides to each nonconflict were computed. The set of nonconflicts was separately combined with each of the five different sets of conflict-events used earlier in the study. The two independent variables correlated significantly with involvement in conflict for each combination of nonconflict and conflict-events. When the independent variable was logged to reduce the effect of extreme outliers, the coefficients ranged from .27 to .34. The highest correlations were registered when nonconflicts were combined with conflict-events that always included the threat of or actual use of force.

When change in the power capabilities relationship, irrespective of direction, was correlated with involvement in intense conflict, the resulting correlation coefficients were in the postulated direction and statistically significant for each combination of nonconflict and conflict-events, and for all time lags. The highest correlation coefficients occurred when the independent variable was logged and when nonconflicts were combined with conflict-events that always involved the threat or actual use of force. For this condition coefficients ranged from .26 to .45. In terms of time lags, the highest coefficients were registered for intervals of ten, fifteen, and twenty years, and especially for the last.

The correlation of change in the power capabilities relationship with involvement in intense conflict and taking into account direction of change, indicated that a widening in the power capabilities relationship is more important in terms of explaining the occurrence of intense conflict, with the exception of the three-year lag. A narrowing or closing of the gap in the power capabilities relationship does, however, also account for some variation in the occurrence of intense conflict and is equally if not slightly more important for the three-year lag.

An additional important finding brought to light by the correlation of change in the power capabilities relationship with the occurrence of intense conflict is that change in the power capabilities of states is primarily important in terms of each state's relationship to other states with which it interacts. No relationship was found when we correlated change rates in the power capabilities of states, as treated severally and including a control group of states not involved in military hostilities, with whether or not they became involved in hostilities. But relationships were discovered when change in the power capabilities of specific states relative to certain other specific states was computed. The lesson suggested by these results is that substantial change in a state's capabilities is not likely to promote its involvement in intense conflict unless that change significantly detracts from or enhances its power capabilities position vis-à-vis other states in its immediate environment.

Having verified the existence of relationships of power capabilities disparity and change in the power capabilities relationship with involvement in intense conflict, we then sought to determine whether or not the former two are independently associated with involvement in intense conflict, and whether their joint interaction is importantly related to involvement in intense conflict. The answer to the first was solidly affirmative. The multiple correlation of the two independent variables with the dependent variable produced important increases in the magnitude of the correlation coefficients and their levels of statistical significance. The coefficients ranged from .32 to .48.

The answer to the latter question was that the joint interaction of the two variables does not appreciably add to the amount of variation explained by the two when treated independently and additively. The fact that level of the power capabilities disparity is often independently associated with involvement in intense conflicts and not dependent upon previous change in the relationship suggests that power capabilities themselves can have an important effect on the disposition of decision-makers to contemplate involvement in intense conflict, including the resort to military force.

The last stage of the research analysis was directed to controlling for the effect of number of participants to a conflict. We reasoned that statesmen might find it increasingly difficult to ascertain clearly the net effect of particular power capabilities relationships as more states become relevant to their calculations. An augmented element of uncertainty could serve as a constraint, so that states already involved in conflicts might be less inclined to become engaged in military hostilities. And it might even serve as a constraining factor in terms of whether states permit themselves to become involved in an intense conflict.

To examine this notion we eliminated from the conflict inventories all events that involved more than one state on either side of a conflict and retested all of the hypotheses centering on escalation to military hostilities and involvement in intense conflict. Regarding the former, no appreciable difference was registered for relationships between power capabilities disparity and escalation to the level of military hostilities when controlling for the number of participants. And, with few exceptions, no appreciable differences were manifested in correlating change in the power capabilities relationship and escalation to the level of military hostilities. The exceptions were in a direction opposite that predicted, indicating that as change increased, involvement in military hostilities decreased. But the number of meaningful correlation coefficients was so few as to indicate that they probably arose from chance variation.

Regarding the dependent variable, involvement in intense conflict, none of the correlation coefficients changed appreciably when the independent variable examined was power capabilities disparity. However, virtually all of the coefficients improved somewhat when change in the power capabilities relationship was correlated with involvement in intense conflict, thus lending slight support to the idea that states are less likely to become involved in an intense conflict as the number of states relevant to the considerations of the decision-makers increases.

Suggestions for Further Research

The findings forthcoming from this study suggest several possible areas of inquiry for future research aimed at reinforcing and further extending their breadth and scope. The power capabilities scores generated in the course of this study have opened new avenues to inquiry that formerly were inaccessible. We will discuss briefly some of the more prominent possibilities that come to mind.

Our first suggestion concerns studies aimed at examining power capabilities in greater depth. The power capabilities scores are an objective measure. Equally important to an understanding of their role is the subjective estimation of power capabilities made by the decision-makers of nation-states. It will be remembered that a key assumption of the elementary model outlined in Chapter 3 was that statesmen are capable of accurately judging the power capabilities at the disposal of various states and actually seek to do so. A research finding to the contrary would certainly be an important one, suggesting that war involvement is an irrational process. Half of the data requisite for a testing of this assumption are now at hand. In order to examine the validity of the assumption, it is not necessary to assemble information on the perceptions of the leaders of all states in the international system vis-à-vis all other states. A more feasible and equally fruitful approach would be to collect data on the perceptions of decision-makers for those states involved in the conflicts utilized in the course of this study. Furthermore, perception data would only be required for each state's evaluation of the power capabilities situation describing its relationship to the other state participants to the conflict. It may be that some of the conflicts that were described by a low level of power capabilities disparity and yet escalated to the level of military hostilities were ones in which one or both sides significantly overestimated its own power capabilities relative to those available to the other side.

A second type of perception data may be of importance to our understanding. Alliance with other states is a means by which one state to a conflict can dramatically alter the power capabilities relationship. Some conflicts that escalate to the level of military hostilities and that are characterized by an approximate equality in capabilities available to each side may be conflicts in which one side erroneously felt that a state external to the conflict would not join the fray. For such instances, a recalculation of the power capabilities disparity ratios might result in a substantially improved relationship between disparity and war involvement.

A third type of perception data is required to determine if the nexus between change in the power capabilities relationship and involvement in intense conflict arises from the intentions of the leaders of one or more states to narrow or widen the power capabilities gap in order to improve their ability to resolve conflict situations to their favor. Is change in the power capabilities relationship deliberately effected so that a state can initiate or conclude developing conflicts to its liking? Or is change in the power capabilities relationship frequently an occurrence arising unconsciously from the interplay of many forces, intrastate as well as interstate, the outcome of which is a conscious realization by the leaders of states advantageously affected by the change that they are perhaps capable of exerting power, influence, and authority to an extent greater than previously contemplated, much less attempted? The evidence generated in the course of this study is not sufficient for providing an answer to the question. But the evidence does demonstrate the existence of a relationship and does differentiate intense conflicts in which change is relevant from those in which it is not. With the former specified, it is now possible to seek relevant perception data that would provide an answer to the inquiry.

A second area of importance for future inquiry is that of the value-importance attached by each side of a conflict to the conflicting interest. This is a key variable in our elementary model of the causes of war and one for which variation has not been directly measured in the course of this study. Most, if not all, of the conflicts included herein were described as "intense" conflicts. Presumably, for all of these conflicts, considerable value was attached to the conflicting interest by both sides. It may be that many conflicts that were characterized by a low level of power capabilities disparity yet which escalated to the level of military hostilities are ones in which both sides attached great importance to the conflicting interest. Similarly, conflicts characterized by substantial power capabilities disparity and that did not escalate to the level of military hostilities may be ones in which one or possibly both sides attached only moderate or low importance to the interest in conflict.

In order to explore the import of this variable more systematically, it will be necessary to assemble information on variation in the extent of value-importance attributed by each state-participant to a conflict. It is also desirable that research be undertaken to expand the currently available lists of interstate conflicts. As previously discussed, the conflicts relied upon in this study seemingly are characterized by a high level of intensity or attached value-importance. The inclusion of conflicts described by moderate or low intensity might result in a significant increase in the correlations between power capabilities disparity and involvement in war. At a bare minimum, the current conflict inventories need to be expanded to include conflicts that did not escalate to the level of military hostilities for the 1850-1918 time frame.

A third area of concern for future research endeavors centers on the threshold level for identifying war events. Two thresholds were utilized in this study, one requiring a minimum of 317 fatalities, the other one thousand battle-connected fatalities. As has been apparent throughout this study report, only a small number of interstate conflicts qualify at either level. Yet, as earlier noted, Richardson observed that there are a relatively large number of interstate conflicts in which battle-related deaths resulting from the application of military force total more than a few but less than 317. A thorough investigation of the validity of hypotheses examined in this study requires the incorporation of these conflict events into the analysis.

Our final thoughts concern the relationship between threat or actual use of force, on the one hand, to involvement in intense conflict and to the escalation of conflict to the level of military hostilities. Neither power capabilities disparity nor change in the power capabilities relationship were significantly more associated with intense conflict or military hostilities when the conflicts examined always included the threat or actual use of force. This finding is perhaps suspect, however, since it is not clear to what extent the conflict inventories that do not always involve the threat or use of force include many conflicts not involving the threat or use of force. Further research in this area is required.

Policy Implications

Recognizing that the broad focus of this study has necessarily been restricted, that the importance of other variables must be accounted for, and that other studies with a similar if not identical focus to that employed herein may yield disparate findings, it is nonetheless relevant to inquire whether any policy implications are suggested by the findings of the study. In view of the above considerations, and also because so many of our research hypotheses were unsupported, it is difficult to draw recommendations for the policy-maker from this analysis. One is tempted, in fact, to look elsewhere, particularly in the psychopolitical realm, for the answers to questions about war and peace, and as was intimated in the previous section, additional research in such areas is required to ascertain clearly relationships between power capabilities variables and involvement in conflict and war.

Nevertheless, the power capabilities of nation-states must be counted among the conditions that facilitate or militate against armed conflict in the presence of more potent motivational factors. Evidence resulting from this study indicates that relative parity in power capabilities does have deterrent value in precluding the onset of intense conflict. Moreover, few wars result between states that are closely balanced in power capabilities available to each. Thus, there appears to be some merit in the policy of statesmen who seek to approximate parity in capabilities relative to specific nations that are perceived with distrust and as potential adversaries in military conflict. Yet states that seek to narrow the disparity between themselves and other specific states, as well as those that aim at widening an established gap, are to be cautioned. The evidence indicates that such change increases the probability of becoming involved in intense conflict with those nations disadvantaged by the alteration. It seems especially true for states that widen an already existing capabilities gap at the expense of other nations. Consequently, although parity tends to promote noninvolvement in both intense conflict and in war, states that enjoy a marked advantage vis-à-vis other nations might be well advised to preserve their edge, since change in the direction of parity is a destabilizing factor associated with the occurrence of intense conflict. Leaders of states are unable to maintain the status quo need to be alert to the prospects of increased conflict and be prepared to formulate policies aimed at minimizing its likelihood.

Moreover, the evidence in this study indicates that once an intense conflict is underway, power capabilities are not sufficient for preventing escalation to the level of military hostilities. Statesmen who believe they are capable of orchestrating both change in power capabilities relationships *and* whether or not conflict that might result from such change escalates to the level of hostilities are to be forewarned. In the interest of security they may succeed in closing or widening the gap separating them from other states only to become involved in a war they hoped to avoid.

Once a war is underway, the evidence suggests that power capabilities are efficacious for winning. However, the very considerable number of wars that have been won by the side with lesser capabilities indicates that power capabilities alone are not adequate to ensure success. Equally if not more important, states with superior capabilities that are prepared to risk loss in war provided that the duration or devastation be minimized are also to be cautioned. There is no evidence that superior capabilities, as measured in this study, leads to either a shorter (or for that matter longer) war or to less devastation (or for that matter more), as measured in terms of battle-connected fatalities.

Appendixes

Appendix A: Identification of the Universe of Sovereign Nation States for the Time Frame of the Study

To date the field of international politics has been supplied with three inventories that seek to identify the sovereign nation state members of the international system and that are applicable to the time frame of this study.[1] The first to appear was coauthored by J. David Singer and Melvin Small and covers the period between 1815 and 1940. The second was a somewhat revised edition of the first, focuses only on the 1900-1968 years, and includes as an additional coauthor Bruce Russett. The third was a version by Arthur Banks, highly similar to but not identical to the first two inventories, and covers the period of time between 1815 and 1966.

The initial Singer-Small inventory was based on a set of explicit criteria for classifying whether political entities qualify for membership in the international system of independent states. Two criteria were proposed, a population threshold and a standard of diplomatic recognition. With respect to the former, the authors sought a threshold that would " 'objectify' the intuitively reasonable" by excluding such insignificant political entities as Monaco, Andorra, and Liechtenstein, or the smaller preunification German and Italian states. In their judgment a threshold of 500,000 best met this standard for the 1815-1940 period. Regarding the latter, the authors sought, on the basis of number or rank of diplomatic recognitions, to differentiate between independent entities, on the one hand, and colonies, protectorates, and more ambiguously independent actors, on the other. Different yardsticks were applied to different periods of time in furtherance of this objective. For the 1815-1919 years the authors originally intended that a state be recognized by at least half of the nations that qualified as system members during the previous five years, but in its place substituted a simpler criterion which had the same practical effect, namely, recognition by two "legitimizers," France and Great Britain. For the 1920-1940 years the standard employed was that a state be judged independent according to historical consensus. Moreover, insistence on the population threshold of 500,000 was dropped for the 1920-1940 period if a state was a member of the League of Nations during any portion of that time.[2]

The Singer-Small inventory represents an important contribution to the study of international politics, but is not beyond criticism. Employing a population threshold of 500,000 results in the exclusion of ten states from membership in the international system for some portion of the 1815-1920 time period. The ten states are: Dominican Republic (to 1887), El Salvador (to 1875), Hanover (to 1838), Mecklenburg (to 1843), Honduras (to 1899), Modena (to 1847), Parma (to 1851), Nicaragua (to 1900), Paraguay (to 1896), and Uruguay (to

1882). Six of these are Latin American states that have remained in the system until the present day. This presents a problem for a longitudinal analysis involving interrelationships among the states of Latin America. The population threshold of 500,000 excludes from the analysis as much as one-third of the Latin American states for portions of the nineteenth century. A perhaps more realistic cut-off point, and one perhaps equally reasonable on intuitive grounds, would be a threshold of 100,000. It results in the inclusion of the aforementioned states, while simultaneously excluding, at least for the post-1850 time period, most of the globally insignificant entities cited by the authors.

Regarding the criterion of diplomatic recognition, the choice of France and Britain as "legitimizers" for the 1815-1919 time frame may result in the exclusion of some states that were independent and that did participate in interstate relationships on an important scale, albeit not on a global scale. What is ambiguous in such cases is not their independence, but rather the *degree* to which they are integrated into a global pattern of interstate relationships. The criterion of recognition by *half* the members in the system or by France and Great Britain is somewhat arbitrary. If one wishes to generalize about the behavior of interacting independent states, should he exclude from his purview a state that has relationships with one-third of the members of the system? There is perhaps no definitive solution to the question.

The modified version of the original Singer-Small inventory covers only the twentieth century. It includes territorial national political units of the dependent as well as independent variety and relies on a set of criteria for identifying members that are both different in some respects and less explicit. All entities whose population has never exceeded ten thousand people were eliminated, thus allowing for the inclusion of such entities as Andorra, Monaco, and Liechtenstein. States were designated as independent if they enjoyed "some measure of diplomatic recognition" and "effective control" over their armed forces.[3] In describing the resulting inventory of states, the authors admit:

Problems of error and ambiguity remain, especially in regard to the date at which a given unit achieved or lost a given political status, or even reached (or fell from) the 10,000 population figure. The termination of a military occupation, a mandate, or other status of dependency is seldom well defined, and the same holds true for the date of annexation, federation, or disunion. Our general rule was to use the politically effective date rather than that which reflected a declaration of independence or the mere signing of a treaty or convention. Thus, despite careful investigation and our preference for dates which are politically operational, there will certainly be room for disagreement on occasion, and there may even be discrepancies of more than a year or two.[4]

Given the problems experienced by this group of investigators, it is perhaps not surprising that Arthur Banks did not seek to provide a more explicit set of operational criteria for identifying independent national political entities. Banks did not discuss this problem nor explicitly specify the criteria a political entity had to satisfy in order to qualify as a state. His inventory is to a large extent a replication of the original Singer-Small list, with subsequent additions for the post-1940-to-1966 period. Even so, there are numerous differences between the two inventories which Banks partially explains by implication in a series of footnotes. The differences appear to arise from Banks's willingness to set a population threshold less than 500,000 (but beyond that not identifiable), unwillingness to exclude states only because they do not enjoy recognition by the "legitimizers," France and Britain, and differences of interpretation about exactly when a state attains de facto independence. Thus, although Singer and Small set Uruguayan qualification as a state at 1882, when it crossed the threshold of 500,000, Banks uses 1828. Banks recognizes Bulgaria as achieving "effective autonomy" in 1878, while noting that the Singer-Small date of Bulgaria's membership in the international system, 1908, was when it became "fully independent." What the difference is between "effective autonomy" and "fully independent" Banks does not say.[5]

Since Banks is primarily a student of comparative politics, while Singer and Small have specialized in international politics, one might suspect that the latter's inventory would be more applicable to a study of international political relationships. Unfortunately, the evidence in favor of this proposition is not self-evident because Banks has not been explicit in defining his criteria, because the footnoted entries to Banks's list in some cases imply superior evidence for identifying the moment a state attains or loses independence, and because Singer and Small (and Banks to a lesser extent) have specified a number of states as entering the system *on or before* a particular date. With respect to the latter point, the implication of such entries is that the state did qualify before the particular year cited and that sufficient evidence for identifying exactly when the moment of qualification occurred has not been found.

For the purpose of this study we have relied primarily on the Singer-Small and Singer-Small-Russett inventories. Where differences exist between these two lists, we have utilized the more recently prepared list. Where differences exist with the Banks inventory, and in the absence of definitive information that would resolve the differences between the two inventories, we have selected entries from either of the two lists on the basis of what evidence was available for making a decision. Table A-1 presents the final list of states included in the scope of this study. The list is contrasted with the Banks, Singer-Small, and Singer-Small-Russett lists.

As did Banks, we have included states falling below the 500,000 population threshold. The cut-off point for excluding a potential member is 100,000. Some entries are unique in comparison to both Singer, Small and Russett and Banks as based on evidence judged superior to that of Banks and Singer, Small and Russett. In all discrepancies the rationale underlying our choice has been footnoted. Overall, the list of states relied on in this study is basically a replication of the Singer-Small and Singer-Small-Russett inventories, with some modifications arising from evidence supplied by Banks or gleaned by independent investigation of our own.

It was necessary to omit several states from the present study because of insufficient variable data for the analysis phase of the study. Entirely excluded are Modena (1850-1861), Mongolia (1920-1966), Nepal (pre-1900-1966), Yemen (1934-1966), Zanzibar (1963-1964). Partially excluded are Afghanistan (pre-1919), Albania (1912-1914), Morocco (1850-1871), and Saudi Arabia (1902-1954).

Two concluding caveats are pertinent to this discussion. In computing power capabilities scores, a state that leaves the system during the time frame of the analysis is actually dropped one year previous to its departure. The reason for employing this criterion is theoretical. The purpose of the inquiry is to measure the *relative* power capabilities of all states in the international system during any given year. Since the method of operationalizing power capabilities does scale each state relative to the performance of all others, the entry or departure of a state will necessarily result in changes in the scorings of all other states in the system. Common sense suggests that these changes should be accounted for as close as possible to the actual occurrence of the change. If a state enters the system in 1875, for example, data on it as a case should be entered for 1875 on the basis of which power capabilities scores for all states are determined. If the state leaves the system in 1875, data on it as a case should not be included for that year even though it actually was a member of the system for some portion of that year. Since the capabilities scores represent a year's duration, and since 1875 is the year in which the change transpired, the effects should be registered for that year. Consequently, where Banks and Singer, Small and Russett identify a state as leaving the system in a given year, we always drop the state from the system for that year when computing the power capabilities scores.

Finally, the country identification numbers utilized are identical to those used by Banks. In the case of the Republic of China, which is not in Banks's inventory, we have supplied a new number consistent with his scheme.

Table A-1
Independent States in the International System: 1850-1966[a]

ID	Country	Qualifies as State (Banks)[b]	International System Member (S/S/R)[c]	International System Member (Ferris)	Loses Membership	Regains Membership
0010	Afghanistan	1919[d]	1900[d]	1919[d]		
0020	Albania	1913[e]	1912[e]	1921[e]	1914[e] / 1939	1921[e] / 1944
0030	Algeria	1962	1962	1962		
0040	Argentina					
0050	Australia	1901	1920	1920		
0060	Austria-Hungary				1918	
0061	Austria	1918	1918	1918	1938	1955
0062	Hungary	1918	1918	1918		
0070	Barbados	1966	1966	1966		
0080	Belgium				1940	1945
0100	Bolivia					
0110	Botswana	1966	1966	1966		
0120	Brazil					
0130	Bulgaria	1878[f]	1908[f]	1878[f]		
0140	Burma	1948	1948	1948		
0150	Burundi	1962	1962	1962		
0160	Cambodia	1953	1953	1953		
0170	Cameroun	1960	1960	1960		
0180	Canada	1867	1920	1920		
0190	Central African Rep.	1960	1960	1960		
0200	Ceylon	1948	1948	1948		

Table A-1 (cont.)

ID	Country	Qualifies as State (Banks)[b]	International System Member (S/S/R)[c]	International System Member (Ferris)	Loses Membership	Regains Membership
0210	Chad	1960	1960	1960		
0220	Chile			1860		
0230	China		1860	1860		
0231	Republic of China	No entry	1949	1949		
0240	Colombia					
0250	Congo (Brazzaville)	1960	1960	1960		
0260	Congo (Kinshasha)	1960	1960	1960		
0270	Costa Rica		pre-1900[g]	1851		
0280	Cuba	1902	1902	1902		
0290	Cyprus	1960	1960	1960		
0300	Czechoslovakia	1918	1918	1918	1939	1945
0310	Dahomey	1960	1960	1960		
0320	Denmark				1940	1945
0330	Dominican Republic		1887[h]		1861[h]	1865[h]
0340	Ecuador		1854	1854		
0350	El Salvador		1875[h]			
0360	Estonia	1918	1918	1918	1940	
0370	Ethiopia	1898[i]	1898[i]	1941[i]		
0380	Finland	1919	1919	1919		
0390	France				1942	1944
0400	Gabon	1960	1960	1960		
0410	Gambia	1965	1965	1965		

132

Code	Country					
0420	Germany	1867[j]	1867[j]	1945	1867[j]	1944
0421	Baden			1870		
0422	Bavaria			1870		
0423	Hanover			1867		
0424	Hesse, Electorate			1867		
0425	Hesse, Grand Duchy			1867		
0426	Mecklenburg			1867		
0427	Prussia			1867[j]		
0428	Saxony			1867		
0429	Wurtemberg			1870		
0430	German Dem. Rep.[k]	1949	1955			
0431	German Fed. Rep.[k]	1949	1955			
0440	Ghana	1957	1957			
0450	Greece			1941		
0460	Guatemala					
0470	Guinea	1958	1958			
0480	Guyana	1966	1966			
0490	Haiti	1859[l]				
0500	Honduras	1899[h]				
0510	Iceland	1944	1944			
0520	India	1947	1947			
0530	Indonesia	1949	1949			

Table A-1 (cont.)

ID	Country	Qualifies as State (Banks)[b]	International System Member (S/S/R)[c]	International System Member (Ferris)	Loses Membership	Regains Membership
0540	Iran		1855	1855		
0550	Iraq	1932	1932	1932		
0560	Israel	1948	1948	1948		
0570	Italy	1861[m]		1860[m]		
0572	Papal States				1860[m]	
0573	Parma				1860[m]	
0574	Sardinia				1860[m]	
0575	Tuscany				1860[m]	
0576	Two Sicilies				1861	
0580	Ivory Coast	1960	1960	1960		
0590	Jamaica	1962	1962	1962		
0600	Japan		1860	1860	1945	1952
0610	Jordan	1946	1946	1946		
0620	Kenya	1963	1963	1963		
0630	Korea	1895[n]	1888[n]	1895[n]	1905	
0631	Korean People's Rep.	1948	1948	1948		
0632	Korean Republic	1948	1948	1948		
0640	Kuwait	1961	1961	1961		
0650	Laos	1954	1954	1954		
0660	Latvia	1918	1918	1918	1940	
0670	Lebanon	1946	1946	1946		
0680	Lesotho	1966	1966	1966		

Code	Country	(1)	(2)	(3)	(4)	(5)
0690	Liberia			pre-1900[o]		
0700	Libya	1952	1952	1952	1940	
0710	Lithuania	1918	1918	1918		
0720	Luxembourg			pre-1900[o]	1914 / 1940	1918 / 1944
0730	Malagasy Republic	1960	1960	1960		
0740	Malawi	1964	1964	1964		
0750	Malaysia	1957	1957	1957		
0770	Mali	1960	1960	1960		
0780	Malta	1964	1964	1964		
0790	Mauritania	1960	1960	1960		
0810	Mexico					
0830	Morocco[p]	No entry	1872	pre-1900	1911	1956
0850	Netherlands				1940	1945
0860	New Zealand	1920		1920		
0870	Nicaragua		1920	1900[h]		
0880	Niger	1960	1960	1960		
0890	Nigeria	1960	1960	1960		
0900	Pakistan	1947	1947	1947		
0910	Panama	1903	1903	1903		
0920	Paraguay			1896[h]		
0930	Peru					

Table A-1 (cont.)

ID	Country	Qualifies as State (Banks)[b]	International System Member (S/S/R)[c]	International System Member (Ferris)	Loses Membership	Regains Membership
0940	Philippines	1946	1946	1946		
0950	Poland	1919	1919	1919	1939	1945
0960	Portugal					
0970	Rumania	1859	1878	1878		
0980	Rwanda	1962	1962	1962		
0990	Saudi Arabia[q]	1902	1902	1955		
1000	Senegal	1960	1960	1960		
1010	Sierra Leone	1961	1961	1961		
1020	Singapore	1965	1965	1965		
1030	Somali Republic	1960	1960	1960		
1040	South Africa	1910	1920	1920		
1060	Spain					
1070	Sudan	1956	1956	1956		
1090	Sweden-Norway				1905	
1091	Norway	1905	1905	1905		
1092	Sweden	1905	1905	1905		
1100	Switzerland					
1110	Syria	1946	1946	1946	1958	1961
1120	Tanzania	1961	1961	1961		
1130	Thailand	1887	1887	1887		
1140	Togo	1960	1960	1960		
1150	Trinidad	1962	1962	1962		

No.	Country					
1160	Tunisia	1956	1956	1956		1961
1170	Turkey					
1180	Uganda	1962	1962	1962		
1190	Russia/USSR					
1200	Egypt/UAR	1951	1922	1922	1958	
1201	United Arab Rep.[r]	1958	1958	1958	1961	
1210	United Kingdom					
1212	Ireland	1922	1922	1922		
1220	United States					
1230	Upper Volta	1960	1960	1960		
1240	Uruguay		1882			
1250	Venezuela					
1261	Vietnam People's Rep.	1954	1954	1954		
1262	Vietnam Republic	1954	1954	1954		
1270	Western Samoa	1962	1962	1962		
1290	Yugoslavia	1919[s]	1919[s]	1919[s]	1941	1944
1291	Montenegro	1878[t]	No entry[h]	1878[t]	1919	
1292	Serbia	1878	1878	1878	1919	
1300	Zambia	1964	1964	1964		

Table A-1 (cont.)

ᵃIn most instances the year entries in the Ferris column are based on the Singer-Small-Russett inventories. Where differences exist, the entries are footnoted with an explanation. Data entries in the Loses Membership and Regains Membership columns are also from the aforementioned inventories unless otherwise noted. A blank in the Banks, S/S/R, or Ferris columns indicates that the state entered the system or qualified as a member in or prior to 1850.

ᵇArthur S. Banks, *Cross-Polity Time-Series Data* (Cambridge: The MIT Press, 1971), pp. 297-99. The country identification numbers employed in the table are also according to Banks's notation.

ᶜPre-1900 entries are according to J. David Singer and Melvin Small, "The Composition and Status Ordering of the International System: 1815-1940," *World Politics*, 18 (January 1966), pp. 236-82. Post-1899 entries are according to the same, as well as to: J. David Singer, Melvin Small and Bruce M. Russett, "National Political Units in the Twentieth Century: A Standardized List," *The American Political Science Review*, 62 (September 1968), pp. 932-51. See text for further clarification.

ᵈAccording to Banks and Singer, Small and Russett, Afghanistan qualified on or before the date specified. We have chosen the year 1919 because of the absence of adequate power capabilities variable data prior to that year.

ᵉAccording to Singer, Small and Russett, Albania entered the system in 1912, departed in 1914, and reentered in 1921. We have entered Albania in 1921 because of insufficient power capabilities variable data prior to 1921.

ᶠThe Singer-Small-Russett entry is based on the recognition of Bulgaria by the "legitimizers," France and Great Britain. According to Banks, Bulgaria acquired effective autonomy in 1878. We have adopted Banks's entry.

ᵍAccording to the Singer-Small-Russett inventory, Costa Rica acquired membership in the international system sometime previous to 1900. Banks dates Costa Rica's independence as occurring in 1838. We have included Costa Rica in this study from 1851, when it crossed the population threshold of 100,000.

ʰSinger and Small exclude the country previous to this year because of population less than 500,000. We have included the country, preferring to adopt a population threshold of 100,000. (The entries for Loses Membership and Regains Membership for the Dominican Republic are from Banks's list on qualification as an independent state.)

ⁱBanks sets Ethiopia's qualification as an independent state on or before 1898. Singer and Small mark Ethiopia's entry as 1898, based on recognition by the two "legitimizers." Ethiopia left the system in 1936 and returned in 1941. We have entered Ethiopia in 1941 because of insufficient power capabilities data prior to that year.

ʲThe Singer-Small inventory treats Germany as a continuation of Prussia. We prefer to follow Banks's distinction in which the emergence of the North German Confederation in 1867 is regarded as a qualitatively new political entity, namely, Germany. Five states in addition to Prussia were absorbed into the North German Confederation: Hanover, Hesse Electorate, Hesse Grand Duchy, Mecklenburg, and Saxony. The addition of three more states in 1870 is treated as an expansion of Germany.

ᵏ1955 has been selected as the year when the German Federal Republic (GFR) and the German Democratic Republic (GDR) qualified as sovereign states. The GFR did not acquire effective control over its armed forces until ratification of the Paris Pacts in 1955, by which it became a member of NATO and the Western European Union. West German rearmament was not allowed to begin until 1955. Indications are that the Soviet Union did not allow the GDR effective control over its armed forces until 1955. See *Britannica Book of the Year*, 1953-1956, sections on "Germany" and "Armed Forces."

ˡIn the Singer-Small inventory, Haiti enters the international system in 1859 as a result of recognition by both "legitimizers," France and Britain. We have chosen to include Haiti in the international system from 1850. According to editions of the *Almanach De Gotha*, eleven or more states maintained a consul or consul-general in Haiti between 1854 and 1859. See, for example, *Almanach De Gotha*, 1854 (p. 462), 1855 (pp. 476-77), 1856 (p. 475).

Table A-1 (cont.)

[m]Singer and Small treat Italy as a continuation of Sardinia. Banks treats Italy as a qualitatively new political entity, arising from the unification of six separate states, and entering the system in 1861. The six states are Parma, Tuscany, Modena, the Papal States, Sardinia, and the Two Sicilies. Banks apparently regards the defeat of the Two Sicilies in early 1861, along with its annexation to Sardinia, and the proclamation of the kingdom of Italy in February 1861 as signifying the creation of the new state. We, however, have treated Sardinia's absorption of Modena, Parma, Tuscany, and the Papal States in 1860 as more correctly representing the birth of a qualitatively new political entity, which is formally recognized as Italy in early 1861. See "Italian Independence, Wars of," *The Encyclopaedia Britannica* (Chicago: Encyclopaedia Britannica, Inc., 1968), pp. 709-11. Modena has not been included in the study because of insufficient power capabilities variable data.

[n]The Singer-Small entry is based upon Korea's recognition by the "legitimizers." Banks's entry is based upon Japanese and Chinese recognition of Korea's independence. We have used Banks's reference point.

[o]Singer, Small and Russett identify the state as entering the system at some unspecified point in time prior to 1900. We have treated the state as a member from the beginning of the time frame of this study, 1850.

[p]Banks has no entry for Morocco previous to 1955. According to the Singer-Small-Russett inventory, Morocco qualified as a member of the international system prior to 1900; beyond that, no further specification is supplied. We have included Morocco in the analysis from 1872; prior to that year sufficient power capabilities variable data was not available.

[q]We have not entered Saudi Arabia until 1955 because of insufficient power capabilities variable data prior to 1955.

[r]Singer, Small and Russett use "United Arab Republic" to characterize Egypt from 1922-1958 and from 1961 on, as well as to identify the union of Egypt and Syria between 1958 and 1961. Banks has done the same, except in his inventory Egypt does not qualify as an independent state until 1951. To avoid confusion we have used "United Arab Republic" to refer only to the union of Egypt and Syria.

[s]Singer, Small and Russett treat Yugoslavia as a continuation of Serbia. We prefer to treat Yugoslavia as a qualitatively new entity, as does Banks.

[t]We have adopted Banks's criterion: recognition of Montenegro's independence by the Treaty of Berlin.

Appendix B: Inventory of War Events

The list of wars is from J. David Singer and Melvin Small, *The Wages of War*, pp. 61-69. All interstate wars identified by the authors for the 1850-1965 years are included, with one exception: the Spanish-Moroccan War of 1859 was not used in the present study, since power capabilities data for Morocco was unavailable.

For the purpose of the present study, participants to the wars identified by Singer and Small were included in the analysis only if they entered the war within six months of its inception. A basic assumption underlying the hypotheses framed for testing is that statesmen generally evaluate power capabilities relationships prior to reaching a decision as to whether to resort to the use of military force in pursuit of their objectives. Assuming that this is in fact the case, and that their evaluations are usually sound, we would expect that the line-up of participants to a war does not change shortly after a war gets underway. In fact, this is the case for most of the wars in the Singer-Small inventory for the 1850-1965 period. Of forty-three wars, only four are ones in which all of the participants had not become actively involved within six months of the onset of war. The four are the Crimean, World War I, World War II, and the Korean. Since a principal focus of the hypotheses in this study is on how power capabilities relationships, and implicitly the perception of such relationships, prior to the occurrence of conflict are related to later developments or outcomes of such conflicts, it seemed the best test of the validity of the hypotheses would be one that took into account the actual line-up of participants in the early stages of conflicts. For the Singer-Small list of wars it was possible to apply this standard, since the authors identify the month, and at times even day of the month, when participants became actively involved in a war.

Table B-1
War Events: 1850-1965

War ID	War Name	Year War Began
0080	La Plata	1851
0090	Crimean	1853
0100	Anglo-Persian	1856
0110	Italian Unification	1859
0130	Italo-Roman	1860
0140	Italo-Sicilian	1860
0150	Franco-Mexican	1862
0160	Ecuadorian-Colombian	1863
0170	Second Schleswig-Holstein	1864

Table B-1 (cont.)

War ID	War Name	Year War Began
0180	Spanish-Chilean	1865
0190	Seven Weeks	1866
0200	Franco-Prussian	1870
0210	Russo-Turkish	1877
0220	Pacific	1879
0230	Sino-French	1884
0240	Central American	1885
0250	Sino-Japanese	1894
0260	Greco-Turkish	1897
0270	Spanish-American	1898
0280	Russo-Japanese	1904
0290	Central American	1906
0300	Central American	1907
0310	Spanish-Moroccan	1909
0320	Italo-Turkish	1911
0330	First Balkan	1912
0340	Second Balkan	1913
0350	World War I	1914
0360	Hungarian-Allies	1919
0370	Greco-Turkish	1919
0380	Manchurian	1931
0390	Chaco	1932
0400	Italo-Ethiopian[1]	1935
0410	Sino-Japanese	1937
0420	Russo-Japanese[2]	1939
0430	World War II[2]	1939
0440	Russo-Finnish	1939
0450	Palestine	1948
0460	Korean	1950
0470	Russo-Hungarian	1956
0480	Sinai	1956
0490	Sino-Indian	1962
0500	Second Kashmir	1965

Appendix C: Inventory of International Conflicts Involving Force

The conflicts are from K.J. Holsti, "Resolving International Conflicts: A Taxonomy of Behavior and Some Figures on Procedures," *Journal of Conflict Resolution*, 10 (September 1966), pp. 293-96. A conflict is defined by Holsti as a "situation where one or more governments have made demands upon another state, backed up with the threat of force, or where they have taken planned military or confiscatory actions which were a threat to the interests of other states." Holsti distinguishes conflicts from "disputes," which involve specific grievances rather than incompatible collective objectives, and from "tensions," which involve widespread and deep-seated feelings of hostility between two or more societies. For further elaboration, see Holsti, pp. 272-73, 282. Conflicts in the Holsti inventory which do not include at least one member state of the international system (as defined in Appendix A of this study) to each side of the conflict are not included. Nor are participants included which do not qualify as members of the international system.

Table C-1

International Conflicts Involving the Threat of or Actual Use of Force, Including Military Hostilities: 1919-1939 and 1945-1965

Conflict	Sides and Participants	Occurrence of Military Hostilities[1]
1. Allied Intervention in Russia, 1919-1921[2]	Russia	
	Czechoslovakia	
	France	
	Great Britain	
	Japan	
	United States	Yes
2. Finland-Sweden (Aaland Islands), 1919-1923	Finland	
	Sweden	No
3. Lithuania-Poland (Vilna), 1919-1923	Lithuania	
	Poland	Yes
4. Allies-Turkey-Greece (Smyrna), 1919-1922[3]	Greece	
	Turkey	Yes
5. Poland-Germany (Silesia), 1920-1923	Germany	
	Poland	No

143

Table C-1 (cont.)

Conflict	Sides and Participants	Occurrence of Military Hostilities[1]
6. Finland-Russia (Karelia), 1920-1923	Finland	
	Russia	No
7. Poland-Czechoslovakia (Jawarzina District), 1920	Czechoslovakia	
	Poland	No
8. Poland-Russia 1920-1921	Poland	
	Russia	Yes
9. Hungary-Austria (Burgenland), 1921-1922	Austria	
	Hungary	No
10. Chile-Bolivia-Peru (Tacna-Arica), 1921-1924	Chile	
	Bolivia	
	Peru	No
11. Hungary-Rumania, 1922-1930	Hungary	
	Rumania	No
12. France-Germany (Rhineland Occupation), 1923	France	
	Germany	No
13. Italy-Albania-Greece (Corfu), 1923[4]	Greece	
	Italy	No
14. US-Nicaragua-Mexico, 1923-1927	United States	
	Mexico	
	Nicaragua	No
15. England-Egypt, 1924	Egypt	
	Great Britain	No
16. Greece-Bulgaria 1925	Bulgaria	
	Greece	No
17. Bolivia-Paraguay (Chaco War), 1928-1935	Bolivia	
	Paraguay	Yes
18. Japan-China 1931-1933	China	
	Japan	Yes
19. Japan-China (Jehol, 1933)	China	
	Japan	No
20. Peru-Colombia (Leticia) 1932-1934	Colombia	
	Peru	Yes

Table C-1 (cont.)

Conflict	Sides and Participants	Occurrence of Military Hostilities[1]
21. France-Germany (Saarland), 1934-1935	France Germany	No
22. Italy-Abyssinia 1934-1935	Abyssinia (Ethiopia) Italy	Yes
23. Black Seas Straits Rearmament, 1936[5]	Great Britain Russia/USSR	No
24. Germany-Allies (Rhineland Occupation), 1936[6]	France Germany	No
25. Spanish Civil War, 1936-1939[7]	Germany Italy Spain Soviet Union	Yes
26. Germany-Austria 1937-1938	Austria Germany	No
27. Germany-Czechoslovakia 1938	Czechoslovakia Germany	No
28. Poland-Czechoslovakia (Teschen), 1938	Czechoslovakia Poland	No
29. Hungary-Czechoslovakia (Ruthenia), 1939	Czechoslovakia Hungary	No
30. Germany-Czechoslovakia 1939	Czechoslovakia Germany	No
31. Germany-Lithuania (Memel), 1939	Germany Lithuania	No
32. Italy-Albania, 1939	Albania Italy	No
33. USSR-Estonia, 1939[8]	Estonia USSR	No
34. USSR-Latvia, 1939[8]	Latvia USSR	No
35. USSR-Lithuania, 1939[8]	Lithuania USSR	No

Table C-1 (cont.)

Conflict	Sides and Participants	Occurrence of Military Hostilities[1]
36. USSR-Finland, 1939-1940	Finland	
	USSR	Yes
37. Germany-Poland, 1939	Germany	
	Poland	Yes
38. USSR-Iran, 1945-1946	Iran	
	USSR	No
39. Trieste, 1946-1953[9]	Italy	
	Yugoslavia	No
40. Korean Reunification, 1946[10]	USSR	
	United States	No
41. Great Britain-Albania (Corfu), 1946-1949	Albania	
	Great Britain	No
42. Great Britain-Egypt, 1947-1954	Egypt	
	Great Britain	No
43. Palestine, 1948[11]	Israel	
	Egypt Iraq Jordan Lebanon Syria	Yes
44. Pakistan-India (Kashmir), 1948	India	
	Pakistan	Yes
45. Pakistan-India (Hyderabad), 1948	India	
	Pakistan	No
46. USSR-Allies (Berlin), 1948-1949[12]	France Great Britain United States	
	USSR	No
47. German Reunification 1949[13]	France Great Britain United States	
	USSR	No
48. Honduras-Nicaragua, 1949-1963	Honduras	
	Nicaragua	No

Table C-1 (cont.)

Conflict	Sides and Participants	Occurrence of Military Hostilities[1]
49. USSR- Yugoslavia, 1949-?	USSR Yugoslavia	 No
50. North Korea, China-South Korea, US, UN, 1950-1953[1][4]	China North Korea Australia Belgium Canada France Greece Netherlands Philippines South Korea Thailand Turkey United Kingdom United States	 Yes
51. Iran- Great Britain, 1951-1953	Great Britain Iran	 No
52. Indonesia- Netherlands (West Iran), 1954-1962	Indonesia Netherlands	 No
53. Honduras- Nicaragua- Guatemala, 1954	Guatemala Honduras Nicaragua	 No
54. Nicaragua- Costa Rica, 1955	Costa Rica Nicaragua	 No
55. Israel, France Great Britain- Egypt, 1956	Egypt France Great Britain Israel	 Yes
56. Hungary- USSR, 1956	Hungary USSR	 Yes
57. Egypt-Jordan- US, 1957	Egypt Jordan United States	 No
58. Communist China- Nationalist China, United States (Quemoy), 1958	Communist China Nationalist China United States	 No

148

Table C-1 (cont.)

Conflict	Sides and Participants	Occurrence of Military Hostilities[1]
59. Lebanon-Jordan-United States-Great Britain, 1958[15]	Great Britain Jordan Lebanon United States	
	United Arab Republic	No
60. USSR-Allies (Berlin), 1958[16]	USSR France German Federal Republic Great Britain United States	No
61. Thailand-Cambodia, 1960-1963	Cambodia Thailand	No
62. India-Portugal (Goa), 1955-1961	India Portugal	No
63. USSR-Allies (Berlin), 1961[17]	USSR Britain German Federal Republic France United States	No
64. US-Cuba, 1961	Cuba United States	Yes
65. France-Tunisia, 1961-1962[18]	France Tunisia	Yes
66. China-India, 1955-1962	China India	Yes
67. USSR, Cuba-US, 1962	Cuba USSR United States	No
68. Morocco-Algeria, 1962-1963	Algeria Morocco	No
69. Panama-US, 1963-1964	United States Panama	No
70. Greek Civil War, 1946-1951[19]	Greece Albania Bulgaria Yugoslavia	Yes
71. Lithuania-Germany, 1923	Germany Lithuania	No

Appendix D: Inventory of International Political Disputes and Military Hostilities

Political disputes and hostilities are from Wright, *A Study of War*, pp. 1429-31, 1544-47, and 1553-57. The political disputes are conflicts brought before the League of Nations or United Nations. The conflicts involving military hostilities were frequently, but not always, brought before either the League or United Nations. Wright explicitly states that conflicts specified as military hostilities during the 1945-1964 period involved a minimum of 317 fatalities, but he does not state the same with reference to the 1920-1939 period. According to accounts in *The Annual Register of World Events* reviewed by this author, at least some of the latter conflicts did not result in at least 317 fatalities. For the purpose of the present study these events were coded as involving military hostilities only if other sources verified the 317 threshold level.

Conflicts listed by Wright that do not include at least one member state of the international system (as defined in Appendix A of this study) to each side of the conflict are not included. Nor are participants' included which do not qualify as members of the international system.

Some of the conflicts in Wright's inventories have not been included because of incomplete information as to the participants. Other conflicts, also incomplete in terms of participants, have been documented by referencing other sources and consequenly included. These are footnoted accordingly.

Presumably, many of the conflicts drawn from Wright did not involve a threat or actual use of force, since Holsti's inventory which was restricted to such types of conflicts covers essentially the same period of time yet has considerably fewer entries (see Appendix C).

Table D-1
International Political Disputes and Military Hostilities: 1920-1939 and 1945-1965

Conflict	Sides and Participants	Occurrence of Military Hostilities
1. Eupen and Malmedy, 1920-1921	Belgium	
	Germany	No
2. Enzeli, 1920	Iran	
	USSR	No
3. Aaland Islands, 1921	Finland	
	Sweden	No

149

Table D-1 (cont.)

Conflict	Sides and Participants	Occurrence of Military Hostilities
4. Vilna, 1920-1931	Lithuania	
	Poland	Yes
5. Tacna-Arica, 1920-1921	Bolivia Peru	
	Chile	No
6. Coto, 1921	Costa Rica	
	Panama	No
7. Albanian Frontier, 1921-1924	Albania	
	Yugoslavia Greece	No
8. Austrian Estates 1921	Austria	
	Yugoslavia	No
9. Upper Silesia, 1921-1922	Germany	
	Poland	No
10. Eastern Carelia, 1921-1923	Finland	
	USSR	No
11. Insurance Funds, 1921-1925	France Poland	
	Germany	No
12. Burgenland, 1922	Austria	
	Hungary	No
13. Bulgarian Frontier, 1922	Bulgaria	
	Greece Rumania Yugoslavia	No
14. Hungarian Frontier, 1922	Hungary	
	Yugoslavia	No
15. St. Naoum Monastery, 1922-1925	Albania	
	Yugoslavia	No
16. Salgo Tarzan, 1923	Hungary	
	Czechoslovakia	No
17. Tunis Nationality Decrees, 1922	France	
	Great Britain	No

Table D-1 (cont.)

Conflict	Sides and Participants	Occurrence of Military Hostilities
18. Hungarian Optants, 1923-1930	Hungary	
	Rumania	No
19. Jaworzina, 1923	Czechoslovakia	
	Poland	No
20. Corfu, 1923	Greece	
	Italy	No
21. Koritza, 1924	Albania	
	Yugoslavia	No
22. Ottoman Public Debt, 1924-1925	Bulgaria France Greece	
	Turkey	No
23. Mosul, 1924-1926	Great Britain	
	Turkey	No
24. Ecumenical Patriarch, 1925	Greece	
	Turkey	No
25. Demir Kapu, 1925-1926	Bulgaria	
	Greece	No
26. Maritza, 1926	Greece	
	Turkey	No
27. Memel, 1923-1932[1]	Lithuania	
	Germany	No
28. Succession to Railroads, 1926-1935	Austria Hungary	
	Czechoslovakia Rumania Yugoslavia	No
29. Danube Commission, 1926-1933	Rumania	
	France Great Britain Italy	No
30. Albanian Minorities, 1924-1928	Albania	
	Greece	No
31. Cruiser "Salamis," 1927-1928	Greece	
	Germany	No

Table D-1 (cont.)

Conflict	Sides and Participants	Occurrence of Military Hostilities
32. Bahrein Islands, 1927	Great Britain	
	Iran	No
33. Szent-Gotthard Arms, 1928	Hungary	
	Czechoslovakia	
	Rumania	
	Yugoslavia	No
34. Unequal Treaties, 1929	China	
	France	
	Great Britain	
	Netherlands	
	Norway	
	United States	No
35. Gran Chaco, 1928-1935	Bolivia	
	Paraguay	Yes
36. Rhodope Forests, 1930-1934	Bulgaria	
	Greece	No
37. Austro-German Customs Union, 1931	Austria	
	France	
	Great Britain	No
38. Bulgarian-Greek Debts, 1931	Bulgaria	
	Greece	No
39. Iraq-Syrian Frontier, 1931-1933	France	
	Great Britain	No
40. Finnish Vessels, 1931-1935	Finland	
	Great Britain	No
41. Manchuria, 1931-1933	China	
	Japan	Yes
42. Assyrians, 1932-1937	Great Britain	
	Iraq	No
43. Anglo-Persian Oil Co., 1932-1933	Great Britain	
	Iran	No
44. Leticia, 1932-1935	Colombia	
	Peru	Yes

Table D-1 (cont.)

Conflict	Sides and Participants	Occurrence of Military Hostilities
45. Arms Smuggling, 1933	Austria	
	Czechoslovakia Rumania Yugoslavia	No
46. Swiss War Losses, 1934	Switzerland	
	Germany France Great Britain Italy	No
47. Hungarian Frontier, 1934	Hungary	
	Yugoslavia	No
48. Marseilles Crime, 1934-1935	Hungary	
	Yugoslavia	No
49. German Rearmament, 1935	Germany	
	France Italy Great Britain	No
50. Ethiopia, 1935-1938	Ethiopia	
	Italy	Yes
51. Iraq Frontier 1934	Iran	
	Iraq	No
52. Burma Frontier, 1935	China	
	Great Britain	No
53. Saar Valley, 1935[2]	Germany	
	France	No
54. Uruguay, Soviet Relations, 1936	USSR	
	Uruguay	No
55. Rhineland Occupation, 1936-1938	Belgium France	
	Germany	No
56. Spanish Civil War, 1936-1939	Italy Germany	
	Russia[3] Spain	Yes
57. Alexandretta, 1936-1937	France	
	Turkey	No

Table D-1 (cont.)

Conflict	Sides and Participants	Occurrence of Military Hostilities
58. Partition of Czechoslovakia, 1938	Czechoslovakia	
	Germany	No
59. China, 1937-1939	China	
	Japan	Yes
60. Aaland Islands, 1939	Finland	
	Sweden	No
61. Albania, 1939	Albania	
	Italy	No
62. Russo-Finnish War, 1939	Finland	
	USSR	Yes
63. Forces in Iran, 1946	Iran	
	USSR	No
64. Greek Border, 1946-1950	Greece	
	Albania Bulgaria Yugoslavia	Yes
65. Spanish Threat, 1946	Poland	
	Spain	No
66. Trieste, 1947	Italy	
	Yugoslavia	No
67. Corfu Channel, 1947	Albania	
	United Kingdom	No
68. Forces in Egypt, 1947	Egypt	
	United Kingdom	No
69. Palestine Partition, 1948[4]	Israel	
	Egypt Iraq Jordan Lebanon Syria	Yes
70. Korean Status, 1947	USSR	
	United States	No
71. Kashmir Status, 1948-1949[5]	India	
	Pakistan	No

Table D-1 (cont.)

Conflict	Sides and Participants	Occurrence of Military Hostilities
72. Czechoslovakia, 1948	Czechoslovakia	
	USSR	No
73. Soviet Wives, 1948	Chile	
	USSR	No
74. Berlin-Blockade, 1948-1949	France Great Britain United States	
	USSR	No
75. Greek Children, 1948-	Greece	
	Albania Bulgaria Yugoslavia	No
76. Application of Peace Treaties, 1949	France Great Britain United States	
	Bulgaria Hungary Rumania	No
77. Italian Colonies, 1949	France Great Britain United States	
	USSR	No
78. North Borneo, 1963	Indonesia Philippines	
	Malaysia	No
79. Intervention in China, 1949	Nationalist China	
	USSR	No
80. Chinese Representation in UN 1950-	Nationalist China	
	USSR	No
81. Korean Hostilities, 1950-1953[6]	China North Korea	
	Australia Belgium Canada France Greece South Korea Netherlands Philippines Thailand Turkey United Kingdom United States	Yes

Table D-1 (cont.)

Conflict	Sides and Participants	Occurrence of Military Hostilities
82. Threats to Communist China, 1950	USSR United States	No
83. Intervention in Korea, 1950-1953	South Korea United States Communist China	 No
84. Prisoners of War, 1950-	France Great Britain United States USSR	 No
85. Suez Canal Navigation, 1951-	France Israel United Kingdom Egypt	 No
86. Threats to Yugoslavia, 1951	Yugoslavia USSR	 No
87. Free Elections in Germany, 1951	France Great Britain United States USSR	 No
88. Propaganda in Eastern Europe, 1951	USSR United States	 No
89. Bacteriological War, 1952	USSR United States	 No
90. Apartheid Laws, 1952[7]	South Africa Afghanistan Burma Egypt India Indonesia Iraq Iran Lebanon Pakistan Philippines Syria	 No

Table D-1 (cont.)

Conflict	Sides and Participants	Occurrence of Military Hostilities
91. Moroccan Independence 1952-1956[8]	France	
	Afghanistan	
	Burma	
	Egypt	
	India	
	Indonesia	
	Iraq	
	Iran	
	Lebanon	
	Pakistan	
	Philippines	
	Syria	No
92. Tunisian Independence, 1952-1957[9]	France	
	Afghanistan	
	Burma	
	Egypt	
	India	
	Indonesia	
	Iraq	
	Iran	
	Lebanon	
	Pakistan	
	Philippines	
	Syria	
	Thailand	No
93. Prisoners of War, 1952	USSR	
	North Korea	
	South Korea	
	United States	No
94. Status of Austria, 1952	USSR	
	United States	No
95. Forces in Burma, 1953	Burma	
	Nationalist China	No
96. Guatemalan Revolution, 1954	USSR	
	United States	No
97. Quemoy-Matsu, 1954-1956[10]	Communist China	
	Nationalist China	
	United States	Yes
98. Quemoy and Matsu, 1955	USSR	
	United States	No

Table D-1 (cont.)

Conflict	Sides and Participants	Occurrence of Military Hostilities
99. Suez Hostilities, 1956[11]	Egypt	
	France	
	Great Britain	
	Israel	Yes
100. Hungarian Hostilities, 1956	Hungary	
	USSR	Yes
101. West Irian, 1957	Indonesia	
	Netherlands	No
102. Oman and Muscat, 1957[12]	United Kingdom	
	Egypt	
	Iraq	
	Jordan	
	Lebanon	
	Libya	
	Morocco	
	Saudi Arabia	
	Sudan	
	Syria	No
103. Cyprus, 1957	Greece	
	Turkey	
	United Kingdom	No
104. Berlin Ultimatum, 1958	USSR	
	United States	No
105. Southwest African Mandate, 1958-	Ethiopia	
	Liberia	
	South Africa	No
106. Sheikh Abdullah Imprisonment, 1959	India	
	Pakistan	No
107. Cambodian Border, 1959	Cambodia	
	Thailand	No
108. Panamanian Border, 1959	Nicaragua	
	Panama	No
109. Tunisian Border, 1959	France	
	Tunisia	No
110. Tibet Invasion, 1959	Communist China	
	India	No

Table D-1 (cont.)

Conflict	Sides and Participants	Occurence of Military Hostilities
111. Congo Civil Strife, 1960-1965	Belgium Congo	Yes
112. Eichmann Kidnapping, 1960	Argentina Israel	No
113. Cuban Bay of Pigs, 1961-1963	Cuba United States	Yes
114. Vietnam, 1961-	South Vietnam United States North Vietnam	Yes
115. Kuwait Status, 1961	Iraq Great Britain Jordan Saudi Arabia UAR United States	No
116. Goa Invasion, 1961	India Portugal	No
117. Venezuelan Boundary, 1962	United Kingdom Venezuela	No
118. Cuban Quarantine, 1962	Cuba USSR United States	No
119. Invasion of India, 1962	Communist China India	Yes
120. Senegal Border, 1963	Portugal Senegal	No
121. Rwanda-Burundi, 1962-1963	Burundi Rwanda	Yes
122. Ethiopian Border, 1963	Ethiopia Somali	No

Appendix E: Inventory of Randomly Generated Hypothetical Nonconflict Events

The inventory of hypothetical nonconflict events was constructed as follows. Each state in the international system between 1850 and 1966 was selected at random for one of the total number of years during which it enjoyed membership. Each state was then randomly paired with one of its adjacent neighbors for that year. Only adjacent states that were members of the international system for the point of time selected were considered as a possible partner. States were paired with adjacent nations, since most international conflicts involve neighboring states. Adjacent states were almost always defined as those sharing a common frontier. However, exceptions were made for island states, such as Australia and New Zealand, in which case the nearest state was regarded as a neighbor.

A few states that were members of the international system during the 1850-1966 period do not appear in the "State" column, because the year for which they were randomly selected was one in which less than three years had elapsed since entry of the state into the international system.

Table E-1
Hypothetical Nonconflict Events: 1850-1966

Nonconflict ID	State	Neighboring State Randomly Selected	Year Randomly Selected
0010	Afghanistan	Iran	1937
0020	Albania	Greece	1937
0040	Argentina	Brazil	1921
0050	Australia	New Zealand	1955
0060	Austria-Hungary	Turkey	1887
0061	Austria	Hungary	1930
0062	Hungary	Rumania	1946
0080	Belgium	France	1870
0100	Bolivia	Chile	1917
0120	Brazil	Venezuela	1908
0130	Bulgaria	Rumania	1889
0140	Burma	Laos	1957
0160	Cambodia	Laos	1963
0180	Canada	United States	1958
0200	Ceylon	India	1966

Table E-1 (cont.)

Nonconflict ID	State	Neighboring State Randomly Selected	Year Randomly Selected
0220	Chile	Peru	1913
0230	China	Russia	1870
0231	Rep. of China	Communist China	1959
0240	Colombia	Brazil	1904
0270	Costa Rica	Panama	1907
0280	Cuba	Haiti	1943
0300	Czechoslovakia	Hungary	1930
0320	Denmark	Sweden-Norway	1898
0330	Dominican Republic	Haiti	1938
0340	Ecuador	Colombia	1896
0350	El Salvador	Honduras	1918
0360	Estonia	Russia/USSR	1933
0370	Ethiopia	Saudi-Arabia	1963
0380	Finland	Norway	1966
0390	France	Italy	1899
0420	Germany	Austria-Hungary	1897
0421	Baden	Wurtemberg	1857
0422	Bavaria	Wurtemberg	1862
0423	Hanover	Mecklenberg	1858
0424	Hesse Electorate	Bavaria	1864
0425	Hesse Grand Duchy	Prussia	1866
0426	Mecklenburg	Hanover	1859
0427	Prussia	Saxony	1863
0428	Saxony	Prussia	1865
0429	Wurtemberg	Prussia	1861
0430	German Dem. Republic	Czechoslovakia	1965
0431	German Fed. Republic	Netherlands	1964
0450	Greece	Turkey	1868
0460	Guatemala	Honduras	1900
0490	Haiti	Dominican Republic	1875
0500	Honduras	El Salvador	1908
0510	Iceland	United Kingdom	1958
0520	India	Communist China	1958
0530	Indonesia	Thailand	1963
0540	Iran	Russia/USSR	1943
0550	Iraq	Iran	1963
0560	Israel	Egypt/UAR	1954
0570	Italy	Switzerland	1877

Table E-1 (cont.)

Nonconflict ID	State	Neighboring State Randomly Selected	Year Randomly Selected
0572	Papal States	Tuscany	1854
0573	Parma	Tuscany	1856
0574	Sardinia	Austria-Hungary	1856
0575	Tuscany	Parma	1858
0576	Two Sicilies	Papal States	1855
0600	Japan	China	1890
0610	Jordan	Iraq	1964
0630	Korea	China	1899
0631	Korean People's Rep.	Korean Republic	1957
0632	Korean Republic	Korean People's Rep.	1961
0650	Laos	Cambodia	1957
0660	Latvia	Estonia	1939
0670	Lebanon	Syria	1954
0700	Libya	Chad	1964
0710	Lithuania	Latvia	1938
0720	Luxembourg	Belgium	1887
0750	Malaysia	Indonesia	1964
0810	Mexico	Guatemala	1878
0830	Morocco	Algeria	1965
0850	Netherlands	Belgium	1904
0860	New Zealand	Australia	1960
0870	Nicaragua	Costa Rica	1928
0900	Pakistan	Burma	1965
0910	Panama	Costa Rica	1926
0920	Paraguay	Brazil	1888
0930	Peru	Brazil	1892
0940	Philippines	Indonesia	1955
0950	Poland	Germany	1931
0960	Portugal	Spain	1910
0970	Rumania	Bulgaria	1900
0990	Saudi Arabia	Egypt/UAR	1964
1060	Spain	Portugal	1890
1070	Sudan	Ethiopia	1960
1090	Sweden-Norway	Russia	1890
1091	Norway	Sweden	1922
1092	Sweden	Denmark	1917
1100	Switzerland	Baden	1854
1110	Syria	Lebanon	1964

Table E-1 (cont.)

Nonconflict ID	State	Neighboring State Randomly Selected	Year Randomly Selected
1160	Tunisia	Libya	1960
1170	Turkey	Russia	1900
1190	Russia/USSR	Turkey	1885
1200	Egypt/UAR	Sudan	1956
1210	United Kingdom	Ireland	1927
1212	Ireland	United Kingdom	1953
1220	United States	Mexico	1858
1240	Uruguay	Brazil	1906
1250	Venezuela	Colombia	1903
1261	Vietnam People's Rep.	Laos	1962
1262	Vietnam Republic	Cambodia	1962
1290	Yugoslavia	Rumania	1964
1291	Montenegro	Turkey	1891
1292	Serbia	Bulgaria	1886

Notes

Chapter 1
Power and the Power Capabilities
of Nation States

1. Harold D. Lasswell and Abraham Kaplan, *Power and Society: A Framework for Political Inquiry* (New Haven: Yale University Press, 1950), pp. xiv, 74.

2. Charles A. McClelland, *Theory and the International System* (New York: The Macmillan Company, 1966), p. 63. See also: Hans J. Morgenthau, *Politics Among Nations: The Struggle for Power and Peace* (New York: Alfred A. Knopf, 1963), pp. 3-15.

3. See, for example: Robert A. Dahl, "Power," *International Encyclopedia of the Social Sciences*, editor-in-chief David A. Sills (New York: The Macmillan Company and the Free Press, 1968), pp. 405-15; David A. Baldwin, "Inter-Nation Influence Revisited," *Journal of Conflict Resolution*, 15 (December 1971), pp. 471-86; Jack H. Nagel, "Some Questions About the Concept of Power," *Behavioral Science*, 13 (March 1968), pp. 129-37; J. David Singer, "Inter-Nation Influence: A Formal Model," *American Political Science Review*, 57 (June 1963), pp. 420-30; Peter Bachrach and Morton S. Baratz, "Decisions and Non-Decisions: An Analytical Framework," *American Political Science Review*, 57 (September 1963), pp. 632-42; K.J. Holsti, "The Concept of Power in the Study of International Relations," *Background*, 7 (February 1964), pp. 105-18; Roderick Bell, David V. Edwards, and R. Harrison Wagner, eds., *Political Power; A Reader in Theory and Research* (New York: The Free Press, 1969).

4. Dahl, p. 407.

5. Inis L. Claude, Jr., *Power and International Relations* (New York: Random House, 1962), pp. 11-39; Ernst B. Haas, "The Balance of Power: Prescription, Concept, or Propaganda," *International Politics and Foreign Policy*, ed. James N. Rosenau (New York: The Free Press of Glencoe, 1961), pp. 318-29.

6. Dahl, p. 407.

7. Nagel, p. 129.

8. Bachrach and Baratz.

9. See, for example, Singer, p. 422; Baldwin, p. 477.

10. Dahl, p. 407.

11. Jack H. Nagel, "Some Questions About the Concept of Power," *Behavioral Science*, 13: 2 (March 1968), by permission of James G. Miller, M.D., Ph.D., editor.

12. Dahl, p. 411.

13. Per Maurseth, "Balance-of-Power Thinking from the Renaissance to the French Revolution," *Journal of Peace Research*, 1: 1 (1964), pp. 120-33; Harold

Sprout and Margaret Sprout, *Foundations of International Politics* (Princeton: D. Van Nostrand Co., 1962), p. 138; Klaus Knorr, *The War Potential of Nations* (Princeton: Princeton University Press, 1956), p. 48.

14. Robert C. North, "Conflict Political Aspects," *International Encyclopedia for the Social Sciences*, editor-in-chief David A. Sills (New York: The Macmillan Company and The Free Press, 1968), p. 226. The author is grateful to the Macmillan Company for permission to quote from copyrighted works.

15. The criteria for sovereignty and membership in the international system for the most part are synonymous with those outlined by J. David Singer and Melvin Small and are discussed more fully in Chapter 4 and Appendix A.

16. See, for example, Lasswell and Kaplan, pp. 55-102.

17. The following sources are particularly instructive: Lasswell and Kaplan, pp. 55-102; Robert Bierstedt, "An Analysis of Social Power," *American Sociological Review*, 15: 6 (December 1950), pp. 730-37; Talcott Parsons, "On the Concept of Political Power," *Proceedings of the American Philosophical Society*, 107: 3 (June 1963), pp. 232-62; Carl Friedrich, ed. *Authority* (Cambridge: Harvard University Press, 1958), pp. 28-48; E.V. Walter, "Power and Violence," *American Political Science Review*, 58: 2 (June 1964), pp. 350-60. Peter Bachrach and Morton S. Baratz, "Decisions and Nondecisions: An Analytical Framework," *American Political Science Review*, 57: 3 (September 1963), pp. 632-42.

18. Bachrach and Baratz, pp. 632-42.

19. Ibid., pp. 633-36.

20. Ibid., pp. 637-38.

21. Ibid., pp. 638-39.

22. Nagel, pp. 130-34; Baldwin, pp. 478-79; Herbert A. Simon, "Notes on the Observation and Measurement of Political Power," *Journal of Politics*, 15 (November 1953), pp. 500-16

23. See, for example: Peter Wallenstein, "Characteristics of Economic Sanctions," in William D. Coplin and Charles W. Kegley, Jr. (eds.), *A Multi-Method Introduction to International Politics* (Chicago: Markham Publishing Co., 1971), pp. 128-54.

24. See Paul G. Swingle and Brian MacLean, "The Effect of Illusory Power in Non-Zero-Sum-Games," *Journal of Conflict Resolution*, 15 (December 1971), p. 514.

25. Cited by David A. Baldwin, "The Power of Positive Sanctions," *World Politics*, 24 (October 1971), p. 24.

26. Ibid., pp. 27-37; Singer, p. 429.

27. Lewis Richardson, *Statistics of Deadly Quarrels*. Edited by Quincy Wright and C.C. Lienau (Pittsburgh: Boxwood Press, 1960), pp. 32-112.

28. Ibid., pp. 111-112.

29. Quincy Wright, *A Study of War* (2nd ed., Chicago: University of Chicago Press, 1965), p. 1544.

30. The Singer-Small inventory is the most recent effort to delineate a comprehensive inventory of war events for a sizable length of time. It is also the most thorough in terms of explicitly defining and defending the theoretical and methodological criteria that were devised to ensure, as best as possible, validity of the results. Consequently, it is heavily relied upon in the present study. See J. David Singer and Melvin Small, *The Wages of War 1816-1965 A Statistical Handbook* (New York: John Wiley & Sons, 1972), pp. 17-39.

31. The figures are not fully comparable. For example, Richardson's estimates were based on military and civilian deaths resulting from armed hostilities, whereas Singer and Small exclude civilian fatalities because of validity and reliability considerations. At the same time the latter note that "civilian deaths were quantitatively negligible in most of the international (as distinguished from civil) wars" during the time span they studied (Singer and Small, pp. 47-49). Of course, as the threshold size is increased, the likelihood that individual participants will sustain some minimum level of fatalities or have some minimum number of troops engaged in the war theater increases, and in this sense there is a greater likelihood that individual states will meet a minimum level of involvement.

32. For example, inventories of conflicts compiled by Quincy Wright and K.J. Holsti and which cover the 1919-1965 period include about ten conflicts that qualify according to the 317 threshold but not according to the criteria established by Singer and Small. See Appendixes B, C, and D in this volume.

Chapter 2
Theoretical Overview:
Power Capabilities and War

1. Quincy Wright, *A Study of War* (2nd ed., Chicago: University of Chicago Press, 1965).

2. Lewis Richardson, *Statistics of Deadly Quarrels.* Edited by Quincy Wright and C.C. Lienau (Pittsburgh: Boxwood Press, 1960).

3. Singer, J. David and Melvin Small, *The Wages of War 1816-1965: A Statistical Handbook* (New York: John Wiley & Sons, 1972).

4. The three volumes cited are not the only nor the first studies to compile inventories of war events, but they are the most important. For an identification of other relevant works, see Singer and Small, pp. 9-11.

5. The authors of a recent reader on the causes of war note that the empirical selections in their book are among the very few in existence. See Dean G. Pruitt and Richard C. Snyder, eds., *Theory and Research on the Causes of War* (Englewood Cliffs, N.J.: Prentice-Hall, 1969), p. 113. There is reason to believe, however, that this situation may be reversed in the not too distant future. A not inconsiderable number of studies have appeared very recently,

indicative of growing interest in the subject. Their appearance is directly related to the generation of data banks pertinent to the subject that are rapidly widening opportunities for serious research. This being the case, it is perhaps not an exaggeration to project the possible proliferation of research studies in this area over the course of the next five to ten years.

Among recent studies are: Russell J. Leng and Robert A. Goodsell, "Behavioral Indicators of War Proneness in Bilateral Conflicts." Paper delivered at the 1972 Annual Meeting of the American Political Science Association, Washington, D.C., September 5-9, 1972 (mimeographed); Bruce M. Russett (ed.), *Peace, War, and Numbers* (Beverly Hills, Calif.: Sage Publications, 1972); J. David Singer and Melvin Small, "Foreign Policy Indicators: Predictors of War in History and in the State of the World Message." Paper delivered at the 1972 Annual Meeting of the American Political Science Association, Washington, D.C., September 5-9, 1972 (mimeographed); J. David Singer and Melvin Small, *The Wages of War 1816-1965: A Statistical Handbook* (New York: John Wiley & Sons, 1972); and Harvey Starr, *War Coalitions* (Lexington, Mass.: D.C. Heath and Company, 1972).

6. Rudolph J. Rummel, "U.S. Foreign Relations: Conflict, Cooperation, and Attribute Distances," *Peace, War, and Numbers*. Edited by Bruce M. Russett. (Beverly Hills, Calif.: Sage Publications, 1972), pp. 82-83.

7. Richardson.

8. Wright.

9. Richardson, pp. 32-112.

10. Ibid., pp. 7, 19-26.

11. Ibid., p. 23. Richardson's classification of these two variables quite possibly was based solely on a review of histories relevant to his list of deadly quarrels.

12. Singer and Small, pp. 60-69, 82-128; Richardson, pp. 32-112.

13. Rudolph J. Rummel has implicitly hinted at some of these findings in "Dimensions of Dyadic War, 1820-1952," *Journal of Conflict Resolution*, 11 (June 1967), pp. 176-83. In view of these results, it is perhaps surprising that Richardson devoted as much attention as he did to a study of arms races. It is possible, of course, that Richardson's findings are in error. He may have incorrectly read the sources consulted; some of the sources may have been inaccurate or incomplete with respect to relevant information about the variables. For example, it appears that Richardson did not collect definitive information of a Yes-No variety with respect to each of the variables and all of the conflicts. In other words, if a particular variable was mentioned in an account of a conflict, it was recorded; if a variable was not mentioned, it was assumed not to have been present and hence causally irrelevant with respect to the occurrence of the conflict.

14. Wright, p. 756.

15. Claude, passim; Ernst B. Haas, "The Balance of Power: Prescription,

Concept, or Propaganda," *World Politics*, 5 (1953), pp. 442-77; Per Maurseth, "Balance-of-Power Thinking from the Renaissance to the French Revolution," *Journal of Peace Research*, 1:1 (1964), pp. 120-33.

16. G.H. Snyder, "Balance of Power in the Missile Age," *Journal of International Affairs*, 14 (1960), pp. 21-34; Stanley Hoffmann, "Balance of Power," *International Encyclopedia of the Social Sciences*, editor-in-chief David A. Sills (New York: The Macmillan Company and The Free Press, 1968), pp. 506-10; Partha Chatterjee, "The Classical Balance of Power Theory," *Journal of Peace Research*, 1 (1972), pp. 51-61.

17. See Chapter 1, pp. 1-2.

18. Inis L. Claude, Jr., *Power and International Relations* (New York: Random House, 1962), p. 88.

19. Hans J. Morgenthau and Kenneth W. Thompson, *Principles and Problems of International Politics* (New York: Alfred A. Knopf, 1950), p. 103.

20. Morgenthau, p. 167.

21. See, for example, Chatterjee, p. 51; Claude, pp. 42-43.

22. Morton A. Kaplan, *System and Process in International Politics* (New York: John Wiley & Sons, 1957), p. 23.

23. Two very recent exceptions are: Singer and Small, "Foreign Policy Indicators: Predictors of War in History and in the State of the World Message." Paper delivered at the 1972 Annual Meeting of the American Political Science Association, Washington, D.C., September 5-9, 1972 (mimeographed); J. David Singer, Stuart Bremer, and John Stuckey, "Capability Distribution, Uncertainty, and Major Power War, 1820-1965," *Peace, War, and Numbers*, ed. Bruce M. Russett, pp. 19-48.

24. Morgenthau declares that the balance of power system frequently contains a number of subsystems that are interrelated but each of which maintains within itself a balance of power of its own. See Hans J. Morgenthau, *Politics Among Nations: The Struggle for Power and Peace* (New York: Alfred A. Knopf, 1963), p. 198.

25. Claude, pp. 56, 61-64, 66.

26. Morgenthau, pp. 168-69.

27. Wright, pp. 754-56.

28. A.F.K. Organski, *World Politics* (New York: Alfred A. Knopf, 1958), p. 292.

29. Ibid.

30. Rummel, "U.S. Foreign Relations," pp. 91-92.

31. Raoul Naroll, "Deterrence in History," in *Theory and Research on the Causes of War*, ed. Dean G. Pruitt and Richard Snyder (Englewood Cliffs, N.J.: Prentice-Hall, 1969), pp. 150-64.

32. Quincy Wright, "The Escalation of International Conflict," *Journal of Conflict Resolution*, 9 (December 1965), pp. 434-49.

33. Wright did not specify his operational criteria for military hostilities.

Rather, he referred the reader to separate inventories of conflicts in *A Study of War*. Of these, one identifies military hostilities during the 1945-1965 years and defines military hostilities as a conflict involving 317 or more casualties. Another identifies military hostilities for the 1919-1939 period, but these appear to include conflicts involving less than 317 casualties. For further clarification of this point, see Appendix D and Appendix C. See also Wright, *A Study of War*, pp. 1429, 1544, and 1552.

34. Wright, "The Escalation of International Conflict," pp. 437-42.

35. Singer and Small, "Foreign Policy Indicators." Six indicators were used to measure power capabilities: steel production, energy consumption, urban population, the square root of total population, armed forces size, and military expenditure.

36. Singer, Bremer, and Stuckey, pp. 19-48.

37. John R. Raser and Wayman J. Crow, " A Simulation Study of Deterrence Theories," in *Theory and Research on the Causes of War*, ed. Pruitt and Snyder, pp. 136-49.

38. Paul G. Swingle and ·Brian MacLean, "The Effect of Illusory Power in Non-Zero-Sum Games," *Journal of Conflict Resolution*, 15 (December 1971), pp. 513-22.

39. Johan Galtung, "A Structural Theory of Aggression," *Journal of Peace Research*, 1:2 (1964), pp. 95-118.

40. Ibid., pp. 98-100.

41. Michael D. Wallace, "Power, Status, and International War," *Journal of Peace Research*, 8:1 (1971), pp. 23-35.

42. Ibid., p. 35. Another study, by Maurice East, has also provided confirmatory evidence of Galtung's thesis. The East analysis focuses on the 1948-1964 period of time and employs some different operational indices. See "Status Discrepancy and Violence in the International System: An Empirical Analysis," *The Analysis of International Politics*, ed. James A. Rosenau, Vincent Davis, and Maurice East (New York: The Free Press, 1972), pp. 299-319.

43. Michael D. Wallace, "Status, Formal Organization, and Arms Levels as Factors Leading to the Onset of War, 1820-1965," *Peace, War, and Numbers*, ed. By Bruce M. Russett, pp. 49-70.

Chapter 3
Power Capabilities Related to the
Occurrence and Resolution of War:
A Theoretical Model

1. K.J. Holsti has differentiated six modes of conflict resolution: avoidance or voluntary withdrawal; violent conquest; forced submission or withdrawal; compromise; award; and passive settlement. See "Resolving International Con-

flicts: A Taxonomy of Behavior and Some Figures on Procedure," *Journal of Conflict Resolution*, 10 (September 1966), pp. 272-96.

2. The idea that the behavior of nations is determined in part by the attributes of states has been propounded by other international theorists. Rummel's field theory, for example, hypothesizes that similarities and differences in the attributes of states act as a force causing social behavior. See Rudolph J. Rummel, " A Field Theory of Social Action with Application to Conflict Within Nations," *General Systems Yearbook,* 10 (1965), pp. 183-96. See also Sang-Woo Rhee, *China's Cooperation, Conflict and Interaction Behavior; Viewed from Rummel's Status Theoretic Perspective*, (Hawaii: Dimensionality of Nations Project, 1972), pp. 1-4 (mimeographed).

3. Glenn H. Snyder, "Deterrence and Power," *Journal of Conflict Resolution*, 4:2 (June 1960), pp. 163-78, by permission of the publisher, Sage Publications, Inc. See also: Clinton F. Fink, "More Calculations About Deterrence," *Journal of Conflict Resolution*, 9 (March 1965), pp. 54-65; Lars Porsholt, "On Methods of Conflict Resolution," *Journal of Peace Research*, 3:2 (1966), pp. 178-93; John R. Raser, "Deterrence Research: Past Progress and Future Needs," *Journal of Peace Research*, 3:4 (1966), pp. 297-327.

4. Empirical evidence on this point is contradictory. Theodore Abel examined twenty-five wars and concluded that the decision to wage war was a rational undertaking. Ole R. Holsti's detailed study of communications among the primary participants to the start of World War I and prior to the outbreak of the war indicates the opposite. See Theodore Abel, "The Element of Decision in the Pattern of War," *American Sociological Review*, 6 (1941), pp. 853-59; and Ole R. Holsti, "The 1914 Case," *Basic Issues in International Relations*, ed. Peter A. Toma and Andrew Gyorgy (Boston: Allyn and Bacon, 1967), pp. 140-47. See also Singer, "Inter-Nation Influence: A Formal Model," *American Political Science Review*, 57 (June 1963), p. 425.

5. As previously suggested (Chapter 1, note 13), some theorists assume otherwise. See also: Partha Chatterjee, "The classical Balance of Power Theory," *Journal of Peace Research*, 1 (1972), p. 52; Morgenthau, *Politics Among Nations*, pp. 206-07; Wright, *A Study of War*, pp. 753-54.

6. The model outlined in this chapter is compatible in many respects with models outlined by other international theorists. See, for example, Fink, pp. 54-65; Porsholt, pp. 178-93; Glenn Snyder, "Deterrence and Power," pp. 163-78; Wright, "The Escalation of International Conflicts"; Bruce M. Russett, "The Calculus of Deterrence," *Journal of Conflict Resolution*, 7 (June 1963), pp. 97-109.

7. Chatterjee, p. 53.

8. For a similar point of view, see Russell J. Leng and Robert A. Goodsell, "Behavioral Indicators of War Proneness in Bilateral Conflicts." Paper delivered at the 1972 Annual Meeting of the American Political Science Association, Washington, D.C., September 5-9, 1972 (mimeographed).

9. Wright, *A Study of War*, p. 1285.

10. Morgenthau, *Politics Among Nations*, pp. 211-13.

11. Wright, *A Study of War*, pp. 1291-92, 744 (n. 4). See also Abel, pp. 853-55.

12. Abel, p. 854; John H. Herz, *International Politics in the Atomic Age* (New York: Columbia University Press, 1959), p. 154; Wright, *A Study of War*, pp. 1245-46.

13. For a similar viewpoint, see Porsholt, p. 184. Morgenthau argues that this was an important factor accounting for the occurrence of World War I (*Politics Among Nations*, p. 111).

Chapter 4
Operationalizing the Hypotheses

1. For a useful introductory discussion of the importance of operational definitions in scientific research see Fred N. Kerlinger, *Foundations of Behavioral Research* (New York: Holt, Rinehart and Winston, Inc., 1964), pp. 33-38. This volume can serve as a valuable reference in general for those readers who find themselves on unfamiliar ground with respect to the overall methodological approach employed in the present study.

2. J. David Singer and Melvin Small, "The Composition and Status Ordering of the International System: 1850-1940," *World Politics*, 18 (January 1966), pp. 236-82.

3. J. David Singer, Melvin Small, and Bruce M. Russett, "National Political Units in the Twentieth Century: A Standardized List," *The American Political Science Review*, 62 (September 1968), pp. 932-51.

4. Arthur S. Banks, *Cross-Polity Time-Series Data* (Cambridge: The MIT Press, 1971), pp. 297-99.

5. See Appendix B for a listing of the war events selected from the Singer-Small inventory. For a few of these events not all of the participants designated by Singer and Small are incorporated in the present analysis. See Appendix B for clarification.

6. K.J. Holsti, "Resolving International Conflicts: A Taxonomy of Behavior and Some Figures on Procedures," *Journal of Conflict Resolution*, 10 (September 1966), pp. 273-96. See Appendix D for a report on the conflicts selected from Holsti for analysis in this study and for a listing of these conflicts. The conflicts, presented by Wright in the form of several inventories, have been aggregated into a single inventory for the purpose of this study. For a description of the procedures followed in selecting conflicts from the Wright inventories for analysis in this study and a listing of the conflicts, see Appendix C.

7. Quincy Wright, *A Study of War*, (2nd ed., Chicago: University of Chicago Press, 1965), p. 753.

8. Harold and Margaret Sprout, *Foundations of International Politics* (Princeton: D. Van Nostrand Co., 1962), p. 137.

9. Klaus Knorr, *The War Potential of Nations* (Princeton: Princeton University Press, 1956), p. v.

10. Sprout and Sprout, pp. 167-74. The elements from which national power capabilities are derived, as identified by Hans Morgenthau, include a combination of many of those discussed above: geography, natural resources (food, raw materials), industrial capacity, military preparedness (technology, leadership, quantity and quality of the armed forces), population, national character, national morale, the quality of diplomacy, the quality of government. See Morgenthau, *Politics Among Nations*, pp. 110-48.

11. The collection and preparation of data for this study required about two years of time and the efforts of seventeen individuals.

12. Knorr, p. 63.

13. Adam Przeworski and Henry Teune, *The Logic of Comparative Social Inquiry* (New York: John Wiley & Sons, 1970), pp. 113-31.

14. Air force personnel were not included because cross-time indicators applicable to the entire 1850-1966 time period were desired. Naval personnel were not included because the available data for many countries of the world was clearly insufficient. Possible error introduced by the omission of these two indicators, especially the latter, is compensated for, in part at least, by the inclusion of the indicator of defense expenditure. A country that fields a large navy or air force will necessarily spend a larger amount of money on defense than otherwise. Hence, it will score higher relatively on this indicator than another country that maintains a smaller navy or air force.

15. Knorr, p. 199.

16. Original data were compiled on government revenue, defense expenditure, imports, exports, and exchange rates for nearly all sovereign nation-states between 1850 and 1945, and on armed forces personnel for nearly all states between 1850 and 1966. Data on area and population were largely secured from a recent volume by Arthur Banks, as well as government revenue, defense expenditure, imports, and exports for the 1946-1966 years. The original data compiled for the purpose of the present study, and the power capabilities variable data generated in the course of the analysis, are being published in a separate volume. The sources drawn upon and the procedures observed in gathering the data, and the methods developed and used for estimating missing data, are likewise reported in the companion study. See Wayne H. Ferris, *Nation-State Power and Economic Variable Data 1850-1966* (Lexington, Mass.: D.C. Heath and Co., forthcoming).

17. The following sources are instructive. Milton Gilbert and Irving B. Kravis, *An International Comparison of National Products and the Purchasing Power of Currencies* (Paris: The Organization for European Cooperation, 1954), pp. 21-26. Economic Research Institute, Economic Planning Agency (Japan),

"Analysis of Price Comparisons in Japan and the United States," *Economic Bulletin*, 13 (September 1963). William W. Hollister, *China's Gross National Product and Social Accounts, 1950-1957* (Illinois: The Free Press, 1958). Morris Bornstein, "A Comparison of Soviet and United States National Product," *Comparisons of the United States and Soviet Economies* (Washington: U.S. Government Printing Office, 1959), pp. 384-89. United States Arms Control and Disarmament Agency, *World Military Expenditures 1969* (Washington: U.S. Government Printing Office, 1968), pp. 17, 25-26. Wilfred Beckerman, "International Comparisons of Income Levels: A Suggested New Measure," *Economic Journal* (September 1966), pp. 519-36.

18. The reader unfamiliar with this technique will find the following instructive: Rudolph J. Rummel, "Understanding Factor Analysis," *Journal of Conflict Resolution*, 11:4 (December 1967), pp. 444-80; and by the same author, *Applied Factor Analysis* (Evanston: Northwestern University Press, 1970).

19. Rudolph J. Rummel, "Dimensions of Conflict Behavior Within and Between Nations," *General Systems Yearbook*, 8 (1963), p. 9.

20. The BMDX72 program was used for the principal components analysis. Unities were inserted in the principal diagonal, since we wanted to account for as much of the total variance of the variables as possible.

21. Singer and Small, *The Wages of War*, pp. 363-70.

22. Fatality figures are from Singer and Small, *The Wages of War*, pp. 61-70. The calculations were made using population data from Banks's *Cross-Polity Time-Series Data*. Population was scored for the year of the outbreak of war.

23. The data are from Singer and Small, *The Wages of War*, pp. 61-70.

26. The data reported by Wright do not guarantee that the year preceding the outbreak of the conflict is always represented. Most of the conflicts in his inventory are ones that were brought before the League of Nations or United Nations, and Wright has dated them accordingly. However, some of these conflicts were underway for more than a year prior to being formally brought before one of the organizations.

27. Data on number of states in wars underway, number of nation-months-war underway, number of nation-months-war begun, and number of war entrants are from Singer and Small, *The Wages of War*, pp. 156-59. The number of states in the international system in each year, which was used for normalizing, is according to the inventory of states used in the present study. See Appendix A.

Chapter 5
Findings: The Empirical Evidence Regarding Relationships
Between Power Capabilities and Conflict

1. Rudolph J. Rummel, "Dimensions of Conflict Behavior Within and Between Nations," *General Systems Yearbook*, 8 (1963), p. 6.

2. For examples in political science, see: Norman Z. Alcock and Alan G. Newcombe, "The Perception of National Power," *Journal of Conflict Resolution*, 14 (September 1970), p. 335; A.F.K. Organski, *World Politics* (New York: Alfred A. Knopf, 1958).

3. The power capabilities scores and change rates in these scores for all states and all years between 1850 and 1966 are being published under separate cover. See Wayne H. Ferris, *Nation-State Power and Economic Variable Data 1850-1966* (Lexington, Mass.: D.C. Heath and Co., forthcoming). Elsewhere Singer and Small, et al. are experimenting with a variety of combinations and weightings of six indicator-variables: steel production, energy consumption, urban population, the square root of total population, armed forces size, and military expenditure. As is readily apparent, there is dissimilarity as well as overlap between their choice of indicators and that employed in this study. Certain findings already forthcoming from their endeavors were referred to in Chapter 2.

4. For an extended elaboration of this view, see Margaret J. Hagood, *Statistics for Sociologists* (New York: Reynal and Hitchcock, 1941), pp. 425-32, 612-16.

5. Robert F. Winch and Donald T. Campbell, "Proof? No. Evidence? Yes. The Significance of Tests of Significance," *The American Sociologist*, 4:2 (May 1969), pp. 140-43.

6. Whether tests of significance are appropriate is a subject that has occasioned much debate. The favorable interpretations cited above do not exhaust the question. For a comprehensive review of both pros and cons attendant to the controversy, see Denton E. Morrison and Ramon E. Henkel, eds., *The Significance Test Controversy–A Reader* (Chicago: Aldine Publishing Company, 1970).

7. Sidney Siegel, *Nonparametric Statistics for the Behavioral Sciences* (New York: McGraw-Hill Book Company, 1956), pp. 42-47.

8. Evidence of a stronger relationship between strength and victory was reported in a recent study by Steven Rosen in "War Power and the Willingness to Suffer," in *Peace, War, and Numbers*, ed. Bruce M. Russett (Beverly Hills, California: Sage Publications, 1972), pp. 167-84. Rosen examined forty-one wars from the Singer-Small inventory, covering the period between 1815 and 1945, and found that 79 percent of the wars were won by the side with higher government revenue and 70 percent by the side with greater population. For reasons earlier discussed in Chapter 4, the aggregation of multiple indicators into a single index was the strategy selected in the present study for operationalizing power capabilities. It is conceivable, however, that only a few indicators that most directly represent power capabilities, particularly in the sense of military capabilities available for immediate use, may be better predictors of war outcome than a single index based on a wider variety of indicator variables. To determine whether or not the difference between Rosen's result and that reported in the text above is principally due to such an effect, we separately

examined the variable data for government revenue, defense expenditure, and armed forces compiled for the present study. Of the forty-one wars studied between 1850 and 1965, twenty-six were won by the side with greater defense expenditures in the year prior to the outbreak of war, twenty-three were won by the side with greater armed forces personnel in the year before the onset of war, and twenty-eight were won by the side with greater government revenue. Since twenty-seven of the wars were won by the stronger side when the power capabilities index was used, it is clear that government revenue, armed forces, and defense expenditure, treated severally, do not support the evidence of a stronger relationship as reported by Rosen.

9. The product-moment coefficient becomes the phi coefficient where dichotomous data are concerned and is applicable to both continuous and dichotomous data. See Rummel, "Dimensions of Conflict Behavior Within and Between Nations," p. 10. All of the correlation coefficients reported in this chapter are based on the Pearson Product-Moment Formula.

Appendix A
Identification of the Universe of
Sovereign Nation States for the
Time Frame of the Study

1. J. David Singer and Melvin Small, "The Composition and Status Ordering of the International System: 1815-1940," *World Politics*, 18 (January 1966), pp. 236-82; J. David Singer, Melvin Small and Bruce M. Russett, "National Political Units in the Twentieth Century: A Standardized List," *The American Political Science Review*, 62 (September 1968), pp. 932-51; Arthur S. Banks, *Cross-Polity Time-Series Data* (Cambridge: The MIT Press, 1971), pp. 297-99.

2. Singer and Small, "The Composition and Status," pp. 245-47.

3. Singer, Small and Russett, pp. 933-34.

4. Ibid., p. 933. The author is grateful to the American Political Science Association for permission to quote from copyrighted works.

5. Banks, pp. 297-99.

Appendix B
Inventory of War Events:

1. Ethiopia is not listed in the inventory of independent states, Appendix A, for 1935 because adequate power capabilities data were not available for the years prior to 1934 when it qualified as an independent state. Data was available only for 1934-1935. To include Ethiopia for only two years seemed unwise, since it would cause alterations in the power capabilities scores

for all countries in 1934, the year data was first available. This would have a distortion effect on the computation of change rates in the power capabilities scores for all the other states for the year 1934. Therefore, a separate analysis for computing power capabilities scores and including Ethiopia was run for 1934, the year prior to the outbreak of hostilities. This provided a score for Ethiopia, making it possible to include the Italo-Ethiopian War in the testing of hypotheses 1, 2, and 3.

2. Mongolia is identified by Singer and Small as a participant to this war. Mongolia was not included in the present study because adequate information was not available for the indicator-variables used in the power capabilities analysis. This conflict was still used in the testing of the various hypotheses, but minus Mongolia. For hypotheses 1 through 6 the resulting bias introduced makes confirmation of the hypotheses more difficult, since Mongolia was on the side with greater power capabilities. In other words, if sufficient data becomes available for Mongolia at some future date, the resulting alterations in the power capabilities variables will, if anything, improve the correlation coefficients and in the predicted direction. It is not possible to state what effect inclusion of the war event has on hypotheses 7 through 12, since information is unavailable about the degree of change in Mongolia's power capabilities for the years relevant to the hypotheses.

Appendix C
Inventory of International Conflicts
Involving Force

1. The category "occurrence of military hostilities" is not according to Holsti. He did not classify specific conflicts in terms of whether or not military hostilities occurred. The conflicts have been classified by cross-referencing the events against Lewis Richardson (*The Statistics of Deadly Quarrels*, pp. 32-111) and Quincy Wright (*A Study of War*, pp. 1542-47). In this book conflicts involving armed hostilities are classified as involving "military hostilities" if 317 or more fatalities resulted. (For clarification of this point see Chapter 1.)

It is not clear whether Richardson's and Wright's criteria for fatalities are equivalent, since Wright did not specify his criteria (compare Richardson, pp. 8-9 to Wright, p. 1544). Richardson's list of conflicts is applicable to the 1919-1952 period; Wright's list to the 1945-1965 period. Wright also identified conflicts appearing before the League of Nations and which involved military hostilities, but he did not state whether the threshold for specifying military hostilities was 317 fatalities. According to accounts in *The Annual Register of World Events* reviewed by this author, at least some of these conflicts did not result in 317 or more fatalities. Some conflicts appearing in the Holsti inventory are not included in either the Wright or Richardson list. These events have been cross-referenced against other sources for evidence of whether armed hostilities involving 317 or more fatalities resulted.

2. Holsti did not specify the participants. States listed are according to Richardson.

3. Holsti does not specify the allied participants. Singer and Small identify the conflict as an interstate war with Greece and Turkey as participants. Their classification has been adopted.

4. The parties to this conflict have been redefined to include only Greece and Italy. The conflict does not appear to have included Albania as a participant. See *The Annual Register*, 1923, pp. 223-25.

5. Holsti did not identify the participants. The conflict appears to have been between Great Britain and the USSR. See *Kessing's Contemporary Archives*, 1934-1937, pp. 2166, 2192.

6. Holsti does not identify the participants. States listed are according to Wright, "The Escalation of International Conflicts," p. 447.

7. Ibid., p. 449.

8. Holsti has classified these three instances as one, identified as "USSR-Baltic States, 1939." While Soviet ultimatums to the three states for the installation of puppet regimes were made more or less simultaneously, the three were independent states. It seems only appropriate to classify each as a separate instance.

9. Holsti does not identify participants. States listed are according to Wright, *A Study of War*, p. 1554.

10. Holsti does not identify participants. States listed are according to Wright, *A Study of War*, p. 1554.

11. Holsti does not identify participants. States listed are according to Singer and Small, as is the year in which the conflict is said to have originated.

12. Holsti does not specify the allied states. States listed are according to Wright, *A Study of War*, p. 1554.

13. Holsti does not identify the participants, but they presumably included France, Great Britain, the United States, and Russia.

14. Holsti does not identify the UN participants. States listed are according to Singer and Small with the qualification that states that entered the conflict longer than six months after its inception are not included.

15. States specified by Holsti appear to be on the same side against the United Arab Republic, which he hasn't specified. See *Kessing's Contemporary Archives*, 1958, pp. 16305 ff.

16. Holsti does not specify participants for "Allies," but they presumably include France, Great Britain, the United States, and West Germany.

17. Holsti does not specify participants for "Allies," but they presumably include France, Great Britain, the United States, and West Germany.

18. According to *The Annual Register*, 1961 (p. 339) about one thousand Tunisians and twenty French were killed in hostilities.

19. Holsti does not specifiy the participants. States listed are according to Wright.

Appendix D
Inventory of International Political
Disputes and Military Hostilities

1. Participants identified are according to Holsti. (See Appendix C.)

2. Participants are according to Wright, "The Escalation of International Conflicts," p. 443.

3. Ibid., p. 444.

4. Participants are according to Singer and Small, *The Wages of War*, p. 68.

5. Participants are according to Wright, "The Escalation of International Conflicts," p. 443.

6. Participants are according to Singer and Small, *The Wages of War*, p. 68.

7. Participants are according to *Kessing's Contemporary Archives*, 1952-1954, p. 12024.

8. Ibid., 1950-1952, p. 12185; 1952-1954, p. 12024.

9. Ibid.

10. Conflict is according to Wright, "The Escalation of International Conflicts," p. 443.

11. Participants are according to Singer and Small, *The Wages of War*, p. 69.

12. Participants are according to *Kessing's Contemporary Archives*, 1957-1958.

Bibliography

Abel, Theodore. "The Element of Decision in the Pattern of War." *The American Sociological Review*, 6 (1941), pp. 853-59.

Alcock, Norman Z. and Alan G. Newcombe. "The Perception of National Power." *Journal of Conflict Resolution*, 14 (September 1970), pp. 335-43.

Almanach de Gotha: annuaire genealogique, diplomatique et statistique. Gotha: Justus Perthes, 1850-1941.

Bachrach, Peter and Morton S. Baratz. "Decisions and Non-Decisions: An Analytical Framework." *American Political Science Review*, 57:3 (September 1963), pp. 632-42.

Baldwin, David A. "Inter-Nation Influence Revisited." *Journal of Conflict Resolution*, 15 (December 1971), pp. 471-86.

_____. "The Power of Positive Sanctions." *World Politics*, 24 (October 1971), pp. 19-38.

Banks, Arthur S. *Cross-Polity Time-Series Data.* Cambridge: The MIT Press, 1971.

Bell, Roderick, David V. Edwards, and R. Harrison Wagner (eds.). *Political Power: A Reader in Theory and Research.* New York: The Free Press, 1969.

Beckerman, Wilfred. "International Comparisons of Income Levels: A Suggested New Measure." *Economic Journal* (September 1966), pp. 519-36.

Bierstedt, Robert. "An Analysis of Social Power." *American Sociological Review*, 15:6 (December 1950), pp. 730-37.

Bornstein, Morris. "A Comparison of Soviet and United States National Products." *Comparisons of the United States and Soviet Economics.* Washington, D.C.: U.S. Government Printing Office, 1959, pp. 384-89.

Britannica Book of the Year. Chicago: Encyclopaedia Britannica, 1938-1967.

Chatterjee, Partha. "The Classical Balance of Power Theory." *Journal of Peace Research*, 1 (1972), pp. 51-61.

Claude, Inis L., Jr. *Power and International Relations.* New York: Random House, 1962.

Dahl, Robert A. "Power." *International Encyclopedia of the Social Sciences.* New York: The Macmillan Company and The Free Press, 1968, pp. 405-18.

East, Maurice. "Status Discrepancy and Violence in the International System: An Empirical Analysis." *The Analysis of International Politics.* Edited by James A. Rosenau, Vincent Davis, and Maurice East. New York: The Free Press, 1972, pp. 299-319.

Economic Research Institute, Economic Planning Agency (Japan). "Analysis of Price Comparisons in Japan and the United States." *Economic Bulletin*, 13 (September 1963).

Ferris, Wayne H. *Nation-State Power and Economic Variable Data 1850-1966.* Lexington, Mass.: D.C. Heath and Company, forthcoming.

Fink, Clinton F. "More Calculations about Deterrence." *Journal of Conflict Resolution*, 9 (March 1965), pp. 54-65.

Friedrich, Carl (ed.). *Authority*. Cambridge: Harvard University Press, 1958.

Galtung, Johan. "A Structural Theory of Aggression." *Journal of Peace Research*, 1:2 (1964), pp. 95-119.

Gilbert, Milton and Irving Kravis. *An International Comparison of National Products and the Purchasing Power of Currencies*. Paris: The Organization for European Economic Cooperation, 1954.

Haas, Ernst B. "The Balance of Power: Prescription, Concept, or Propaganda." *International Politics and Foreign Policy*. Edited by James N. Rosenau. New York: The Free Press of Glencoe, 1961, pp. 318-29.

Hagood, Margaret J. *Statistics for Sociologists*. New York: Reynal and Hitchcock, 1941.

Herz, John H. *International Politics in the Atomic Age*. New York: Columbia University Press, 1959.

Hoffman, Stanley. "Balance of Power." *International Encyclopedia of the Social Sciences*. Edited by David A. Sills. The Macmillan Company and the Free Press, 1968, pp. 506-10.

Hollister, William W. *China's Gross National Product and Social Accounts, 1950-1957*. Illinois: The Free Press, 1958.

Holsti, K.J. "The Concept of Power in the Study of International Relations." *Background*, 7 (February 1964), pp. 105-18.

_____. "Resolving International Conflicts: A Taxonomy of Behavior and Some Figures on Procedures." *Journal of Conflict Resolution*, 10 (September 1966), pp. 272-96.

Holsti, Ole R. "The 1914 Case." *Basic Issues in International Relations*. Edited by Peter A. Toma and Andrew Gyorgy. Boston: Allyn and Bacon, 1967, pp. 140-47.

"Italian Independence, Wars of." *The Encyclopaedia Britannica*. Chicago: Encyclopaedia Britannica, Inc., 1968, pp. 709-11.

Kaplan, Morton A. *System and Process in International Politics*. New York: John Wiley & Sons, 1957.

Kerlinger, Fred N. *Foundations of Behavioral Research*. New York: Holt, Rinehart and Winston, Inc., 1964.

Kessing's Contemporary Archives: Weekly Diary of World Events. London: Kessing's Ltd., 1931-1967.

Knorr, Klaus. *The War Potential of Nations*. Princeton: Princeton University Press, 1956.

Lasswell, Harold D. and Abraham Kaplan. *Power and Society: A Framework for Political Inquiry*. New Haven: Yale University Press, 1950.

Leng, Russell J. and Robert A. Goodsell. "Behavioral Indicators of War Proneness in Bilateral Conflicts." Paper delivered at the 1972 Annual Meeting of the American Political Science Association, Washington, D.C., September 5-9, 1972 (mimeographed).

McClelland, Charles A. *Theory and the International System.* New York: The Macmillan Company, 1966.

Maurseth, Per. "Balance-of-Power Thinking from the Renaissance to the French Revolution." *Journal of Peace Research*, 1:1 (1964), pp. 121-33.

Morgenthau, Hans J. and Kenneth W. Thompson. *Principles and Problems of International Politics.* New York: Alfred A. Knopf, 1950.

Morgenthau, Hans J. *Politics Among Nations: The Struggle for Power and Peace.* New York: Alfred A. Knopf, 1963.

Morrison, Denton E. and Ramon E. Henkel (eds.). *The Significance Test Controversy–A Reader.* Chicago: Aldine Publishing Company, 1970.

Morrison, Donald F. *Multivariate Statistical Methods.* New York: McGraw-Hill Book Company, 1967.

Nagel, Jack H. "Some Questions About the Concept of Power." *Behavioral Science*, 13 (March 1968), pp. 129-37.

Naroll, Raoul. "Deterrence in History." *Theory and Research on the Causes of War.* Edited by Dean G. Pruitt and Richard Snyder. Englewood Cliffs, N.J.: Prentice-Hall, 1969.

North, Robert C. "Conflict Political Aspects." *International Encyclopedia for the Social Sciences*, editor-in-chief David A. Sills. New York: The Macmillan Company and The Free Press, 1968.

Organski, A.F.K. *World Politics.* New York: Alfred A. Knopf, 1958.

Parsons, Talcott. "On the Concept of Political Power." *Proceedings of the American Philosophical Society*, 107:3 (June 1963), pp. 232-62.

Porsholt, Lars. "On Methods of Conflict Resolution." *Journal of Peace Research*, 3:2 (1966), pp. 178-93.

Pruitt, Dean G. and Richard C. Snyder (eds.). *Theory and Research on the Causes of War.* Englewood Cliffs, N.J.: Prentice-Hall, 1969.

Przeworski, Adam and Henry Teune. *The Logic of Comparative Social Inquiry.* New York: John Wiley & Sons, 1970.

Raser, John R. and Wayman J. Crow. "A Simulation Study of Deterrence Theories." *Theory and Research on the Causes of War.* Edited by Dean G. Pruitt and Richard C. Snyder. Englewood Cliffs, N.J.: Prentice-Hall, 1969, pp. 136-49.

Raser, John R. "Deterrence Research: Past Progress and Future Needs." *Journal of Peace Research*, 3:4 (1966), pp. 297-327.

Rhee, Sang-Woo. *China's Cooperation, Conflict and Interaction Behavior: Viewed from Rummel's Status-Field Theoretic Perspective.* Hawaii: Dimensionality of Nations Project, 1972 (mimeographed).

Richardson, Lewis. *Statistics of Deadly Quarrels.* Edited by Quincy Wright and C.C. Lienau. Pittsburgh: Boxwood Press, 1960.

Riker, William. "Some Ambiguities in the Notion of Power." *American Political Science Review*, 58 (June 1964), pp. 341-49.

Rosen, Steven. "War Power and the Willingness to Suffer." *Peace, War, and*

Numbers. Edited by Bruce M. Russett. Beverly Hills, Calif.: Sage Publications, 1972, pp. 167-84.

Rummel, Rudolph J. " A Field Theory of Social Action with Application to Conflict Within Nations." *General Systems Yearbook,* 10 (1965), pp. 183-96.

_____. *Applied Factor Analysis.* Evanston: Northwestern University Press, 1970.

_____. "Dimensions of Conflict Behavior Within and Between Nations." *General Systems Yearbook,* 8 (1963), pp. 1-50.

_____. "Dimensions of Dyadic War, 1820-1952." *Journal of Conflict Resolution,* 11 (June 1967), pp. 176-83.

_____. "Understanding Factor Analysis." *Journal of Conflict Resolution,* 11:4 (December 1967), pp. 444-80.

_____. "U.S. Foreign Relations: Conflict, Cooperation, and Attribute Distances." *Peace, War, and Numbers.* Edited by Bruce M. Russett. Beverly Hills, Calif.: Sage Publications, 1972.

Russett, Bruce M. "The Calculus of Deterrence." *Journal of Conflict Resolution,* 7 (June 1963), pp. 98-109.

_____. *Peace, War, and Numbers.* Beverly Hills, Calif.: Sage Publications, 1972.

Siegel, Sidney. *Nonparametric Statistics for the Behavioral Sciences.* New York: McGraw-Hill Book Company, 1956.

Simon, Herbert A. "Notes on the Observation and Measurement of Political Power." *Journal of Politics,* 15 (November 1953), pp. 500-16.

Singer, J. David, Stuart Bremer, and John Stuckey. "Capability Distribution, Uncertainty, and Major Power War, 1820-1965." *Peace, War, and Numbers.* Edited by Bruce M. Russett. Beverly Hills, Calif.: Sage Publications, 1972, pp. 19-48.

Singer, J. David. "Inter-Nation Influence: A Formal Model." *American Political Science Review,* 57 (June 1963), pp. 420-30.

Singer, J. David and Melvin Small. "Foreign Policy Indicators: Predictors of War in History and in the State of the World Message." Paper delivered at the 1972 Annual Meeting of the American Political Science Association, Washington, D.C., September 5-9, 1972 (mimeographed).

_____. "Patterns in International Warfare." *Annals of the American Academy of Political and Social Science,* 391 (September 1970), pp. 145-55.

_____. "The Composition and Status Ordering of the International System: 1815-1940." *World Politics,* 18 (January 1966), pp. 236-82.

_____. *The Wages of War 1816-1965: A Statistical Handbook.* New York: John Wiley & Sons, Inc., 1972.

Singer, J. David, Melvin Small, and Bruce M. Russett. "National Political Units in the Twentieth Century: A Standardized List." *The American Political Science Review,* 62 (September 1968), pp. 932-51.

Snyder, G.H. "Balance of Power in the Missile Age." *Journal of International Affairs,* 14 (1960), pp. 21-34.

185

_____. "Deterrence and Power." *Journal of Conflict Resolution*, 4 (June 1960), pp. 164-78.

Sprout, Harold and Margaret Sprout. *Foundations of International Politics.* Princeton: D. Van Nostrand Co., 1962.

Starr, Harvey. *War Coalitions.* Lexington, Mass.: D.C. Heath and Company, 1972.

Swingle, Paul G. and Brian MacLean. "The Effect of Illusory Power in Non-Zero-Sum Games." *Journal of Conflict Resolution*, 15 (December 1971), pp. 514-22.

United States Arms Control and Disarmament Agency. *World Military Expenditures 1969.* Washington, D.C.: U.S. Government Printing Office, 1968.

Wallace, Michael D. "Status, Formal Organization, and Arms Levels as Factors Leading to the Onset of War, 1820-1964." *Peace, War, and Numbers.* Edited by Bruce M. Russett. Beverly Hills, Calif.: Sage Publications, 1972.

_____. "Power, Status, and International War." *Journal of Peace Research*, 1 (1971), pp. 23-35.

Wallenstein, Peter. "Characteristics of Economic Sanctions." *A Multi-Method Introduction to International Politics.* Edited by William D. Coplin and Charles W. Kegley, Jr. Chicago: Markham Publishing Co., 1971, pp. 128-54.

Walter, E.V. "Power and Violence." *American Political Science Review*, 58:2 (June 1964), pp. 350-60.

Weede, Erich. "Conflict Behavior of Nation-States." *Journal of Peace Research*, 3 (1970), pp. 229-35.

Winch, Robert F. and Campbell, Donald T. "Proof? No. Evidence? Yes. The Significance of Tests of Significance." *The American Sociologist*, 4:2 (May 1969), pp. 140-43.

Wright, Quincy. *A Study of War*, 2nd ed. Chicago: University of Chicago Press, 1965.

_____. "The Escalation of International Conflict." *Journal of Conflict Resolution*, 9 (December 1965), pp. 434-49.

Index

Index

About the Author

Wayne H. Ferris is a professional staff member of International Research Group, Ltd., Washington, D.C. He received the Ph.D. in Political Science from the University of Pennsylvania. He is a former research associate of the Foreign Policy Research Institute, Philadelphia, and a contributor to *Eastern Europe and European Security* by William R. Kintner and Wolfgang Klaiber.